300 best taco recipes

DISCARD

Kelley Cleary Coffeen

Robert
ROSE

300 Best Taco Recipes
Text copyright © 2011 Kelley Cleary Coffeen
Photographs copyright © 2011 Robert Rose Inc.
Cover and text design copyright © 2011 Robert Rose Inc.

For complete cataloguing information, see page 376.

Design and Production: Daniella Zanchetta/PageWave Graphics Inc.
Editor: Carol Sherman
Recipe Editor: Jennifer MacKenzie
Copy Editor: Karen Campbell-Sheviak
Indexer: Gillian Watts
Photographer: Colin Erricson
Associate Photographer: Matt Johannsson
Food Stylist: Kathryn Robertson
Prop Stylist: Charlene Erricson

Cover image: Chipotle Pork Tacos with Onion Apple Salsa (page 180)

We acknowledge the financial support of the Government of Canada through the Book Publishing Industry Development Program (BPIDP) for our publishing activities.

Published by Robert Rose Inc.
120 Eglinton Avenue East, Suite 800, Toronto, Ontario, Canada M4P 1E2
Tel: (416) 322-6552 Fax: (416) 322-6936
www.robertrose.ca

Printed and bound in Canada

1 2 3 4 5 6 7 8 9 SP 19 18 17 16 15 14 13 12 11

Contents

Acknowledgments

WOW, TACOS, TACOS, tacos… what a year it has been. A culinary journey that started with 85 tacos and grew to more than 300! The fun and worry; the frustrating yet rewarding exhaustion of late-night testing; the trips to the grocery store; and the calls to experts and hours of research have finally paid off. Thanks to these special people it has been a fun and rewarding experience.

To my beautiful daughter Brooke Elizabeth, your happy face, sweet smile and heartwarming encouragement made every taco adventure worthwhile. Thank you to my son, Daniel. I enjoyed and needed your "You can do it!" attitude. Thank you for your trips to the grocery store and culinary insight on healthy eating and nutrition. You both make me a proud mom. To my husband, Roger, a thousand thank-yous for balancing and taking care of our daily life while I was testing, writing and tasting. Your words of encouragement and calmness kept me focused.

This project has helped me grow in so many ways. I have Lisa Ekus, my literary agent, to thank for that. Lisa, you have remarkable vision and a keen sense of what your authors can do. Thank you for challenging me. Thank you, Sally Ekus for your enthusiasm and support in keeping me connected and on track. I am also grateful to Bob Dees, who saw the potential for this book. A huge thank-you to my editor Carol Sherman, who patiently led me through the editing process; you are amazing. To Karen Campbell-Sheviak for her copy editing and Jennifer MacKenzie for recipe testing. Thank you Daniella Zanchetta and everyone at PageWave for designing such a beautiful book. And to everyone who had a hand in making this book usable and inviting.

Thank you to my family for your constant hugs, laughs and encouragement. To my brother Chris, thank you for your genuine interest when talking tacos with me. You are always there for me and I appreciate you so much. To my sister, Katie, for our weekly chats on food, life and kids.

To Mesilla Valley Kitchen's entire staff, a very dedicated team, from the front of the house — servers, cashiers and bussers — to the prep and line cooks, thank you for allowing me to rely on your patience and support during this project.

To my dear friends and cooking pals, Sherley O'Brien, Julie Peach, Carrie Gaddy, Maureen Brenner and Maria Pacheco, thanks for listening, testing and tasting. You all are the best. Now, back to the margaritas!

To my other team of recipe testers, a huge thank-you for the information you provided; Chris Cleary and Art Johnson, two true culinary heros. Larry Hieber, my culinary spice guy; Scot Martin, my wine and fish/seafood guy; Kyle Branche, my high school pal and bartender to the stars. Thank you all!

Thank you to dear Nora Camunez, an elegant tortilla lady, 91 years young; Marion Lawrence, my chocolate lady (big hugs for you); and June Jenkins, my salsa queen!

A final thank you to Lorenzo Liberto, Louis Samaniego, Tom and Jerean Hutchinson, and Ken Bookman for your culinary expertise and inspiration.

To Roger, with love, my partner and friend.

Introduction

THE ONLY TACOS I knew growing up in the late '60s were stale store-bought corn tortilla taco shells filled with a big spoonful of greasy ground beef, garnished with shredded iceberg lettuce and topped off with a dab of grated Cheddar cheese and chunks of tomatoes. Even at the tender age of nine, I was looking for more in a taco. It wasn't until my family moved to Southern Arizona that I started to experience the rich authentic flavors of Mexico and the fun, wild and creative culinary style of west coast cooking as we traveled back and forth to California. I lived along the border and grew up around fields of fresh fruits and vegetables that were harvested daily. It was there that I learned about the Mexican culture and food. My dad would take us on Saturdays to the "camp" where "Cucka" (the Mexican cook) would prepare a huge lunch for all the workers. That is where I learned to appreciate Mexican food and the love they all shared for the robust flavors and fresh ingredients. I would listen to these hardworking men and women as they savored their food, truly enjoying what they were eating. Bits of culinary knowledge such as salsa is a fine balance of tomatoes, onion and peppers; freshly diced onion is good but diced onion soaked in a bath of citrus juice is heaven; and tortillas, well that is a long story which we will get to (page 7). They were proud of the food and flavors that came from their homeland, Mexico. There we would enjoy the best, authentic Mexican tacos, burritos, beans and rice one could imagine.

I have a passion for tacos. This basic little street snack from south of the border represents an entire culture that has made its way into the North American mainstream. Originating with the early settlers deep in the heart of Mexico, highly flavored meats wrapped in tortillas became a cultural and culinary mainstay handed down from generation to generation. Bertha Haffner-Ginger wrote the first-known English-language taco recipe in her cookbook, *California Mexican-Spanish Cookbook* in 1914. She wrote: "…made by putting chopped cooked beef and chili sauce in a tortilla made of meal and flour; folded edges sealed together with egg; fried in deep fat, chile sauce served over it." Well, the basics of the taco have stayed the same, but *300 Best Taco Recipes* expands North America's vision of the Mexican taco.

The taco, a festive version of the North American sandwich, is aromatic, juicy, flavorful, spicy, textured and simple in presentation but complex in flavor. According to the Tortilla Industry Association (Food Product Design, 2009), tortilla sales are poised to surpass sandwich bread for the first time in the United States, with annual sales projected to grow beyond $6 billion this year. The taco is replacing the North American sandwich!

I offer taco recipes inspired by authentic Mexican dishes along with truly creative and, sometimes, crazy variations. The way I see it, tacos should be filled with the highest quality spiced meats, seasoned poultry and fresh seafood, veggies and even sweet, fresh fruits. Accents of flavor are added with hints of artisanal cheeses, fresh produce, spicy sauces, sweet glazes and tasty salsas. But most importantly, my tacos are fun, crazy and comforting, with bright, bold colors and intriguing flavors all folded, wrapped and rolled into a tasty little bundle.

I have included an array of tacos, including vegetarian, chicken and turkey, seafood, beef and pork — and wait, yes, even dessert tacos. They are flavorful, inviting and inventive. These tacos are stuffed with the most tantalizing fillings and topped with the freshest produce you can imagine. This is North America's new comfort food, seasoned with contemporary flavor! Tacos are inexpensive, creative, quick to make and easy to serve. They can be grilled, deep-fried, broiled or baked. You can spice them up or cool them down, customize your tacos anyway you like. Personally, I like tacos with a little kick.

I want people to experience the Mexican culture and have fun with it. It's a celebration, a fiesta! This book brings together what we admire about our southern neighbors: their love for family, friends and food. It celebrates the beautiful culture that has spilled over the border into our way of life through music, design, art, food, hospitality and fiestas.

It's a culture — a community of appreciation and enjoyment. In my kitchen I often look at the words inscribed above my range, *Aqui Celebramos, Familia, Amigos y Amore!* Here We Celebrate, Family, Friends and Love! My wish is that you do the same, creating tasty, tantalizing tacos for those you hold dear.

History and Evolution of Tacos

In the early 1500s, the Spaniards discovered on their explorations to North America that ground corn bread, a small flatbread, was a staple item in the diet of the Aztec people. Some indigenous settlers living near water wrapped small fish in the flatbread while others chose meats roasted over open fires. Spaniards renamed the small breads tortillas. For centuries, the taco has been a dietary mainstay in many tribes and cultures throughout Mexico. The Mexican people serve tacos in the early morning hours, in the evening and late into the night, enjoying the earthy flavor of the tortilla stuffed with a special filling.

Love for the cultural foods of Mexico continued to grow in the first half of this century, eventually spilling over the border into the southern United States.

For many years, artisans used a simple tortilla press or hand pressed their tortillas. It was not until the 1960s that the development of a mechanical process led to the invention of a small-scale tortilla-making machine. This little mechanical system could turn out hot steaming tortillas every few seconds, revolutionizing what we know today as the tortilla industry.

In the 1950s, as the fast food concept started to grow, a former marine with a passion for Mexican food started selling 19-cent tacos at his small family restaurant in California. Eventually, in the early '60s, Glenn Bell established the first franchised Mexican fast food restaurant, known as Taco Bell. This chain of restaurants gave national recognition for the first time to the beloved taco of Mexico.

Over the years, the taco has evolved into an international symbol of Mexican food. It has become a focus of interest everywhere in the culinary world from neighborhood line cooks to high-end chefs and TV food personalities. From the familiar to the most bizarre adaptations, the taco has taken on a life of its own.

Development of tortillas in niche markets adds new customers and fans to the tortilla and taco world. Today, you will find low-sodium, high-fiber, whole-grain, low-fat and gluten-free tortillas, addressing the health concerns of many. Flavored tortillas add another niche that continues to grow and creates more opportunity for delicious and desirable taco creations.

Today's tacos are packed with flavor; they are fun and immediate, inexpensive and healthy. They are palate pleasing, refreshing and satisfying. They are a comfort food that speaks to the world. Today, the taco has earned a place in culinary history as a true treasure.

Taco Fillings

Taco fillings can encompass an array of flavors, textures and cooking methods, all depending upon your personal taste. The wide range of ingredients that you can fill tacos with make them the perfect entrée for breakfast, lunch or dinner. And the versatility in cooking methods allows you to create incredibly delicious tacos year round. I am sure you will find a delicious taco or two, filled and cooked however you want, to call your very own.

There are four elements to every delicious taco: the wrap or tortilla, the filling, the garnish and the salsas and sauces. They are all equally important and demand attention. We want to taste all of the elements that create the perfect balance in flavor and texture.

Fillings for tacos come in a wide variety of flavors and choices. Again, we are only limited by our imaginations and culinary desires. I offer beefy fillings that are baked, boiled, marinated, broiled, grilled, sautéed or slow-cooked. In Chipotle Tenderloin Tacos (page 125) or Chile-Rubbed Steak Tacos (page 126) I chose spiced meats. Enjoy tacos stuffed with pan-seared steak, slow-roasted shredded beef or grilled Kobe beef.

Pork offerings include Classic Carnita Tacos with Fresh Lime (page 175), Grilled Pork Loin Tacos with Apple, Onion and Garlic Relish (page 171) and Zesty Orange Pork Tacos (page 186). Breakfast tacos are packed full of flavor in Bacon and Avocado Breakfast Tacos (page 183) and Scrambled Sausage Tacos with New Mexico Green Chile Sauce (page 199).

On a lighter note, whether grilled, stir-fried or roasted, chicken and turkey are a popular choice for tacos. Teamed with beans, whole grains and veggies, poultry makes a wise choice for tasty tacos. Enjoy Rosemary Chicken Tacos (page 54), Margarita Chicken Tacos (page 77) and Curried Turkey Tacos (page 98).

Fish and seafood tacos continue to grow in popularity. Fresh succulent shellfish and fish fillets make the perfect filling for a light, healthy taco. Pile it high with fresh veggies, salsa and creamy sauce… delicious! So I offer you a smorgasbord of fish tacos that are deep-fried, sautéed, grilled, chilled, stir-fried, naturally marinated or baked. Try a bite of Crispy Coconut Shrimp Tacos with Orange Salsa (page 209), Ceviche Fresco Tacos (page 212), and Fresh Baja Fish Tacos with Mexican White Sauce (page 206), just to name a few.

My vegetarian tacos encompass veggies, legumes and eggs. So dive in and whip up some tacos with light and tasty fillings that are marinated, tossed, grilled, stir-fried, sautéed, deep-fried, chilled, dressed, glazed or refried. Share taco delights such as Sautéed Spinach, Veggie and Garlic Tacos (page 245) and Fried Tomato and Green Chile Tacos (page 251).

Lastly, just remember that tacos are merely a flatbread stuffed with a filling. So I say why can't it be sweet? You will be smacking your lips over Apple-Caramel Flautas (page 338), Sundae Tacos with Mexican Chocolate Sauce (page 354) and Mango-Raspberry Cupitas (page 352).

Toppings

Salsas and Sauces

Salsas and sauces are the crowning moment, the last chance for culinary inspiration. After we have warmed our fresh tortillas, scooped up our taco filling and layered fresh greens and veggies on top, it is time to lavish our taco with an exquisite tasting salsa or sauce. A well-made salsa will elevate the combination of flavor in even the best-made tacos. Gone are the days when there were only a few salsas to choose from. We have moved on to explore all the opportunities that fresh vegetables, herbs, chile and fruits can give the salsa world.

There are relish-style salsas that are big on texture, such as Pico de Gallo (page 305), Apple, Onion and Garlic Relish (page 313), Jalapeño Relish (page 310), and some that are roasted and smoked like Roasted Tomato Salsa (page 299).

There are herb sauces with intense flavor that are easy to make with a few ingredients, such as Chimichurri Sauce (page 328) and Poblano Sauce (page 320). Rich hot sauces make a lasting impression with their intense level of savory flavors and heat. Try Fresh Red Chile Sauce (page 318), Ancho Bourbon Sauce (page 330) and Creamy Wasabi Sauce (page 316).

Fruit salsas like Sweet Pineapple Salsa (page 309) and Strawberry Salsa (page 308) range in flavor from tangy and spicy to earthy and sweet. The non-traditional, contemporary combinations like Jicama Salsa (page 309) and Tomatillo Avocado Salsa (page 304) are refreshing and fun.

A new trend is dairy sauces made from fresh yogurt and sour cream, which can add delightful highlights to a fresh fish taco.

The collection of recipes in the Salsas, Relishes and Sauces chapter will enliven the flavor of the perfect taco. So enjoy, and surprise your taste buds with new adventures and flavor combinations.

Fresh Vegetables

Tacos can be adorned with a variety of fresh garnishes, from the familiar flavors of diced tomato, chopped onion and shredded iceberg lettuce to the extraordinary taste and textures of jicama, pineapple and tomatillos.

Taste, texture and freshness are the key elements in selecting the garnish for the perfect tacos. Buy good-quality vegetables at the very last minute to ensure freshness and taste. Fresh vegetables lend themselves to the light and healthy characteristics of a fish or seafood taco. Rich flavors from avocados and the sharpness of a fresh onion heighten the taste of a beefy taco or add extra texture and flavor to a shredded chicken taco.

I like lots of fresh greens, chopped or shredded, on many of my tacos. Investigate the varieties of salad mix and greens in your produce department. Look for interesting, unusual vegetables and greens. Try a few fresh herbs as well. Fresh cilantro, chives or basil are delightful thrown in with a chopped salad mix.

Cheese

Cheese is an important part of many North American tacos. We love our tacos piled high with shredded Cheddar and Monterey Jack cheeses, two of the most popular choices. But traditionally the authentic tacos of Mexico are garnished with a hint of cheese. Even though they have a shorter shelf life than American or European cheeses, I encourage you to explore the cheeses of Mexico, such as Cotija, Asadero and Queso Fresco. The Mexican cheeses are worth every ounce of cream. These fresh cheeses, melting cheeses or hard/semifirm cheeses are readily available in most markets. A creamy soft cheese, such as Asadero, can be melted inside a warm taco, while a fresh cheese, such as Queso Fresco can be crumbled and sprinkled on top of garnishes. The firmer cheeses like Cotija, add intense pungent flavors and a little goes a long way (see also Cheese Varieties, page 26).

Not all tacos need cheese. Many can stand with only garnishes and salsa. However, additions of Cheddar, Monterey Jack, hints of blue cheese, feta and, of course, the Mexican ones, add unmatched flavor to the perfect taco.

Homemade Tortillas

As tortilla sales continue to climb, there are more and more tortilla factories taking care of the demand. Fresh corn and flour tortillas are easier to find these days at your local market and tortilla factory. The perfect size tortilla for a taco is 6 inches (15 cm). It is generally more available in corn rather than flour. If I am purchasing flour tortillas, I buy 8-inch (20 cm) ones and trim them with a pair of kitchen shears to 6 inches (15 cm) using a corn tortilla as a template. If your tortillas are too big, it will create an imbalance in your filling portions. The perfect taco is made from a 6-inch (15 cm) corn or flour tortilla, filled with 2 to 3 tablespoons (30 to 45 mL) of filling. For an 8-inch (20 cm) tortilla, 3 to 4 tablespoons (45 to 60 mL) of filling is the right amount. The taco recipes offered here are based on a 6-inch (15 cm) tortilla. This can be a difficult size to find so I have offered the option of 8-inch (20 cm) ones as well. You can use them this size and enjoy tacos with a bit more tortilla than authentic tacos or trim to 6 inches (15 cm). I also use 4-inch (10 cm) corn tortilla for appetizer-style tacos.

Even though tortillas are aplenty in the market place, homemade tortillas are easier to make than most would think. Whether you're making corn tortillas or flour tortillas fresh is better. The warm, soft, lightly grilled flatbread wraps around any taco filling and melts in your mouth.

Basic Corn Tortillas

*Masa harina is a finely
ground corn flour made
from corn that is dried,
cooked in water and
treated with calcium
hydroxide or lime. Then
it is ground and dried
again. By mixing it
with water, it forms a
dough called "masa,"
which is what we use
to make corn tortillas.
These tortillas will add
texture and flavor to
any taco.*

Tip
Fresh corn tortillas do not
stay fresh. They need to
be used within hours of
making them.

- 16 sheets wax paper, cut into 10-inch (25 cm)
  squares
- Tortilla press

2 cups	masa harina	500 mL
1¼ cups	very warm (almost hot) water	300 mL

1. In a large bowl, mix together masa marina and water.
   Knead with your hands to form the masa or dough.

2. Pinch off a golf ball size piece of masa and roll into
   a smooth ball. Place balls in an airtight container as
   you make each one until ready to use for up to 1 hour.
   Continue with remaining masa to make 16 balls.

3. To press tortillas, place a piece of wax paper in tortilla
   press and place masa ball on top. Place another piece
   of wax paper on top of masa ball and press to a 6-inch
   (15 cm) circle. Continue with remaining masa balls,
   stacking uncooked tortillas on a platter with wax
   paper sheets in between each one.

4. Heat a dry nonstick or cast-iron skillet over medium
   heat. Remove wax paper and transfer tortillas to
   skillet, one at a time, and cook, turning once, for
   about 45 seconds per side or until bubbling and
   lightly browned. Transfer tortillas to a towel-lined
   platter. Wrap in towel to keep warm.

Simple Corn Tortillas

**Makes 16
tortillas**

*Tortillas with a hint
of salt are perfectly
balanced with the
flavor of the corn.
The soda adds an
extra light texture
to these tortillas.*

Tip
Fresh corn tortillas do not
stay fresh. They need to
be used within hours of
making them.

- 16 sheets wax paper, cut into 10-inch (25 cm)
  squares
- Tortilla press

2 cups	masa harina	500 mL
1/2 tsp	salt	2 mL
1/4 tsp	baking soda	1 mL
1 1/2 cups	very warm (almost hot) water	375 mL

1. In a large bowl, mix together masa harina, salt, baking soda and water. Knead with your hands to form the masa or dough.

2. Pinch off a golf ball size piece of masa and roll into a smooth ball. Place balls in an airtight container as you make each one until ready to use for up to 1 hour. Continue with remaining masa to make 16 balls.

3. To press tortillas, place a piece of wax paper in tortilla press and place masa ball on top. Place another piece of wax paper on top of masa ball and press to a 6-inch (15 cm) circle. Continue with remaining masa balls, stacking uncooked tortillas on a platter with wax paper sheets in between each one.

4. Heat a dry nonstick or cast-iron skillet over medium heat. Remove wax paper and transfer tortillas to skillet, one at a time, and cook, turning once, for about 45 seconds per side or until bubbling and lightly browned. Transfer tortillas to a towel-lined platter. Wrap in towel to keep warm.

Authentic Flour Tortillas

Makes 16 tortillas

Authentic Mexican tortillas are made with lard. I know some people object to using lard but it adds flavor and it really isn't all that bad for you in moderation. It has less cholesterol and saturated fat than an equal amount of butter by weight! It is the secret ingredient that makes these tortillas delicious.

Tips

Substitute ¼ cup (60 mL) vegetable oil for the lard.

Refrigerate uncooked tortillas with wax paper between layers in an airtight container for up to 8 hours. Otherwise, the dough starts to dry out.

Cooked tortillas can be stored in an airtight container and kept in the refrigerator for up to 3 days or frozen for up to 3 months.

- 16 sheets wax paper, cut into 10-inch (25 cm) squares

3 cups	all-purpose flour (approx.)	750 mL
1 tbsp	salt	15 mL
½ cup	lard (see Tips, left)	125 mL
1¼ cups	very warm (almost hot) water	300 mL

1. In a large bowl, combine flour and salt. Using your fingers, slowly work lard into flour. Add small amounts of water and continue to work with hands until dough is smooth. Form a large ball. Turn out onto a floured surface. Knead the dough thoroughly.

2. Divide dough into 16 small balls. Sprinkle each with flour and place in an airtight container. Cover and let dough stand for at least 15 minutes or for up to 1 hour.

3. On a lightly floured work surface, using a rolling pin, roll each ball out to a 6-inch (15 cm) circle. (The trick here is to turn your dough one-quarter turn each time you roll it. That will ensure you get a round tortilla.) Transfer to a wax paper square. Repeat with each dough ball and stack uncooked tortillas on a platter.

4. Heat a dry nonstick or cast-iron skillet over medium heat. Peel off wax paper from tortillas, one at a time, and cook tortillas, turning once, for about 45 seconds per side or until bubbling and lightly browned. Transfer tortillas to a towel-lined platter. Wrap in towel to keep warm.

Homemade Flour Tortillas

Makes 16 tortillas

This is a favorite from the borderland among my circle of friends. These small tortillas are perfect for my tacos — full of texture and flavor.

Tips

Traditionally, flour tortillas are rolled out with a rolling pin. However, since we are making smaller 6-inch (15 cm) tortillas here, a tortilla press would also work well. Follow Steps 1 and 2. Then place a 7-inch (18 cm) square of wax paper in the press. Place a ball of dough in the press and cover dough with another 7-inch (18 cm) square of wax paper and press. Transfer to a wax paper square. Repeat with each dough ball and stack uncooked tortillas on a platter.

Refrigerate uncooked tortillas with wax paper between layers in an airtight container for up to 8 hours.

Cooked tortillas can be stored in an airtight container and kept in the refrigerator for up to 3 days or frozen for up to 3 months.

- 16 sheets wax paper, cut into 10-inch (25 cm) squares

4 cups	all-purpose flour (approx.)	1 L
1 tsp	salt	5 mL
1¾ cups	very warm (almost hot) water	425 mL
⅓ cup	olive oil	75 mL

1. In a large bowl, combine flour and salt. Using your fingers, slowly work water and oil into flour. Work with hands until dough is smooth. Turn out onto a floured surface and knead several times until smooth.

2. Divide dough into 16 small balls. Sprinkle each with flour and place in an airtight container. Cover and let dough stand for at least 15 minutes or for up to 1 hour.

3. On a lightly floured work surface, using a rolling pin, roll each ball out to a 6-inch (15 cm) circle. (The trick here is to turn your dough one-quarter turn each time you roll it. That will ensure you get a round tortilla.) Transfer to a wax paper square. Repeat with each dough ball and stack uncooked tortillas on a platter.

4. Heat a dry nonstick or cast-iron skillet over medium heat. Peel off wax paper from tortillas, one at a time, and cook, turning once, for about 45 seconds per side or until bubbling and lightly browned. Transfer tortillas to a towel-lined platter. Wrap in towel to keep warm.

Variation

For whole wheat tortillas, substitute the 4 cups (1 L) all-purpose flour with 1 cup (250 mL) all-purpose flour and 3 cups (750 mL) whole wheat flour.

Folded Taco Shells

Makes 8 taco shells

I like to make my own taco shells. They have a light crispy texture. They won't crumble and fall apart making them easy to stuff with filling. The secret to making the perfect shape is to make a foil mold, which helps keep the tortilla wide enough to insert your delicious fillings.

Tips

Kitchen gloves or grilling mitts are heat resistant, with a long form-fitting cuff that gives you protection when grilling or deep-frying. You can find these online or in most kitchen supply stores.

Peanut oil has a higher smoke point than other oils. It tends to crisp tortillas faster and help them retain less oil.

- Heavy-duty foil
- Kitchen gloves (see Tips, left)
- Candy/deep-fry thermometer

8	corn or flour tortillas (pages 11 and 13)	8
	Peanut oil (see Tips, left)	

1. Cut a 4-foot by 12-inch (120 by 30 cm) piece of foil. Fold it in half so you have a 2-foot (60 cm) long piece. Fold edges in toward the center 2 inches (5 cm) on each side. You will have an 2-foot by 8-inch (60 by 20 cm) piece of foil. Fold each end toward the middle every 4 inches (10 cm) three times until both ends meet in the middle. Shape into a narrow "U" shape. This creates a mold that you can wrap your tortilla around.

2. In a deep-fryer or deep heavy pot, heat 3 inches (7.5 cm) of oil to 350°F (180°C). Working with one tortilla at a time, wrap tortilla around foil mold to make the taco shape, holding it at the top of the mold with your thumb and index finger or tongs. Dip center of tortilla (wrapped around the mold) into oil and fry for about 2 minutes until center is crispy and hard. Using tongs, carefully remove foil mold and place on a paper towel. Holding the shell with tongs, immerse one side of the taco shell in oil and fry until crisp and golden brown. Repeat with second side of tortilla, creating a "U" shaped shell. Transfer to a paper towel-lined surface to drain. Adjust heat as necessary between taco shells.

Reheating Tortillas

The freshest homemade tortillas make the best taco wraps. However, it is not often that I have time to make homemade tortillas and cook an entire meal in one evening. I usually make my flour and corn tortillas early in the day. Therefore, I have to reheat them before working with them in my recipes. Even the freshest store-bought tortillas need to be reheated so they are soft, pliable and easy to work with. Heating tortillas is an essential element in the success of my taco recipes. Corn tortillas need a bit more moisture in the reheating process than flour tortillas. Here I offer different methods for each.

Reheating Folded Taco Shells

To reheat fried taco shells or keep freshly fried shells warm, place on a baking sheet and heat in a 200°F (100°C) preheated oven for 8 to 10 minutes.

Reheating Corn and Flour Tortillas

Skillet-Warmed Corn Tortillas

This method gives you a soft, pliable tortilla that is lightly toasted on one or both sides. Place a dry nonstick or cast-iron skillet over medium heat. Place tortilla in skillet and heat each side by turning once until warm and pliable, about 1 minute per side. Place in a tortilla warmer (see page 17) or wrap in foil to keep warm until ready to use.

Tip
You can also spray each side of a corn tortilla with water for a moister consistency. For a slightly toasted texture, lightly spray one or both sides of tortilla with cooking spray before heating.

Micro-Warmed Corn or Flour Tortillas

This method gives you a very pliable and soft tortilla and allows you to roll the tacos tightly so it's perfect for preparing rolled tacos and taquitos. It is also quick and easy for soft tacos.

Place 4 tortillas in a small plastic storage bag and close or fold over the opening. Microwave on High for 25 to 45 seconds (depending on the power of your microwave). Remove from plastic bag. The tortillas should be warm and pliable. If you leave them in too long they will be too hot to handle and will be overdone. Place in a tortilla warmer (see page 17) or wrap in foil to keep warm until ready to use.

Skillet-Warmed Flour Tortillas

In a griddle or skillet over medium-high heat, heat each tortilla on each side until soft and pliable. Place in a tortilla warmer (see page 17) or wrap in foil to keep warm until ready to use.

Oven-Warmed Flour Tortillas

Preheat oven to 275°F (140°C). Wrap 6 to 12 flour tortillas in a large piece of foil, enough to wrap around tortillas once. Seal edges tightly. Heat in preheated oven for 30 to 40 minutes.

Keeping Tortillas Warm

There are several ways to keep tortillas warm while serving. You can simply wrap fresh cooked or heated tortillas in a clean kitchen towel and place in a basket or bowl. There are also small insulated tortilla warmers with lids that are decorative.

As for large amounts of tortillas, keep them warm in an insulated chest, such as an ice chest (cooler) lined with cotton kitchen towels. Remove small amounts as needed and place in tortilla warmers.

Top 10 Tips for Perfect Tacos

1. **The Perfect Tortilla** — The freshest tortillas are the best tortillas. And the best tortillas have to be the right size for your tacos. Whether you make them yourself or buy them from the local taqueria or at your local grocery store, they need to be fresh. For flour tortillas, make them on or one day before serving. Corn tortillas must be made the same day. Find out when tortillas are made or delivered locally. Use the proper reheating directions on page 15.

2. **Know Your Tortilla Press** — If you choose to make your own homemade tortillas, test your recipes ahead of time. Homemade tortillas do take practice. Select a simple hand tortilla press. You can find them in kitchen supply stores or online. Look for one with an easy-to-clean round disk area and simple lever. Tortilla presses are generally used for corn tortillas because the round disks are about 6-inches (15 cm) in diameter. In this book, I also recommend making 6-inch (15 cm) flour tortillas so the tortilla press is ideal for making them as well. To avoid stressful situations, find a recipe that works for you by testing several. Then practise that recipe a couple of times until you feel confident in making it. My family loves having extra tortillas around to snack on. (See also Tortilla press, page 17.)

3. **Know What and When** — Look at each recipe and analyze the time and resources you need to put your meal together. Do the same for the fillings and salsas. If you are making a grilled taco recipe, chances are you will be grilling close to the serving time.

Can all other elements of the meal be prepared around that?

4. **Oh My, Oil** — Use a good-quality oil. I like olive oil for sautéing with herbs and garlic. However, some fillings do not need added flavor, so vegetable or canola oil will do. For deep-frying, I prefer to use peanut oil because it has a higher smoke point. Canola oil and vegetable oil are good oils to use as well.

5. **Fabulous Fillings** — These taco filling recipes do not use a lot of ingredients, therefore cooking is quick. Use the highest quality meats, poultry, and vegetables. Select the best spices and be sure to measure accurately. Taste your fillings as you go and season your fillings toward the end of the cooking process.

6. **Don't Overstuff** — The best taco is a taco balanced in flavor. A 6-inch (15 cm) tortilla with 2 to 3 tbsp (30 to 45 mL) of filling leaves just the right amount of room for fresh garnish and salsas, which results in the perfect folded taco. A rolled taco, using a 6-inch (15 cm) tortilla commands about 2 tbsp (30 mL) of filling. You want to taste all of the elements in your taco, creating the perfect balance in flavor and texture. Don't overfill your tortilla and overwhelm your taste buds.

7. **Cheese to Please** — There are so many varieties of cheese on the market. Be adventurous. Cheese adds yet another layer of flavor to the taco experience. You do not need to pile it on. Just a hint of a high-quality cheese adds intense creamy flavor. The Mexican cheeses are worth a taste (see page 26). They are fresh cheeses that need no aging and are available in most Latin American markets or online. Not all tacos need cheese; many can stand with only garnish and salsa. However, additions of Cheddar, Monterey Jack,

hints of blue cheese and feta add unmatched flavor to the perfect taco.

8. **Fresh Garnish** — Taste, texture and freshness are again the key elements of topping the perfect taco. Be knowledgeable about the shelf life of your produce. Don't slice, tear or dice until the last minute, ensuring freshness from the field to the table. Be creative; texture and flavor can create a whole new twist on a traditional taco. Don't be afraid to try new types of vegetables and greens.

9. **Simply Salsas and Sassy Sauces** — Some salsas take a lot of time, others do not. Made fresh is best, but some may need to sit and infuse in flavor. Try the different varieties paying attention to the prep time and task. Freshen leftover salsas by pulsing in the blender with a squeeze of fresh lime juice. Try sweet salsas with savory meats. Spicy salsas add intense flavor to vegetarian tacos. Experiment and enjoy your salsas but don't forget sauces. Many of my taco recipes use additional sauces that are layered for extra flavor. Occasionally, I will add a creamy sauce instead of cheese to a taco recipe, then top with a flavorful salsa. They are delicious and really heighten the flavors of the fillings, salsas, garnish and cheeses. Make these a day ahead so the herbs and chiles will infuse with the sauce mixture. This will ensure the best-tasting sauces.

10. **Let's Eat!** — Timing and presentation are critical when serving tacos. Every element has to be ready at the same time — tortillas, filling, garnishes and cheese, along with the salsas and/or sauces. Get your timing down. Make your salsas ahead, prep your garnishes and shred your cheese, warm your tortillas, make sure your fillings are hot. Now whip up a taco in seconds and become known as a Master Taquero!

Tools and Equipment for the Best Tacos

Tortilla press

Tortilla presses are available in cast iron that is polished to a chrome finish. This simple kitchen tool has a base, top and handle. It is great for not only pressing out tortillas but also making the perfect dough for tartlets or empanadas. Moist balls of flour tortilla dough or corn masa are placed in the center of the press and then pressed to a thin layer for tortillas or pastries. I use a press to create the perfect corn and flour tortillas.

Tortilla warmer

These small insulated tortilla warmers with lids are decorative and useful for keeping the tortillas warm. They are available in colorful ceramic styles as well as plastic — polyethylene material that keeps fresh tortillas hot. Also fabric tortilla warmers that can be heated in the microwave are available in an array of colors.

Kitchen shears

I use kitchen shears to trim store-bought flour tortillas to a smaller size. It is difficult to find 6-inch (15 cm) flour tortillas, which are the perfect size for many tacos. I trim the 8- or 10-inch (20 to 25 cm) tortilla to a 6-inch (15 cm) size with shears.

Skillet

A large 10- to 12-inch (25 to 30 cm) nonstick heavy skillet that is at least 2-inches (5 cm) deep is perfect for sautéing meats, veggies, chicken or fish, and also pan searing meats.

Deep-fryer

Look for deep-fry sets that include a base, a nonstick pot and basket with a handle. It should heat to at least 375°F (190°C). I prefer an electric deep fryer that has a rectangular shape with a large pot that holds 10 to 12 cups (2.5 to 3 L) of oil and a mesh basket with a heat-resistant handle. You will be frying tacos that are generally 6- to 8-inches (15 to 20 cm) long, making the rectangular basket ideal. There are also round fryers available but they limit how many tacos you can cook at one time.

Thermometers

Digital instant-read thermometer

This is a simple tool that is a necessity for checking the internal temperature of larger pieces of meat and poultry. The oven-safe type can be set to the exact temperature you want. An alarm sounds when the desired temperature is achieved. Some thermometers cannot be put directly in the oven but can measure the temperature by probing the roast once removed from the grill or oven.

Candy/deep-fry thermometer

This thermometer is needed for checking the temperature of oil when deep-frying tacos. It records temperatures from 100 to 400°F (38 to 200°C). It is approximately 12 inches (30 cm) long and clips to the side of the pot for safety.

Grills

Selecting a barbecue grill is a very personal choice. Some people like grilling with gas, others prefer the traditional charcoal grills and still others prefer grilling with wood.

A barbecue grill is perfect for grilling meats, fish, poultry and vegetables. Small thin pieces of meat, fish and vegetables cook quickly and are well suited to grilling at high heat levels. However, larger pieces of meat, poultry and fish can be grilled to perfection at lower heat levels. Grilling is a quick and perfect cooking method for many taco fillings.

Gas Grill

Gas grilling is flame cooking with temperatures of up to 600°F (315°C). Gas grills are quick and convenient, with push button ignition systems. They generally have 2 or 3 cooking zones so you can find the right temperature when cooking. Propane adds no flavor as it burns.

Charcoal grill

These grills burn hotter and dryer than propane or gas grills. This causes the high, dry heat of the charcoal to sear the meat more quickly. The high, dry heat caramelizes the proteins in the meat and fish and caramelizes the plant sugars in vegetables and fruits. You can also add wood chunks to charcoal to add a wood flavor to your meats or fish.

Indoor grill

When outdoor grilling is not an option, indoor grills work nicely. There are a wide variety of indoor electric grills. Small, thin pieces of meat, fish and vegetables cook quickly and are well suited to an indoor grill. Indoor grills are quick to heat up and easy to clean. You may not get all of the authentic flavors of outdoor grilling, but you can compensate for that by using spices, glazes and marinades. There are open grills and contact grills, some large, some small. There are many online resources that review grills. Do some research and find the right grilling method and grill for you.

Grilling mitts

Heat resistant, with a long, form-fitting cuff that gives you protection when grilling or deep-frying (see also Heat-resistant kitchen gloves or mitts, right).

Tongs

A long and a short pair is helpful in deep-frying and grilling. Use the long pair of tongs for deep-frying in order to keep your hands and arms away from the hot oil.

Heat-resistant kitchen gloves or mitts

Keeps hands and arms safe when deep-frying and grilling. Look for mitts made with a heat-resistant fiber and nonslip silicone grip. These are generally good for heat up to 400°F (200°C). I like both mitts and gloves. Gloves allow the use of your fingers for more control. You can find these online or in most kitchen supply stores (see also Grilling mitts, left).

Cutting boards

I like to have several cutting boards on hand. An antibacterial cutting board for raw meats, fish and chicken and a couple of favorite wood boards for veggies and cheeses.

Cheese grater

I like to grate and shred my own cheese when I can. A lot of bulk cheeses seem to have more flavor than pre-shredded varieties. Most of the Mexican cheeses will come in bulk form.

Ice cream scooper

I like to create the perfect scoop for my dessert tacos. I find that the ice cream scoopers with the thumb trigger are sometimes difficult to use. But if you use that type, look for one that holds $1/2$ cup (125 mL). I prefer the old-fashioned aluminum scoopers. You can work the ice cream into a perfect ball with ease.

Heavy-duty foil

Heavy-duty foil, as opposed to regular foil, is perfect for creating molds for shaping taco shells (see page 14). The heaviness creates and holds the perfect shape that will withstand the heat of hot oil when deep-frying.

Dry measuring cups

Use plastic or metal measuring cups with flat rims to measure dry ingredients such as flour, sugar, beans and corn masa. They come in graduated sizes ranging from $1/4$ cup (60 mL) to 1 cup (250 mL). Spoon dry ingredients into the appropriate size cup and level off with the flat side of a knife or spatula. I also use these measuring cups to measure chopped vegetables and cheeses.

Liquid measuring cups

Use standard glass or Pyrex measuring cups with spouts to measure water, oil, milk and juice. Place the cup on a flat surface and add liquid until the desired measurement is reached, bending over while pouring so your eye is level with the measure. There are also angled liquid measuring cups that have the measurement line on the inside of the cup. You can measure without bending over to view the measurement.

Whisks

Use a sturdy whisk for sauces, creams, eggs and fillings in order to get well blended results.

Small whisk — select a small whisk for eggs, sauces and marinades. I also use this for mixing spices for rubs.

Large whisk — use a larger whisk for batters, tempuras and cream fillings. If you only buy one whisk select a sturdy medium whisk, which will work for both.

Mixing bowls

A nested set of glass or ceramic mixing bowls will be used quite often. I use small or medium bowls for marinades, salsas, sauces and tossing spices together. I use large bowls for tossing mixed greens, whipping cream fillings and mixing tortilla dough.

Small serving bowls

When serving "family style" it is nice to have a group of small matching bowls (6 to 10 oz/175 to 300 g) for taco garnishes, cheeses and salsas. I use small glass or Pyrex bowls for fresh herbs and spices. I also have a set of brightly colored ceramic bowls that make the condiments look more festive.

Small chafing dish

I use a 5-quart chafing dish for entertaining and serving "family style." I use them to keep tortillas, taco fillings and queso warm. There are a variety of styles and sizes on the market. You can find electric or Sterno-style (Sterno flame disposable burners) chaffing dishes ranging from 4 to 5 quarts.

Hand-held citrus juicer

I use a lot of fresh citrus juice in my salsas and sauces. I also like to accent grilled meats, chicken and fish with fresh lemon and lime juice. A hand-held juicer comes in handy for a quick zest of flavor. You can find heavy plastic ones in bright, fun colors. They also come in aluminum and other metals.

Zester

A Microplane grater is sharp with a fine grate that is perfect for citrus. It makes adding a bit of zest from limes, lemons and oranges to sauces and salsas quick and easy.

Ingredient Essentials

The ingredients in this book make some assumptions about what is standard when it comes to basic ingredients. For the best results, follow the recipe and use the recommended ingredient, unless other options are indicated in a tip or variation. Here is a list of what is assumed:

- All eggs used are large eggs.
- 2% milk and yogurt unless otherwise specified.
- Butter is salted unless otherwise specified.
- Fresh vegetables and fruits are medium-size unless otherwise indicated. Any inedible peels, skins, seeds and cores are removed unless otherwise indicated.
- "Onions" means regular cooking onions unless otherwise indicated.
- "Mushrooms" means white button mushrooms unless otherwise indicated.
- With canned tomatoes and tomato products, the juice is also used unless the recipe instructs you to drain it.
- When broth (chicken, beef or vegetable) is called for, homemade is the ideal, but ready-to-use broth in Tetra Paks comes a close second. If you can only find canned broth, make sure to dilute it as directed on the can before use.
- Canned soups are used undiluted unless otherwise specified.
- Chopped or minced garlic is freshly chopped or minced, not purchased already minced and preserved.

Common Ingredients

Tortillas

Tortillas are available in corn and flour. Handmade tortillas are delicious and easy to make (see page 9). Store-bought or fresh tortillas made at your local tortilla factory also work well. The key to a great taco is to use the freshest tortillas possible and warm them before using so they are pliable. Available in 4-, 6- or 8-inch (10, 15 or 20 cm) sizes.

Corn tortillas

Corn tortillas are round thin flatbreads made from corn masa or corn flour. They average about 40 calories, less than 1 gram of fat and about 12 grams of carbohydrates. You can buy yellow, white and blue corn tortillas. Blue corn has more protein and less starch than white corn. Corn tortillas can be frozen in an airtight container and defrosted and reheated when ready to use.

Flour tortillas

Flour tortillas are round thin unleavened Mexican flatbreads, made from wheat flour. There is an increasing variety of tortillas on the market, from whole wheat and multigrain to fat-free and carb-balanced. Flavored tortillas such as spinach herb, jalapeño, Cheddar, sun-dried tomato and garlic herb are just a few of the varieties available. Size generally ranges from 4- to 10-inches (10 to 25 cm). Flour tortillas can be frozen in an airtight container and defrosted and reheated when ready to use.

Wonton skins

Thin sheets of dough made of flour, egg and salt used to wrap fillings.

Flour

You can make tortillas with a combination of whole wheat and all-purpose flour.

Masa harina

A dry form of corn, masa is made from white corn that has been treated with mineral lime and then stone ground. It is used to make fresh corn tortillas and tamales.

Oils

Peanut oil

I like to use organic oil derived from peanuts. It's perfect for deep-frying tacos and taco shells because it has a high-smoke point. They fry faster and seem to be crispier.

Vegetable oil

This oil is very versatile. It adds no taste or flavor to foods. It works well for deep-frying tacos and taco shells. I use vegetable oil for sautéing meats and vegetables when I do not want to add additional flavor.

Olive oil

Derived from the olive tree, this oil has health benefits and adds a nice hint of flavor to sautéed meats and vegetables. Flavors are added to salsas and sauces as well. Olive oils range in flavor from mild and extra light, to bold, rich and fruity. I use the bolder flavors when sautéing with garlic and onion and the lighter flavors when adding to sauces, marinades and salsas.

Nonstick cooking spray

I use nonstick cooking spray for a variety of taco techniques. For taco fillings I coat the meat, chicken or fish surface with cooking spray so the spices will stick to it before roasting or grilling and no extra flavor will be added. For some tacos shells and wraps, I spray the corn and flour tortillas lightly before skillet warming for a lightly toasted texture. When making dessert taco shells, I use cooking spray to coat the tortillas before baking to form a shell. There are quite a few flavored sprays such as olive oil and butter. Test them out and see what you prefer. I also use cooking spray to coat skillets and baking sheets. Look for the cooking spray specifically for grilling to coat your barbecue grill.

Chiles

Chipotle chile in adobo sauce
Dried jalapeños marinated in a smoky sauce made of onions, tomato and garlic. It is generally canned and is available in the Mexican food section at the market.

Dried red chile pods
Usually rehydrated and blended and used in sauces. Available in plastic bags in the Mexican food section at the market.

Habanero
Small and orange. Known as one of the hottest chiles in the world. Available fresh in the produce section at the market.

Jalapeño
Small bright green chile. They range from mild to hot, used in salsas, sauces and many Mexican dishes. Available fresh in the produce section at the market.

Pickled jalapeños
Small bright green chile, marinated in an oil, vinegar and herb solution. Available canned or bottled in the Mexican food or condiment section at the market.

New Mexico or Anaheim
Long thin green chile pepper with medium to hot varieties. Used in salsas and sauces. Tastes best when roasted, seeded and peeled (see page 49). Available fresh in the produce section of the market.

Regional crops are in season during the early fall months but imports are available most of the year. Roasted green chile can also be found in most frozen food sections at the market or online.

Poblano
Larger chile used in salsas and sauces. Rich, earthy flavor, mild to medium in heat. Tastes best when roasted, seeded and peeled. Available fresh in the produce section of the market.

Serrano
Small thin green chile, usually hotter than a jalapeño. Available fresh in the produce section of the market.

Yellow chile
Yellow, waxy appearance, mild in flavor. Available fresh in the produce section of the market.

Vegetables

Avocados
This vegetable has a creamy texture and exceptional nutrients, including antioxidants. It adds a natural buttery flavor when used to garnish a taco or thicken a salsa.

Bell peppers
Large peppers that are mild in taste. There is no heat in their flavor. Red bells are sweeter than the green or orange.

Cabbage
Cabbage comes in red and green varieties. This fresh vegetable makes the perfect garnish and is available year round. These two types of cabbage add color and texture to any taco. I like to use red when I think I need more color in my taco recipe. For example a white fish with a white sauce needs a splash of color. So I add Pico de Gallo (page 305) and red and green cabbage.

Corn
This vegetable is a good source of B vitamins and adds fiber to the diet. It has a hint of sweetness and blends well with chile in salsas.

Garlic

Garlic is a pungent bulb that has a sharp and strong flavor. It adds a depth of flavor to sautéed fillings, marinades, sauces and salsas.

Green onion

These little onions, also known as scallions, add a sharp flavor to tacos and salsas. The crunchy texture makes them good to use as a garnish.

Lettuces

Iceberg lettuce

This lettuce is mild in flavor but the crunchy texture adds a refreshing garnish to tacos.

Romaine

This leafy green lettuce adds a lot of color along with texture as a garnish for tacos.

Salad mix

There are a variety of salad mixes with a wide range of flavors on the market. There are red and green lettuce varieties that range in taste from intense bittery spice to sweet and mild. "Living" lettuce and "artisan" lettuce and greens are also available. Many are available prewashed and packaged in your produce section. Taste and compare to find your favorite combination of greens.

Jicama

Jicama is a Mexican root plant that is creamy white with a crisp, distinctive texture. It is mild in taste and adds texture to salsas and fillings.

Onions

Onions are available in yellow, white and red varieties. They vary in taste and flavor. Look for mild-tasting onions, such as white onions, to blend with chile and add to salsas. If you are looking to sweeten a sauce or salsa, use red onions, or onions specifically labeled "sweet onions." They will add a bit of a sweet flavor to your recipes.

Potato

This versatile root vegetable can take on other flavors and make delicious fillings for tacos. I use a basic Russet potato in most taco recipes. However, experiment with golden potatoes for a more buttery flavor or new potatoes for a fresher, sweeter flavor.

Spinach

This leafy green is high in choline and folic acid and is an appetizing garnish for tacos. I team fresh spinach with a variety of meats, vegetables, cheeses and seafood for delicious taco fillings.

Tomatoes, fresh and canned

Fresh and canned are both perfect for fresh salsas, enhancing the flavorful chile and spices. I like ripe greenhouse tomatoes for fresh vegetables salsas, Pico de Gallo and as a garnish for tacos. I use canned tomatoes in cooking sauces and stews. Canned tomatoes are convenient and easy to keep on hand. There is a growing variety of flavors offered in canned tomatoes, such as roasted garlic, balsamic, basil and oil, and green pepper, celery and onions. An unflavored canned diced tomato works best unless otherwise noted.

Tomatillos

A small green tomato-like fruit covered in a green filmy husk. It has a citrusy flavor and is perfect for sauces and salsas.

Zucchini

This vegetable can be eaten raw or cooked. I use it sautéed in taco fillings and uncooked for garnish and in salsas.

Fruits

Apples

A fruit that adds a natural sweetness, fiber and texture to salsas and sauces. I like the sweet-sour tartness of Golden and Delicious Apples along with Granny Smith.

Lemons

A citrusy fruit high in vitamin C and limonene. It adds a sharp taste and complements vegetable and fruit combinations in taco toppings and sweet and savory salsas. Adding a zest of the lemon rind to salsas and sauces adds another hint of fresh flavor. Juicing a fresh lemon generally yields about 2 to 3 tbsp (30 to 45 mL) of fresh juice. Roll a room temperature lemon on the counter a few times to maximize the amount of juice. Fresh lemon juice has a lighter, zestier flavor than bottled juice.

Limes

A fruit high in vitamin C that adds refreshing citrusy flavor to vegetable toppings and salsas. Heightens the taste of chile. Freshly squeezed lime juice has a fresher, lighter taste than bottled juice. Zesting the rind of a lime for salsas and sauces adds flavor and color.

Mangos

A fruit high in vitamin A. It has a sweet pineapple-banana flavor. The texture is smooth and velvety. Select a mango that is firm yet just soft to the touch.

Oranges

Orange is a citrusy fruit high in vitamin C and limonene. It is citrusy, yet sweeter than lemons and limes. Adds flavor to marinades for meats and sauces and makes a good sweet salsa.

Pineapple

A fruit high in vitamin C. It is a very sweet fruit with good texture for sweet salsas. It blends well with a variety of chile peppers. You can use fresh or canned pineapple. Canned pineapple can be a bit sweeter and more consistent than fresh pineapple. There are a variety of cuts available in canned pineapple, such as chunky, tidbits, rings and crushed. Drain if directed in recipe. A fresh pineapple needs to have the skin removed and the center removed, then cut to desired size chunks.

Legumes and Grains

Black beans

Black, shiny kidney-shaped beans with an earthy flavor. They blend well with meats and cook well in stews. You can use dry or canned. Dried black beans are best cooked like pinto beans (page 265). The canned beans are nice and firm and should be rinsed before using.

Pinto beans

Pinto beans are a fat-free, high-protein legume that adds fiber to taco fillings. After being cooked (page 265) they can be smashed and reheated for a popular refried bean filling (page 273). Canned pinto beans are a convenient choice and have good flavor and texture.

Red beans

Also known as kidney beans. They have a good texture and rich flavor when cooked (page 265). Canned kidney beans are available. They are a bit softer but work well in taco fillings.

Rice

Cooked rice adds fiber and taste to taco fillings. It is also an economical way to expand the volume of taco fillings. It lends itself to herbs, spices and flavorings. Nutritional value is abundant in brown rice and can be used as a healthier option. White long-grain rice is more prevalent in Mexican food. It is longer and stays separate, allowing each grain to grab and hold flavors and spices. Short-grain rice is a moister round grain that does not work as well in taco fillings.

Herbs and Spices

Herbs

Cilantro
A leafy green flat-leaf herb that has a distinctive pungent flavor. It is used widely in Mexican cuisine, especially as a garnish and in salsas.

Italian flat-leaf parsley
This is a mild herb that adds color and texture to marinades and sauces.

Rosemary
Rosemary is an aromatic herb that has a pine and citrus flavor. It is used in rubs and marinades.

Spices

Cayenne pepper
This is a chile powder that has a hot edgy flavor to it. It spices up sauces, stews and salsas.

Cinnamon
This is a fragrant spice that blends well with fruits and chocolate. It has a spicy clove flavor to it.

Cumin
Earthy, nutty flavor and aroma. Just a pinch adds flavor to sauces and marinades.

Hot pepper flakes
These flakes come from hot dried red peppers and add heat to salsas, marinades and sauces.

Seasonings and Blends

Cajun seasoning
Cajun seasoning is usually a blend of garlic, pungent chile spices, peppers, sea salt, onion and paprika. Look for spice blends in your market or online.

Caribbean jerk seasoning
There are a variety of seasoning blends on the market. Dry Caribbean spice mix is a blend of dried and minced chile peppers combined with allspice, a variety of salts and peppers. Some are very spicy; others are mild. Test a few until you find a favorite.

Creole seasoning
Creole seasoning, unlike Cajun, is a milder, more traditional flavor from the South. It is usually a blend of cayenne pepper, garlic powder, black pepper, salt and paprika.

Garlic and herb seasoning
Dry garlic and herb blends vary in taste and flavor combinations. Some blends combine up to 20 spices and herbs. Try a few and find your favorite.

Italian seasoning
A combination of dry herbs and spices such as basil, marjoram, oregano and sage.

Margarita mix
Select a liquid margarita mix that is not too tart but evenly balanced in flavor. I like to use Jose Cuervo liquid margarita mix.

Mesquite seasoning blends
There are a variety of mesquite seasoning blends on the market. Most offer a granular blend of spices ranging from sweet to salty with mild heat and smoky flavors. Check your local market or go online.

Cheese Varieties

Soft cheese

Cream cheese is a mild soft white cheese make from cow's cream and milk. Whipped cream cheese, which is a favorite of mine, has air whipped into it. It is easy to use and does not need to be softened.

Semisoft cheese

Feta cheese has a texture that can range from soft to semisoft. It is a brined curd white cheese with a crumbly texture and is traditionally made in Greece.

Panela and Queso Fresco are fresh cheeses with a crumbly texture that taste like a combination of Monterey Jack and mozzarella cheese. Their main characteristic is that they do not melt, but will get soft when warmed. They are mild and differ in taste slightly, but add a lightly salted cheese flavor when used as a garnish for tacos, burritos, beans, casseroles and more.

Semifirm cheese

Cheddar is a semifirm cow's milk cheese that originated in England. Its flavor ranges from mild to sharp depending on the length of aging.

Monterey Jack is an American semifirm cheese that has creamy mild flavor and is white in color. It is a melting cheese.

Swiss cheese is white in color with holes in its texture. It has a mild, buttery, almost fruit-like flavor.

Hard cheese

Añejo enchilado is a firm Mexican aged (añejo means "aged") cheese that is rolled in paprika. It is used as a stuffing or topping for enchiladas, burritos or tacos.

Cotija is a hard Mexican cow's milk cheese, originating in the Mexican town of Cotija. It has a strong flavor and grating properties from its dry crumbly texture. This cheese is salted and then aged for up to one year. It's used to garnish and top tacos, adding a flavorful garnish to Mexican dishes. It's also used to mix in directly with other ingredients to enhance the flavor. It is tagged as the Parmesan of Mexico.

Parmesan is a dense hard Italian cheese that is dry and sharp. It is aged for two or more years. It has a sharp, pungent flavor.

Blue cheese

Blue cheese is a crumbly white cheese that is visibly marbled with blue-green mold. It has a tart, sharp flavor.

Melting cheese

Asadero, Queso Blanco, Queso Quesadilla and Manchego cheeses are among many cheeses that melt easily and are used in quesadillas and many Mexican recipes due to their creamy and rich elements. Asadero cheese has a smooth texture, is yellow in color and has a tangy yet mild flavor. Queso Blanco and Queso Quesadilla cheeses are mild in flavor and white in color. Manchego is a buttery yellow cheese with a salty, nutty flavor.

Mexican Food Definitions

Adobo sauce: A smoky chile-based sauce most often made with garlic, vinegar and chile peppers.

Anaheim chile see Chiles (page 22).

Antojitos: A Mexican street snack that means "little whims" or "craving." It is an appetizer or small portion of something.

Carne: Refers to meats, such as pork and beef.

Carne asada: Means "roasted meat," most-often meat cooked over coals.

Carnitas: Means "little meats" and refers to a simmered pork filling for tacos or burritos.

Ceviche: Raw fish marinated in lime juice accompanied by diced chile, tomato and onion.

Chile rellenos: A large green chile pepper, such as Anahiem or New Mexico, stuffed with cheese, then dipped in an egg batter and lightly fried.

Chipotle see Chiles (page 22).

Cilantro see Herbs (page 25).

Corn masa: A dough of ground corn meal, lime and water, used to make corn tortillas.

Corn masa harina: see Masa harina (page 21).

Cotija see Cheese (page 26).

Crispy folded taco: A corn or flour tortilla deep-fried in the shape of a "U" and filled with taco filling of either beef, chicken, fish or veggies.

Cupitas: Mexican slang for small crispy, corn or flour tortillas shaped into a cup form.

Dulce: Means "sweet" and refers to sweets or candy.

Elote: The Mexican name for fresh corn on the cob.

Empanada: A pastry turnover filled with spicy meat or fruit.

Enchilada: A lightly fried corn or flour tortilla dipped in red or green chile sauce and filled with either cheese, meat or chicken and rolled.

Escabeche: A mixture of oil, vinegar and herbs used to pickle jalapeños, onions and carrots.

Fajita: A traditional Tex-Mex dish of grilled beef, chicken or shrimp, sliced and served with grilled onions and peppers. It is served with fresh tortillas and garnishes on the side. Once served the filling is then placed into the tortillas and garnished with fresh produce.

Flauta: A flour tortilla filled with chicken, beef or beans and rolled and deep-fried.

Folded taco: Flour or corn tortilla folded in half and stuffed with filling. The tortilla can be soft or crispy.

Frijoles: Dried beans. *Rijoles refritos* refers to refried beans (see also Refried Beans).

Guacamole: A creamy dip or garnish made with mashed avocado, onions, chiles, tomato and lime juice.

Habanero chile see Chiles (page 22).

Huevos: Spanish for "eggs."

Jicama see Vegetables (page 23).

Leche: Spanish for "milk."

Mexican chorizo: A locally made fresh sausage with red chiles and pork.

Nachitos: Mexican slang for mini nachos. Nachos are a Mexican appetizer of crispy tortilla chips covered in melted cheese and topped with a jalapeño slice.

Quesadillas: A flour or corn tortilla stuffed with cheese and grilled until the cheese is melted.

Queso: Spanish for "cheese." Referred to as melted cheese.

Refried beans: Cooked and mashed pinto beans sautéed or "refried" with oil or lard.

Rolled taco: A 6-inch (15 cm) corn tortilla filled either with chicken, beef or beans, then rolled and deep-fried.

Salsa: A condiment made of a combination of vegetables, fruits and chiles, served with chips or over Mexican dishes.

Sangria: Spanish wine punch made with brandy, red wine, liqueur and fresh fruit.

Taquito: Miniature rolled tacos.

Tequila: A liquor originating in Mexico made of distilled juice of the agave plant. It is popular in Margaritas.

Tomatillo see Vegetables (page 23).

Chicken and Turkey

Chicken

continued…

Turkey

Poached Chicken

*Lightly poached chicken
breasts seasoned with
garlic and onion make
an uncomplicated
filling for chicken tacos.*

Tips

To reheat chicken: Place
desired amount in a
microwave-safe bowl.
Cover and microwave
on High for 1 minute.
Remove and stir.
Repeat until chicken
is completely warmed
through, 2 to 3 minutes.

Chicken breasts are
generally 5 oz (150 g)
each. Once cooked and
shredded, they yield
about ½ cup (125 mL)
of cooked chicken.
I generally allow for 2 to
3 ounces (60 to 90 g) of
cooked chicken per taco.

1½ lbs	boneless skinless chicken breasts	750 g
3	cloves garlic	3
1	onion, cut into quarters	1

1. Place chicken in a large pot and fill with enough water to cover the chicken by 2 inches (5 cm). Add onion and garlic and bring to a gentle boil over medium heat. Reduce heat and simmer gently until chicken is tender and no longer pink inside, 18 to 20 minutes.

2. Transfer chicken to a bowl. Discard broth, garlic and onions. Use broth in another recipe. Let chicken cool for 10 to 12 minutes. Shred chicken with your fingers or two forks. Use immediately or let cool completely and place in a resealable plastic bag. Refrigerate for up to 2 days or freeze for up to 4 months.

Roasted Chicken

**Makes about
4 cups (1 L)**

*Roasted chicken is a
flavorful filling that is
moist and succulent,
adding texture and
flavor to each taco
recipe.*

Tips

When I am pressed for
time I pick up a roasted
chicken from the deli
section of my grocery
store.

For added robust flavor,
include bits and pieces of
the crispy seasoned skin
of the chicken.

- Preheat oven to 375°F (190°C)
- Roasting pan
- Instant-read thermometer

1	whole chicken (about 4 lbs/2 kg) (see Tips, left)	1
3 tbsp	unsalted butter, melted	45 mL
1 tsp	salt	5 mL
1 tsp	freshly ground black pepper	5 mL

1. Remove giblets and excess fat from chicken. Rinse chicken, pat dry and place in roasting pan. Brush chicken with butter and sprinkle with salt and pepper. Tie legs together with kitchen string and tuck wings underneath chicken.

2. Roast chicken in preheated oven until an instant-read thermometer inserted in the thickest part of the thigh registers 165°F (74°C) and juices run clear, about 1½ hours. Tent with foil and let stand for 20 minutes. Remove and discard skin (see Tips, left) and bones from chicken. Shred chicken with fingers or two forks or cut into about ¼-inch (0.5 cm) dice. Use immediately or let cool completely and place in a resealable plastic bag. Refrigerate for up to 2 days or freeze for up to 4 months.

Classic Shredded Chicken Tacos

Makes 8 tacos

This is an everyday classic found in many Mexican kitchens. The chicken filling is a favorite because it goes well with almost any sauce or salsa. The fresh fried tortillas are both crispy and soft, which adds a distinctive texture to these tacos.

Tips

I prefer making my own crispy taco shells. They will be hot, crispy and delicious. Directions on taco shell "how-tos" are on page 14. However, when I am short on time I do buy high-quality prepared taco shells. Check your local grocery store and test the different brands. I tend to like the true Mexican brands because they taste more authentic to me.

Serve these tacos with Cilantro Chile Sauce (page 325) or Pico de Gallo (page 305).

3 cups	shredded cooked chicken, warmed (see pages 31 and 32 and Tip, page 39)	750 mL
	Salt and freshly ground black pepper	
8	taco shells (see Tips, left)	8
2 cups	shredded lettuce	500 mL
1 cup	shredded Cheddar cheese	250 mL
1	onion, minced	1
1	tomato, seeded and diced	1

1. In a large bowl, toss chicken with salt and pepper to taste.

2. To build tacos, divide chicken equally among taco shells. Top chicken with lettuce, cheese, onion and tomato. Fold tortillas in half.

Classic Rolled Chicken Tacos

Makes 24 rolled tacos

I grew up on rolled tacos; hot, fresh little flute-like tacos we could dip in salsa, refried beans or queso. These tightly rolled tacos are quick to crisp and a perfect taco classic for a crowd.

Tips

Do not overcook these tacos; crispy on the ends and soft in the middle is a perfect rolled taco.

I recommend these sauces and salsas: Fiesta Taco Sauce (page 324), Chimichurri Sauce (page 328) and Chile con Queso (page 315).

Variation

For a fresh, spicy flavor, add ½ cup (125 mL) chopped roasted New Mexico or Anaheim green chile peppers (see page 49) to shredded chicken.

• Candy/deep-fry thermometer

3 cups	shredded cooked chicken (see pages 31 and 32)	750 mL
	Salt	
24	6-inch (15 cm) corn tortillas, micro-warmed (page 15)	24
	Vegetable oil	

1. In a large bowl, thoroughly combine chicken and ¾ tsp (3 mL) salt.

2. To build tacos, place 2 tbsp (30 mL) of chicken at one end of each tortilla. Gently roll tortilla and secure with a toothpick. Deep-fry immediately or place rolled tacos in a resealable plastic bag to keep them moist. Refrigerate until ready to cook for up to 2 days or place in freezer for up to 4 months. Thaw completely before cooking.

3. Fill a deep-fryer, deep heavy pot or deep skillet with 3 inches (7.5 cm) of oil and heat to 350°F (180°C). Using tongs, gently place 3 to 4 tacos into the hot oil and deep-fry, turning once, until golden brown and crispy on the ends and a bit soft in the middle, 2 to 3 minutes. Drain on paper towels. Lightly season tacos with salt. Serve 3 or 4 per person.

Tres Taquitos with Chicken and Guacamole

Makes 36 rolled tacos

A taquito is a fresh, last-minute appetizer that will go quickly. This smaller, skinnier version of the classic rolled taco has a bit less filling and is rolled tighter. I like to serve these tasty little tacos with rich, creamy guacamole or hot bubbling queso.

Tip

I like to pack 12 uncooked tacos in a quart (1 L) size resealable plastic bag and place in the freezer for up to 4 months. When you are ready to cook, thaw completely in the refrigerator and cook as directed.

- Candy/deep-fry thermometer

3 cups	shredded cooked chicken (see pages 31 and 32)	750 mL
	Salt	
36	6-inch (15 cm) corn tortillas, micro-warmed (page 15)	36
	Vegetable oil	
	Guacamole (page 316)	
2 cups	shredded Cheddar cheese	500 mL

1. In a large bowl, thoroughly combine shredded chicken and ¾ tsp (3 mL) salt.

2. To build tacos, place 1 heaping tbsp (15 mL) of chicken at one end of each tortilla. Gently roll tortilla and secure with a toothpick. Deep-fry immediately or place rolled tacos in a resealable plastic bag to keep moist. Refrigerate until ready to cook for up to 2 days.

3. Fill a deep-fryer, deep heavy pot or deep skillet with 3 inches (7.5 cm) of oil and heat to 350°F (180°C). Using tongs, gently place 3 to 4 tacos at a time into the hot oil and deep-fry, turning once, until golden brown and crispy on the ends and a bit soft in the middle, 2 to 3 minutes. Drain on paper towels. Lightly season tacos with salt. To serve, place 3 taquitos side by side on a plate and top with guacamole and sprinkle with cheese.

Sonoran Chicken Flautas

Makes 12 rolled tacos

Creating a deep-fried rolled taco with a flour tortilla is a bit unusual unless you are familiar with Sonoran-style Mexican cuisine. Generations have enjoyed flaky, crisp flautas, another one of Mexico's gifts to the world.

Tips

You do not need to seal the ends. The taco looks like a small flute.

I like to pack 12 uncooked tacos in a quart (1 L) size resealable plastic bag and place in the freezer for up to 4 months. When you are ready to cook, thaw completely in the refrigerator and cook as directed.

Serve with Fiesta Taco Sauce (page 324) or Poblano Sauce (page 320).

Variation

Miniature Sonoran Tacos: Cut six 10-inch (25 cm) flour tortillas into 4 wedges each. Place 1 tbsp (15 mL) of chicken filling in the middle of the widest part of the tortilla wedge, shaping the filling into a short, straight line. Roll up the tortilla and filling and secure with a toothpick. Continue with Step 3. Serve with a variety of dipping sauces.

- Candy/deep-fry thermometer

3 cups	shredded cooked chicken (see pages 31 and 32)	750 mL
	Salt	
12	6-inch (15 cm) flour tortillas (see Tips, page 41), micro- or skillet-warmed (page 15)	12
	Vegetable oil	

1. In a large bowl, combine chicken and ¾ tsp (3 mL) salt.

2. To build tacos, divide shredded chicken equally among tortillas. Place chicken at one end of each tortilla. Gently roll tortilla and secure with a toothpick (see Tips, left). Deep-fry immediately or place rolled tacos in a resealable plastic bag to keep moist. Refrigerate until ready to cook for up to 2 days.

3. Fill a deep-fryer, deep heavy pot or deep skillet with 3 inches (7.5 cm) of oil and heat to 350°F (180°C). Using tongs, gently place 4 tacos at a time in the hot oil and deep-fry, turning once, until crispy and golden brown, about 2 minutes. Drain on paper towels. Lightly season with salt.

Shredded Chicken Crispy Tacos with Cilantro Lime Sour Cream

Folded tacos are simple to master. Fry the shells to perfection and stuff them until they are overflowing with flavor. Cilantro lime sauce is a tantalizing flavor enhancer.

Tip

I prefer making my own crispy taco shells. They will be hot, crispy and delicious. Directions on taco shell "how-tos" are on page 14. However, when I am short on time I do buy high-quality prepared taco shells. Check your local grocery store and test the different brands. I tend to like the true Mexican brands because they taste more authentic to me.

1 cup	sour cream	250 mL
2 tbsp	plain yogurt	30 mL
1 tbsp	minced cilantro	15 mL
	Juice of 1 lime	
3 cups	shredded cooked chicken, warmed (see pages 31 and 32)	750 mL
4	green onions, green part only, minced	4
	Salt and freshly ground black pepper	
8	taco shells (see Tip, left)	8
1½ cups	shredded lettuce	375 mL
1 cup	shredded Monterey Jack cheese	250 mL
1	tomato, seeded and diced	1

1. In a small bowl, combine sour cream, yogurt, cilantro and lime juice. Transfer to an airtight container or squeeze bottle and refrigerate for 30 minutes or for up to 2 hours.

2. In a large bowl, toss chicken with green onions and salt and pepper to taste.

3. To build tacos, divide chicken mixture equally among taco shells. Top with lettuce, cheese and sour cream mixture. Garnish with tomato.

Red Chile Chicken Tacos

Flavors of the southwest transform this taco into a culinary favorite. Chicken coated in a rich, spicy red sauce tempered with a little spice is soulfully satisfying.

Tips

Serve with Garlic Sour Cream (page 321), Fresh Red Chile Sauce (page 318) or Jalapeño Cream Sauce (page 323).

I like to pack 12 uncooked tacos in a quart (1 L) size resealable plastic bag and place in the freezer for up to 4 months. When you are ready to cook, thaw completely in the refrigerator and cook as directed.

- Candy/deep-fry thermometer

1 cup	red enchilada sauce	250 mL
1	clove garlic, minced	1
3 cups	shredded cooked chicken (see pages 31 and 32)	750 mL
	Salt and freshly ground black pepper	
24	6-inch (15 cm) corn tortillas, micro-warmed (page 15)	24
	Vegetable oil	

1. In a large skillet over medium heat, combine enchilada sauce and garlic. Add chicken and sauté until chicken is well coated and heated through, 4 to 6 minutes. Season with salt and pepper to taste. Let cool.

2. To build tacos, place 2 tbsp (30 mL) of chicken at one end of each tortilla. Gently roll tortilla and secure with a toothpick. Deep-fry immediately or place rolled tacos in a resealable plastic bag to keep moist. Refrigerate until ready to cook for up to 2 days.

3. Fill a deep-fryer, deep heavy pot or deep skillet with 3 inches (7.5 cm) of oil and heat to 350°F (180°C). Using tongs, gently place 4 tacos at a time into hot oil and deep-fry, turning once, until crispy and golden brown, 2 to 3 minutes. Drain on paper towels.

Roasted Chicken Tacos with Tomatillo Avocado Salsa

Whether I buy a roasted chicken or cook my own, I always include bits and pieces of the crispy seasoned skin of the chicken for a robust, flavorful filling. The adventurous citrusy taste of the tomatillo salsa adds a delicious topper to this taco.

Tip

When I am pressed for time I pick up a roasted chicken from the deli section of my grocery store. Typically one 4-lb (2 kg) roasted cooked chicken will yield approximately 4 cups (1 L) of cooked diced chicken.

1 tbsp	olive oil	15 mL
1	clove garlic, minced	1
½ cup	chopped onion	125 mL
3 cups	diced roasted chicken (see Tip, left and page 32)	750 mL
	Salt and freshly ground black pepper	
8	6-inch (15 cm) corn tortillas, skillet-warmed (page 15)	8
1 cup	shredded Monterey Jack cheese	250 mL
	Tomatillo Avocado Salsa (page 304)	

1. In a large skillet, heat oil over medium heat. Sauté garlic and onion until onion is translucent, about 5 minutes. Add chicken and sauté until chicken is heated through, about 12 minutes. Season with salt and pepper to taste.

2. To build tacos, divide chicken equally among tortillas. Top with cheese and Tomatillo Avocado Salsa. Fold tortillas in half.

Ten-Minute Chicken Tacos

There are many days that I just don't have enough time to create a delicious meal from scratch. That is why this chicken taco recipe is number one on my list. I just swing by the market and grab a fresh roasted chicken and dinner is ready in minutes.

Tip

Measure out 3 cups (750 mL) of chicken for this recipe. Reserve remaining chicken for future recipes. Place in an airtight container and freeze for up to 4 months.

Variation

Follow Step 1, then toss lettuce mixture with $1/4$ cup (60 mL) Italian dressing and 1 tsp (5 mL) puréed chipotle chile in adobo sauce.

1 cup	chopped romaine lettuce	250 mL
1 cup	chopped fresh spinach	250 mL
3 cups	warm shredded deli-roasted chicken (see Tip, left)	750 mL
8	6-inch (15 cm) corn tortillas, skillet-warmed (page 15)	8
2	ripe avocados, diced	2
1	red onion, minced	1
$1/2$ cup	shredded Monterey Jack cheese	125 mL

1. In a medium bowl, combine lettuce and spinach.

2. To build tacos, divide chicken equally among tortillas. Top with lettuce mixture, avocados, red onion and cheese. Fold tortillas in half.

Grilled Chicken Breast Tacos with Chipotle Ranch Sauce

Light seasoning and grilling add a familiar earthiness to the flavor of these tacos. Spicy, creamy sauce adds a fresh and contemporary flavor.

Tips

Chicken breasts are generally 5 oz (150 g) each. Once cooked and shredded they yield about ½ cup (125 mL) of cooked chicken. I generally allow for 2 to 3 oz (60 to 90 g) of cooked chicken per taco.

The perfect size tortilla for a taco is 6 inches (15 cm). It is generally more available in corn rather than flour. Buy 8-inch (20 cm) flour tortillas and trim them with a pair of kitchen shears to 6 inches (15 cm) using a corn tortilla as a template.

• Barbecue grill

1½ lbs	boneless skinless chicken breasts (see Tips, left)	750 g
	Juice of 1 lemon	
1 tbsp	olive oil	15 mL
1	clove garlic, minced	1
2 tsp	kosher salt	10 mL
1 tsp	cracked black peppercorns	5 mL
8	6- to 8-inch (15 to 20 cm) corn or flour tortillas (see Tips, left)	8
2 cups	chopped salad mix (see Tip, page 53)	500 mL
1 cup	crumbled Cotija or grated Parmesan cheese	250 mL
1	avocado, diced	1
	Chipotle Ranch Sauce (page 326)	

1. Place chicken in a resealable plastic bag. Add lemon juice, oil, garlic, salt and peppercorns. Refrigerate for at least 2 hours or for up to 24 hours.

2. Preheat greased grill to medium-high heat. Remove chicken from marinade and discard marinade. Grill chicken, turning once, until no longer pink inside, 6 to 8 minutes per side. Transfer chicken to a cutting board and let stand for 6 to 8 minutes. Cut into bite-size pieces.

3. To build tacos, skillet warm tortillas (page 15). Divide chicken equally among tortillas. Top with salad mix, cheese and avocado. Drizzle with Chipotle Ranch Sauce. Fold tortillas in half.

Brined Chicken Breast Tacos

Brining provides a juicier, more flavorful filling for this taco. The combination of salt and sugar adds balance in flavor from the inside out.

Tip

If grilling chicken ahead, cover with foil, and keep warm in a preheated 200°F (100°C) oven.

• Barbecue grill

4 cups	water	1 L
3 tbsp	kosher salt	45 mL
3 tbsp	granulated sugar	45 mL
1½ lbs	boneless skinless chicken breasts (see Tip, page 41)	750 g
8	6- to 8-inch (15 to 20 cm) corn tortillas	8
1 cup	sour cream	250 mL
2 tbsp	minced cilantro	30 mL
	Pico de Gallo (page 305)	

1. In a large airtight container, whisk together water, salt and sugar until salt and sugar dissolve. Add chicken. Cover and refrigerate in brine for at least 1½ hours or for up to 4 hours.

2. Preheat greased grill to medium-high heat. Remove chicken from brine and discard brine. Grill chicken, turning once, until no longer pink inside, 6 to 8 minutes per side. Transfer chicken to a cutting board and let stand for 6 to 8 minutes. Cut into bite-size pieces.

3. To build tacos, skillet warm tortillas (page 15). Divide chicken equally among tortillas. Top with sour cream, cilantro and Pico de Gallo. Fold tortillas in half.

Beer-Marinated Chicken Tacos

Marinades are a grand way to import flavor, especially in chicken. This sweet, savory chicken taco is a summer favorite at our house.

Variation
Add 1 tbsp (15 mL) sharp Cheddar cheese on each taco.

- Barbecue grill
- Instant-read thermometer

½ cup	dark beer	125 mL
2 tbsp	liquid honey	30 mL
1 tbsp	olive oil	15 mL
1 tbsp	Dijon mustard	15 mL
2	cloves garlic, minced	2
2 lbs	chicken pieces	1 kg
8	6-inch (15 cm) corn tortillas	8
2 cups	chopped romaine lettuce	500 mL
1	tomato, seeded and diced	1
	Chile Cream Sauce (page 327)	

1. In a large resealable plastic bag, combine beer, honey, oil, mustard and garlic. Add chicken, seal bag and work marinade into chicken with your fingers. Refrigerate for at least 3 hours or for up to 8 hours.

2. Preheat greased grill to medium heat. Remove chicken from marinade and discard marinade. Grill chicken, turning once, until juices run clear for legs and thighs or breasts are no longer pink inside or an instant-read thermometer inserted into the thickest part registers 165°F (74°C), 8 to 12 minutes per side. Let chicken stand for 6 to 8 minutes. Remove chicken from bone and discard bone and skin.

3. To build tacos, skillet warm tortillas (page 15). Divide chicken equally among tortillas. Top with lettuce, tomato and Chile Cream Sauce. Fold tortillas in half.

Sizzlin' Chicken Fajita Tacos

Makes 8 tacos

Fajitas have become a classic in America. These Tex-Mex favorites are loved around the globe. Fajita tacos are even better!

Variations

Add more texture with 1½ cups (375 mL) chopped salad mix divided equally among tacos.

Replace Chile Cream Sauce with Pico de Gallo (page 305).

2 tbsp	olive oil, divided	30 mL
1½ lbs	boneless skinless chicken breasts, sliced into strips (see Tip, page 41)	750 g
1	onion, sliced into ¼-inch (0.5 cm) rings	1
1	red bell pepper, julienned	1
1	orange bell pepper, julienned	1
	Salt and freshly ground black pepper	
8	6- to 8-inch (15 to 20 cm) corn or flour tortillas (see Tip, page 41), skillet-warmed (page 15)	8
1½ cups	shredded sharp Cheddar cheese	375 mL
	Chile Cream Sauce (page 327)	
2	limes, each cut into 6 wedges	2

1. In a large skillet, heat 1 tbsp (15 mL) of the oil over medium heat. Sauté chicken until chicken is no longer pink inside and juices have evaporated, 12 to 14 minutes. Remove chicken from skillet and set aside.

2. Add remaining 1 tbsp (15 mL) of oil to skillet and heat over medium heat. Add onion and red and orange bell peppers. Sauté until onion is translucent and peppers are tender-crisp, 10 to 12 minutes. Add cooked chicken and sauté until chicken starts to char slightly. Season with salt and pepper to taste.

3. To build tacos, divide chicken mixture equally among tortillas. Top with cheese and Chile Cream Sauce. Fold tortillas in half. Serve with lime wedges.

Grilled Chicken and Roasted Veggie Tacos

Makes 8 tacos

This Italian-style taco is lightly flavored with olive oil and lemon juice in the true spirit of Santa Margherita, a little village on the edge of the Italian Riviera. The fresh, seasoned vegetables wrap flavor around the grilled chicken filling.

- Preheat greased barbecue grill to medium-high
- Preheat oven to 200°F (100°C)
- Ovenproof dish
- Vegetable grate or heavy-duty foil

1½ lbs	boneless skinless chicken breasts (see Tip, page 41)	750 g
4 tbsp	olive oil	60 mL
	Kosher salt and freshly ground black pepper	
1	zucchini, cut in half lengthwise	1
1	yellow summer (zucchini) squash, cut in half lengthwise	1
1	onion, cut into ¼-inch (0.5 cm) rings	1
1	red bell pepper, cored and cut in half	1
3	thick asparagus spears, trimmed	3
	Juice of 1 lemon	
2 tbsp	minced fresh basil	30 mL
8	6-inch (15 cm) corn tortillas, skillet-warmed (page 15)	8
1 cup	shredded Mozzarella cheese	250 mL

1. Coat chicken with 2 tbsp (30 mL) of the oil. Season with salt and pepper to taste.

2. Grill chicken, turning once, until no longer pink inside, 6 to 8 minutes per side. Transfer to a cutting board and let chicken stand for 6 to 8 minutes. Cut chicken into bite-size pieces. Transfer to ovenproof dish and keep warm in preheated oven.

3. Coat zucchini, squash, onion, bell pepper and asparagus with remaining 2 tbsp (30 mL) of oil. Place vegetables in vegetable grate or on foil on grill. Grill, turning once, until vegetables are tender-crisp, 4 to 6 minutes per side. Transfer to a cutting board and cut into bite-size pieces.

4. In a large bowl, combine chicken and vegetables and toss with lemon juice and basil. Season with salt and pepper to taste.

5. To build tacos, divide chicken mixture equally among tortillas. Top with cheese. Fold tortillas in half.

Grilled Chicken, Garlic and Lime Shrimp Tacos

Makes 8 tacos

This is a rich buttery filling that has layers of flavor. Accents of garlic and lime bring the chicken and shrimp together for a great taco experience.

Tip

For best results in grilling, brush the grill grate with vegetable oil or coat with a nonstick cooking spray before preheating the grill.

- Preheat greased barbecue grill to medium-high (see Tip, left)
- Preheat oven to 200°F (100°)
- Ovenproof bowl

24	medium shrimp	24
	Juice of 2 limes, divided	
	Salt and freshly ground black pepper	
2	boneless skinless chicken breasts	2
6 tbsp	butter	90 mL
2	cloves garlic, minced	2
1 tbsp	minced cilantro	15 mL
8	6- to 8-inch (15 to 20 cm) corn or flour tortillas, skillet-warmed (page 15)	8
2 cups	chopped salad mix (see Tip, right)	500 mL
1	tomato, seeded and chopped	1

1. Rinse shrimp under cool water, leaving shells on. Drain and blot dry on paper towels. Place in a bowl and add juice of 1 lime and salt and pepper to taste. Toss until shrimp are well coated. Let shrimp marinate at room temperature for 10 minutes.

2. Grill chicken, turning once, until no longer pink inside, 6 to 8 minutes per side. Transfer to a cutting board and let stand for 6 to 8 minutes. Cut chicken into bite-size pieces and transfer to an ovenproof bowl.

3. Remove shrimp from marinade and discard marinade. Using tongs, place shrimp in shells on grill. Grill, turning once, until shrimp is opaque and pink, 2 to 3 minutes per side. Let shrimp cool for 5 to 7 minutes. Remove shells and dice shrimp into bite-size pieces. Add to chicken and mix well. Cover with foil and keep warm in preheated oven.

Tip

There are a variety of salad mixes with a wide range of flavors on the market. There are red and green lettuce varieties that range in taste from intense spice to sweet and mild. "Living" lettuce and "artisan" lettuce and greens are also available. Taste and compare to find your favorite combination of greens.

Variation

For added flavor, divide ½ cup (125 mL) grated Parmesan or Romano cheese equally among tacos.

4. In a small saucepan over medium-low heat, combine butter, remaining lime juice, garlic and cilantro, stirring occasionally, until well blended. Pour over chicken and shrimp.

5. To build tacos, using a slotted spoon, divide chicken and shrimp mixture equally among tortillas. Top with salad mix and garnish with tomato. Fold tortillas in half.

"Low-Carb" Chicken Taco Wraps

Makes 8 to 10 tacos

These tacos epitomize freshness; sautéed chicken filling nestled in a natural wrap: lettuce leaves! This is the perfect guiltless taco.

Tip

I like leafy romaine lettuce with ribs removed, but red leaf and green leaf lettuces are also very good. Be sure to rinse them well and pat dry with paper towels.

Stir-Fry Sauce

2 tbsp	soy sauce	30 mL
2 tbsp	packed brown sugar	30 mL
1½ tsp	red wine vinegar	7 mL
2 tbsp	olive oil, divided	30 mL
1 lb	boneless skinless chicken breasts	500 g
1	clove garlic, minced	1
3 tbsp	minced green onions, white part and a hint of green	45 mL
⅔ cup	minced mushrooms	150 mL
6	leafy lettuce leaves (see Tip, left)	6
	Spicy Asian Sauce (page 325)	

1. *Stir-Fry Sauce:* In a small bowl, combine soy sauce, brown sugar and vinegar, stirring until sugar dissolves. Set aside.

2. In a large skillet, heat 1 tbsp (15 mL) of the oil over medium-high heat. Add chicken and cook, turning once, until no longer pink inside, 6 to 8 minutes per side. Transfer chicken to cutting board and let cool.

3. In same skillet, heat remaining 1 tbsp (15 mL) of oil over medium-high heat. Sauté garlic, green onions and mushrooms until onions are transparent and mushrooms are soft, 4 to 6 minutes. Mince chicken and add to skillet. Add Stir-Fry Sauce and sauté chicken mixture until well blended and heated through, 4 to 6 minutes.

4. Allow guests to build their own wraps by placing chicken mixture in a serving bowl and lettuce leaves on a serving platter. Serve with Spicy Asian Sauce.

Pollo Verde Tacos

Makes 8 tacos

These tacos include a stew-like chicken filling smothered in a green chile sauce. So quick to make, this taco is perfect for last-minute entertaining or a late-night meal.

Tip
When I am pressed for time I pick up a roasted chicken from the deli section of my grocery store. Typically one 4-lb (2 kg) roasted cooked chicken will yield approximately 4 cups (1 L) of cooked diced chicken.

1 tbsp	olive oil	15 mL
1	clove garlic, minced	1
½ cup	chopped roasted New Mexico or Anaheim green chile peppers (2 to 3 depending on size) (see below)	125 mL
1	onion, diced	1
¼ cup	chicken broth	60 mL
2 cups	diced roasted chicken (see page 32 and Tip, left)	500 mL
8	6- to 8-inch (15 to 20 cm) corn or flour tortillas, skillet-warmed (page 15)	8
1½ cups	shredded Cheddar cheese	375 mL
2 cups	chopped salad mix	500 mL

1. In a large skillet, heat oil over medium heat. Sauté garlic until tender, about 1 minute. Add chiles and onion and sauté until onion is translucent, 4 to 6 minutes. Add broth and chicken and simmer, stirring occasionally, until chicken is heated through, 10 to 12 minutes.

2. To build tacos, divide chicken mixture equally among tortillas. Top with cheese and salad mix. Fold tortillas in half.

Roasting Chiles
To roast chiles, such as New Mexico, Anaheim, poblano, jalapeño and habanero: Preheat greased barbecue grill to medium or preheat broiler. Place fresh chiles on barbecue grill or arrange on a baking sheet and place 2 to 3 inches (5 to 7.5 cm) away from heat under broiler. Grill or broil, turning often with tongs, until surfaces of skin are lightly charred and blistered. Immediately place peppers in a paper or plastic bag, or an airtight container and close tightly. Let peppers cool for 12 to 15 minutes. Peel off charred skin and remove stems and seeds. Tear into strips or chop as needed according to the recipe. Wash your hands thoroughly after handling chiles. Refrigerate peppers for up to 3 days or freeze in airtight container for up to 6 months. Yields for chopped medium green chiles: 2 chiles = ¼ cup (60 mL), 4 chiles = ½ cup (125 mL) and 8 chiles = 1 cup (250 mL).

Crisp Chicken and Rice Tacos with Roasted Tomato Salsa

Makes 8 tacos

Layers of flavor in the rice, chicken and cheese offer a variety of complex textures folded into a crispy taco shell.

Tip

I use a quick-cooking rice, which comes in a variety of white and brown flavors.

- Candy/deep-fry thermometer

1½ cups	shredded cooked chicken (see pages 31 and 32)	375 mL
1 cup	cooked rice (see Tip, left)	250 mL
1 cup	shredded Monterey Jack cheese	250 mL
8	6-inch (15 cm) corn tortillas, micro-warmed (page 15)	8
	Vegetable oil	
	Roasted Tomato Salsa (page 299)	

1. In a large bowl, combine chicken, rice and cheese.

2. To build tacos, divide chicken mixture equally among tortillas, placing it on one half of the tortilla. Fold over and secure edges with toothpicks. Deep-fry immediately or place filled tortillas in a large resealable plastic bag and refrigerate until ready to cook for up to 2 days.

3. Fill a deep-fryer, deep heavy pot or deep skillet with 3 inches (7.5 cm) of oil and heat to 350°F (180°C). Using tongs, gently place 2 to 3 tacos at a time in hot oil and deep-fry, turning once, until crispy and golden brown, 1 to 2 minutes. Drain on paper towel. Serve with Roasted Tomato Salsa.

Roasted Chicken, Cheddar and Bacon Tacos

This is a hearty chicken taco with a contemporary twist. It is simple and fun to eat.

Variation
For additional fresh flavor add chopped tomato, minced onion or chopped fresh jalapeños. Have fun with these tacos!

2 cups	diced roasted chicken, warmed (see page 32 and Tip, page 49)	500 mL
½ tsp	seasoned salt	2 mL
8	6- to 8-inch (15 to 20 cm) flour tortillas, skillet-warmed (page 15)	8
1½ cups	shredded sharp Cheddar cheese	375 mL
8	strips bacon, cooked and chopped	8
2 cups	shredded lettuce	500 mL
1 cup	Mexican White Sauce (page 206)	250 mL

1. In a large bowl, combine warm chicken and salt.

2. To build tacos, divide chicken equally among tortillas. Top with cheese, bacon and lettuce. Drizzle with Mexican White Sauce. Fold tortillas in half.

Pollo Asada Tacos

This intensely flavored marinade delivers flavor and texture. Chicken breasts are quick to marinate and easy to grill.

Tip

If you are pressed for time, omit the bell pepper, garlic, sugar and salt. In a small bowl, combine 1 package (0.7 oz/19 g) dry Italian dressing mix with lemon juice, jalapeños and teriyaki sauce. Continue with Step 2.

Variation

For a richer flavor, top each taco with 1 tbsp (15 mL) Guacamole (page 316).

- Barbecue grill

	Juice of 3 lemons	
3	cloves garlic, minced	3
½ cup	drained sliced pickled jalapeños	125 mL
½ cup	teriyaki sauce	125 mL
1 tbsp	minced red bell pepper	15 mL
1 tbsp	granulated sugar	15 mL
1 tsp	kosher salt	5 mL
2 lbs	boneless skinless chicken breasts	1 kg
12	6-inch (15 cm) corn tortillas	12
	Pico de Gallo (page 305)	
2	limes, each cut into 6 wedges	2

1. In a medium bowl, combine lemon juice, garlic, jalapeños, teriyaki sauce, bell pepper, sugar and salt, mixing until sugar and salt dissolve.

2. In a large resealable plastic bag, combine marinade and chicken. Seal bag and work marinade into chicken with your fingers. Refrigerate for at least 2 hours or for up to 6 hours.

3. Preheat greased grill to medium-high heat. Remove chicken from marinade and discard marinade. Grill chicken, turning once, until no longer pink inside, 6 to 8 minutes per side. Transfer chicken to a cutting board and let stand for 6 to 8 minutes. Cut into thin slices.

4. To build tacos, skillet warm tortillas (page 15). Divide chicken equally among tortillas. Top with Pico de Gallo. Fold tortillas in half. Serve each with a lime wedge.

Pollo Piccata Tacos with Citrus Salsa

Makes 8 tacos

Lightly battered and sautéed, this chicken is bathed in a light, zesty sauce. The lemon and butter sauce gives this taco a well balanced zing. Adding the citrus salsa creates an unforgettable taco.

Tip

There are a variety of salad mixes with a wide range of flavors on the market. There are red and green lettuce varieties that range in taste from intense spice to sweet and mild. "Living" lettuce and "artisan" lettuce and greens are also available. Taste and compare to find your favorite combination of greens.

1	egg, lightly beaten	1
3 tbsp	lemon juice, divided	45 mL
¼ cup	all-purpose flour	60 mL
1½ lbs	boneless skinless chicken breasts	750 g
¼ cup	butter	60 mL
½ cup	chicken broth	125 mL
1 tsp	hot pepper flakes	5 mL
8	6-inch (15 cm) corn tortillas, skillet-warmed (page 15)	8
2 cups	chopped salad mix (see Tip, left)	500 mL
	Citrus Salsa (page 301)	

1. In a small bowl, beat egg with 1 tbsp (15 mL) of the lemon juice. Place flour in a shallow dish. Dip each chicken breast in egg mixture then dredge in flour. Discard any excess egg mixture and flour.

2. In a large skillet, melt butter over medium heat. Add chicken and lightly brown on both sides, about 6 minutes per side. Add chicken broth, remaining 2 tbsp (30 mL) of lemon juice and hot pepper flakes. Cover, reduce heat to low, and simmer until chicken is tender and no longer pink inside, about 20 minutes. Transfer chicken to a cutting board and cut into thin slices.

3. To build tacos, divide chicken equally among tortillas. Top with salad mix and Citrus Salsa. Fold tortillas in half.

Rosemary Chicken Tacos

Makes 8 tacos

Rosemary has a distinctive flavor that begs for a little hint of garlic. This herb-crusted chicken is folded into a steamy corn tortilla and topped with a garlic cream sauce and sun-dried tomatoes.

- Preheat greased barbecue grill to medium-high

2 tbsp	minced fresh rosemary	30 mL
2 tsp	kosher salt	10 mL
1 tsp	cracked black peppercorns	5 mL
1½ lbs	boneless skinless chicken breasts	750 g
1 tbsp	olive oil	15 mL
8	6-inch (15 cm) corn tortillas, skillet-warmed (page 15)	8
	Creamy Garlic Spread (page 321)	
½ cup	oil-packed sun-dried tomatoes, drained and chopped	125 mL

1. In a small bowl, combine rosemary, salt and peppercorns.

2. Coat chicken with oil, then rub with rosemary mixture.

3. Grill chicken, turning once, until no longer pink inside, 6 to 8 minutes per side. Transfer chicken to a cutting board. Let stand for 6 to 8 minutes. Cut into thin slices.

4. To build tacos, divide chicken equally among tortillas. Top with Garlic Sour Cream and sun-dried tomatoes. Fold tortillas in half.

Asian Chicken Tacos

This is a chilled taco full of Asian flavors. It is perfect for a light lunch, afternoon snack or appetizer.

Tips

Regular soy sauce is loaded with sodium. I use a reduced-sodium one for a less salty taste whenever I can. Check the label for a true reduced-sodium soy sauce and make sure it's not just additives and colorings.

When I am in a rush I do buy high-quality prepared taco shells. But I prefer to make my own. For directions on taco shell "how-tos," see page 14.

Variations

I also like this taco with skillet-warmed corn tortillas (page 15).

Substitute Creamy Wasabi Sauce (page 316) for the Spicy Asian Sauce.

1½ cups	shredded cooked chicken (see pages 31 and 32)	375 mL
½ cup	finely chopped celery	125 mL
½ cup	chopped sugar snap peas	125 mL
¼ cup	chopped red bell pepper	60 mL
¼ cup	chopped onion	60 mL
1 tbsp	minced drained canned water chestnuts	15 mL
½ cup	rice vinegar	125 mL
2 tbsp	reduced-sodium soy sauce (see Tips, left)	30 mL
1 tsp	granulated sugar	5 mL
8	taco shells (see Tips, left)	8
2 cups	minced cabbage	500 mL
	Spicy Asian Sauce (page 325)	

1. In a large bowl, combine chicken, celery, peas, bell pepper, onion and water chestnuts.

2. In a small bowl, combine vinegar, soy sauce and sugar, stirring until sugar dissolves. Pour over chicken mixture, mix well and refrigerate for 30 minutes or for up to 2 hours.

3. To build tacos, warm taco shells (page 15). Divide chicken mixture equally among taco shells, spooning it in gently. Top with cabbage and Spicy Asian Sauce.

Chicken Club Soft Tacos

This taco is generous with flavor and stuffed full of ham, chicken and turkey. Hints of an intensely flavored cheese add a fresh twist to this taco.

Tip
Even though this taco is served cold, warm the flour tortillas initially so they are more pliable and easier to work with.

Variations
For a spicier version, divide 2 tbsp (30 mL) minced jalapeños evenly among tacos.

¼ cup	mayonnaise	60 mL
¼ cup	crumbled Roquefort or other blue cheese, at room temperature	60 mL
8	6- to 8-inch (15 to 20 cm) flour tortillas, micro-warmed (page 15)	8
8	thin slices deli turkey	8
2 cups	shredded cooked chicken (see pages 31 and 32)	500 mL
6	strips bacon, cooked and crumbled	6
2 cups	chopped romaine lettuce	500 mL
1	tomato, seeded and diced	1
1	avocado, diced	1

1. In a small bowl, combine mayonnaise and Roquefort cheese. Mix well until smooth.

2. To build tacos, spread one side of each tortilla with mayonnaise mixture. Top each tortilla with one slice of turkey. Divide chicken and bacon equally among tortillas. Top with lettuce, tomato and avocado. Fold tortillas in half.

Honey Mustard Chicken Tacos

Honey mustard, a popular condiment among sandwich lovers, makes the perfect taco sauce. It complements the roasted chicken and sautéed onions in this taco.

Tip

If you don't have two large skillets, cook the onions first, transfer to a bowl and cover to keep warm then use the same skillet to heat the chicken mixture.

¼ cup	liquid honey	60 mL
¼ cup	Dijon mustard	60 mL
1 tbsp	mayonnaise	15 mL
2 tbsp	olive oil	30 mL
2	onions, sliced into ¼-inch (0.5 cm) rings	2
1 tbsp	balsamic vinegar	15 mL
2 tsp	Worcestershire sauce	10 mL
¼ tsp	kosher salt	1 mL
¼ tsp	freshly ground black pepper	1 mL
2 cups	diced roasted chicken (see page 32 and Tip, page 49)	500 mL
1 tbsp	minced cilantro	15 mL
8	6- to 8-inch (15 to 20 cm) flour tortillas	8
2 cups	chopped green leaf lettuce	500 mL
1	tomato, seeded and chopped	1

1. In a small bowl, combine honey, mustard and mayonnaise. Set aside.

2. In a large skillet, heat oil over medium heat. Sauté onions, vinegar, Worcestershire, salt and pepper until onions are a deep golden brown, about 20 minutes. Transfer to a bowl.

3. Meanwhile, in another large skillet over medium heat, sauté chicken and cilantro until chicken is heated through, about 10 minutes.

4. To build tacos, spread a thin layer of mustard mixture on one side of each tortilla. Divide chicken equally among tortillas. Top with sautéed onions, lettuce and tomato. Fold tortillas in half.

Pesto Chicken Tacos

Makes 8 tacos

Slightly charred chicken spiked with a pesto sauce of basil and garlic adds a contemporary choice to taco cuisine. Sprinkle with fresh Parmesan cheese and enjoy.

Tips

For best results in grilling, brush the grill grate with vegetable oil or coat with a nonstick cooking spray before preheating the grill.

I typically buy a high-quality pesto at the market when I'm pressed for time. However, it is very simple to make.

To make your own pesto: In a food processor or blender, combine 3 cups (750 mL) fresh basil leaves, $\frac{1}{3}$ cup (75 mL) toasted pine nuts, 3 cloves garlic, $\frac{1}{3}$ cup (75 mL) freshly grated Parmesan cheese and $\frac{1}{2}$ cup (125 mL) olive oil. Pulse until smooth, 45 to 60 seconds. If too thick, add 1 tbsp (15 mL) more olive oil. Season with salt and freshly ground black pepper to taste. Transfer to an airtight container and refrigerate for up to 4 days.

- Preheat greased barbecue grill to medium-high (see Tips, left)

1½ lbs	boneless skinless chicken breasts (see Tips, page 41)	750 g
1 tbsp	olive oil	15 mL
1 tsp	kosher salt	5 mL
1 tsp	freshly ground black pepper	5 mL
¼ cup	basil pesto (see Tips, left)	60 mL
8	6- to 8-inch (15 to 20 cm) flour tortillas, skillet-warmed (page 15)	8
¼ cup	freshly grated Parmesan cheese	60 mL
2 cups	chopped salad mix	500 mL
1	tomato, seeded and diced	1

1. Coat chicken breast with oil and sprinkle all over with salt and pepper.

2. Grill chicken, turning once, until no longer pink inside, 6 to 8 minutes per side. Generously brush pesto over both sides and grill for 1 minute per side. Transfer to cutting board and let stand for 6 to 8 minutes. Cut into thin slices.

3. To build tacos, divide chicken equally among tortillas. Top with cheese, salad mix and tomato. Fold tortillas in half.

Crusted Pecan Chicken Soft Tacos with Green Chile Relish

Makes 8 taco

This taco filling has a crusty texture and nutty flavor wrapped up in a warm flour tortilla. Fresh green chile relish accents this taco perfectly.

Tip

Panko bread crumbs are Japanese bread crumbs that are toasted, giving them a crispy texture. Look for them in grocery stores where the bread crumbs are sold.

1½ lbs	boneless skinless chicken breasts, sliced into ½-inch (1 cm) strips	750 g
1 cup	whole or 2% milk	250 mL
1 cup	finely chopped pecans	250 mL
½ cup	panko bread crumbs (see Tip, left)	125 mL
1 tsp	kosher salt	5 mL
½ tsp	freshly ground black pepper	2 mL
3 tbsp	butter	45 mL
1 tbsp	olive oil	15 mL
8	6- to 8-inch (15 to 20 cm) corn or flour tortillas	8
2 cups	chopped romaine lettuce	500 mL
	Green Chile Relish (page 312)	

1. In a large bowl, soak chicken in the milk, turning occasionally, for 20 minutes.

2. On a large plate, combine pecans, panko bread crumbs, salt and pepper. Remove chicken from milk and dip into dry mixture, pressing to coat well. Discard any excess milk and pecan mixture.

3. In a large skillet over medium-high heat, melt butter and heat oil. Gently place chicken in butter and oil and fry, turning once, until no longer pink inside and golden brown, 4 to 5 minutes per side. Transfer chicken to a cutting board and let stand for 6 to 8 minutes.

4. To build tacos, skillet warm tortillas (page 15). Divide chicken equally among tortillas. Top with lettuce and Green Chile Relish. Fold tortillas in half.

Teriyaki Chicken Tacos

Add a Japanese twist with this intensely flavored chicken sautéed to perfection. Spicy Asian Sauce drizzled over the top kicks up the heat a bit.

Variations

This taco can also be grilled on a barbecue grill over medium-high heat. Skip Steps 2 and 3. Remove chicken from marinade and grill, turning once, until no longer pink inside, 6 to 8 minutes per side. Transfer to a cutting board and let stand for 6 to 8 minutes. Cut into thin slices.

Replace the Spicy Asian Sauce with any of these sweet and tangy salsas: Sweet Pineapple Salsa (page 309), Margarita Melon Salsa (page 310) or Jicama Salsa (page 309).

½ cup	soy sauce	125 mL
⅓ cup	granulated sugar	75 mL
2	cloves garlic, minced	2
2 tsp	minced fresh gingerroot	10 mL
	Juice of 1 lemon	
1½ lbs	boneless skinless chicken breasts	750 g
1 tbsp	olive oil	15 mL
8	6-inch (15 cm) corn tortillas	8
2 cups	chopped salad mix	500 mL
	Spicy Asian Sauce (page 325)	

1. In a small bowl, combine ½ cup (125 mL) water, soy sauce, sugar, garlic, ginger and lemon juice. Stir until sugar dissolves. Place in a large airtight container and add chicken. Cover and refrigerate for at least 6 hours or for up to 24 hours.

2. Transfer chicken to cutting board, discarding marinade. Cut chicken into bite-size pieces.

3. In a large skillet, heat oil over medium-high heat. Sauté chicken until no longer pink inside and slightly charred, 8 to 10 minutes.

4. To build tacos, divide chicken equally among tortillas. Top with salad mix and Spicy Asian Sauce. Fold tortillas in half.

Sweet-and-Sour Chicken Tacos

The filling for this taco is spiced with fruit and mild peppers. It is a contemporary taco with sweet and savory flavor.

- Preheat oven to 200°F (100°C)
- Ovenproof dish

1 tbsp	olive oil	15 mL
1½ lbs	boneless skinless chicken breasts, cut into ½-inch (1 cm) pieces	750 g
1 cup	small pineapple chunks	250 mL
1	red bell pepper, diced	1
½ cup	apple jelly	125 mL
½ cup	rice vinegar	125 mL
2 tbsp	soy sauce	30 mL
1 tbsp	Worcestershire sauce	15 mL
8	6- to 8-inch (15 to 20 cm) flour tortillas, skillet-warmed (page 15)	8
2 cups	chopped salad mix	500 mL
1 cup	bean sprouts	250 mL

1. In a large skillet, heat oil over medium heat. Sauté chicken, pineapple and bell pepper until chicken is no longer pink inside, 12 to 14 minutes. Transfer to ovenproof dish and keep warm in preheated oven.

2. In a small saucepan over medium heat, combine apple jelly, vinegar, soy sauce and Worcestershire sauce. Bring to a boil, stirring constantly, until sauce thickens, 6 to 8 minutes.

3. Pour hot sauce over chicken mixture and stir until chicken is well coated.

4. To build tacos, divide chicken mixture equally among tortillas. Top with salad mix and bean sprouts. Fold tortillas in half.

BBQ Chicken Tacos

Barbecued chicken has been a North American favorite for decades. Adding this traditional dish to my taco cuisine produced a barbecue fiesta that you will love. Simple to make and rich in flavor with tangy toppings, these barbecue tacos can be cooked up in minutes.

Tip

When I am pressed for time I pick up a roasted chicken from the deli section of my grocery store. Typically one 4-lb (2 kg) roasted cooked chicken will yield approximately 4 cups (1 L) of cooked diced chicken.

3 cups	diced roasted chicken (see Tip, left)	750 mL
¾ cup	hickory barbecue sauce	175 mL
2 cups	chopped fresh spinach	500 mL
1	onion, thinly sliced	1
1 cup	shredded Monterey Jack cheese	250 mL
¼ cup	Italian dressing	60 mL
8	6- to 8-inch (15 to 20 cm) flour tortillas, skillet-warmed (page 15)	8

1. In a large skillet over medium heat, sauté chicken and barbecue sauce until chicken is heated through, 8 to 10 minutes.

2. In a large bowl, gently toss together spinach, onion, cheese and Italian dressing.

3. To build tacos, divide chicken equally among tortillas. Top with spinach mixture. Fold tortillas in half.

Crispy Pollo and Chorizo Tacos

Chorizo, a Mexican sausage, is an intensely flavored "chile spiced" pork. It is a great flavor enhancer and is delicious in this taco. Enjoy these crispy corn tortilla shells filled with spicy goodness.

Tips

These tacos can be assembled and frozen for up to 3 months. Thaw completely in the refrigerator and cook as directed.

Serve tacos with Fiesta Taco Sauce (page 324) or Cilantro Chile Sauce (page 325).

• Candy/deep-fry thermometer

6 oz	fresh chorizo sausage	175 g
3 cups	shredded cooked chicken (see pages 31 and 32)	750 mL
8	6-inch (15 cm) corn tortillas, micro-warmed (page 15)	8
	Vegetable oil	

1. In a skillet over medium-high heat, sauté sausage, breaking up with a spoon, until well browned. Drain off excess fat and transfer to a large bowl. Add chicken. Mix well.

2. To build tacos, divide chicken mixture equally among tortillas, placing on one half of the tortilla. Fold over and secure edges with toothpicks. Deep-fry immediately or place filled tortillas in a large resealable plastic bag to keep moist. Refrigerate until ready to cook for up to 24 hours.

3. Fill a deep-fryer, deep heavy pot or deep skillet with 3 inches (7.5 cm) of oil and heat to 350°F (180°C). Using tongs, gently place 2 to 3 tacos at a time in the hot oil and deep-fry, turning once, until crispy and golden brown, 2 to 3 minutes. Drain on paper towels.

Mesquite Chicken Tacos with Citrusy Lime Salsa

Makes 8 tacos

Some flavors and aromas are hard to recreate in the kitchen. Thank goodness there are an abundance of seasonings found in the market today. Mesquite seasoning adds an earthy essence to grilled chicken. A tangy lime marinade combined with the smoky flavor of mesquite and the distinctive flavors of grilling creates a compelling and delicious taco.

Tip

Mesquite flavor traditionally comes from grilling meats and poultry over mesquite wood. However, there are a variety of mesquite seasoning blends on the market that can provide the same flavor. Most offer a granular blend of spices ranging from sweet to salty with mild heat and smoky flavors. Check your local market or go online.

Variation

Substitute Fiery Corn Relish (page 311) for the Citrusy Lime Salsa.

- Barbecue grill

	Juice of 3 limes	
2 tbsp	mesquite seasoning (see Tip, left)	30 mL
2 tbsp	liquid honey	30 mL
1 tbsp	olive oil	15 mL
1½ lbs	boneless skinless chicken breasts	750 g
8	6-inch (15 cm) corn tortillas	8
	Citrusy Lime Salsa (page 307)	
2 cups	chopped salad mix	500 mL
1½ cups	shredded Monterey Jack or Manchego cheese	375 mL

1. In a small bowl, combine lime juice, mesquite seasoning, honey and olive oil. Mix well.

2. In a resealable plastic bag, combine marinade and chicken. Seal bag and work marinade into chicken with your fingers. Refrigerate for at least 2 hours or for up to 4 hours.

3. Preheat greased grill to medium-high heat. Remove chicken from marinade and discard marinade. Grill chicken, turning once, until no longer pink inside, 6 to 8 minutes per side. Transfer chicken to a cutting board and let stand for 6 to 8 minutes. Cut into bite-size pieces.

4. To build tacos, skillet warm tortillas (page 15). Divide chicken equally among tortillas. Top with Citrusy Lime Salsa, salad mix and cheese. Fold tortillas in half.

Grilled Chicken and

Pollo Piccata Tacos
with Citrus Salsa (page 53)

Turkey Taquitos with
Habanero Cream Sauce (page 101)

Grilled Fajita Steak and Shrimp Tacos (page 140)

Chicken Stir-Fry Tacos

The infusion of Asian flavors and fresh veggies adds a contemporary freshness to this taco. It is a hand-held stir-fry delight.

- Preheat oven to 200°F (100°C)
- Ovenproof dish

2 tbsp	olive oil, divided	30 mL
1	clove garlic, minced	1
4	asparagus spears, cut into small pieces	4
1 cup	thinly sliced mushrooms,	250 mL
1	red bell pepper, diced	1
2 tbsp	soy sauce	30 mL
Pinch	granulated sugar	Pinch
1 lb	boneless skinless chicken breasts, cut into ¼-inch (0.5 cm) cubes	500 g
8	6-inch (15 cm) corn tortillas, skillet-warmed (page 15)	8
	Spicy Asian Sauce (page 325)	

1. In a large skillet, heat 1 tbsp (15 mL) of the oil over medium heat. Add garlic, asparagus, mushrooms, bell pepper, soy sauce and sugar. Sauté until vegetables are tender-crisp, 6 to 8 minutes. Transfer to ovenproof dish and keep warm in preheated oven.

2. Add remaining 1 tbsp (15 mL) of oil and chicken to skillet and sauté over medium heat, until no longer pink inside and slightly charred, 10 to 12 minutes.

3. Return vegetables to skillet and mix well with chicken.

4. To build tacos, divide chicken mixture equally among tortillas. Top with Spicy Asian Sauce. Fold tortillas in half.

Santa Fe Chicken Tacos

I like this taco because of the unusual combination, which makes it a bit funky. Also, it has lots of color and texture, which makes it fun. Just like Santa Fe — funky and fun!

Tip

I like to put my sauces in a squeeze bottle for ease of use.

• Barbecue grill

1 cup	canned or cooked black beans, drained and rinsed	250 mL
½ cup	cooked fresh corn kernels	125 mL
1	tomato, seeded and diced	1
½ cup	BBQ sauce (see Tip, left)	125 mL
½ cup	ranch dressing	125 mL
1½ lbs	boneless skinless chicken breasts	750 g
1 tbsp	olive oil	15 mL
	Kosher salt and freshly ground black pepper	
8	6- to 8-inch (15 to 20 cm) flour tortillas	8
2 cups	chopped romaine lettuce	500 mL
1 cup	shredded Pepper Jack cheese	250 mL

1. In a small bowl, combine beans, corn and tomato. Cover and refrigerate for at least 2 hours or for up to 6 hours. In another small bowl, combine barbecue sauce and ranch dressing. Cover and refrigerate for at least 30 minutes or for up to 6 hours.

2. Coat chicken with oil and season with salt and pepper to taste.

3. Preheat greased grill to medium-high. Grill chicken, turning once, until no longer pink inside, 6 to 8 minutes per side. Transfer chicken to a cutting board and let stand for 6 to 8 minutes. Cut into bite-size pieces.

5. To build tacos, divide chicken and bean mixture equally among tortillas. Top with lettuce, cheese and barbecue sauce mixture. Fold tortillas in half.

Hawaiian Chicken Tacos

Makes 8 tacos

The sweetness of the pineapple complements the grilled chicken and creamy Swiss cheese. Tropical salsa crowns this taco with juicy freshness.

- Preheat greased barbecue grill to medium-high
- Preheat oven to 200°F (100°C)

1 tbsp	olive oil	15 mL
	Kosher salt and freshly ground black pepper	
1½ lbs	boneless skinless chicken breasts	750 g
4	canned pineapple rings, drained	4
8	thin slices Swiss cheese	8
8	6- to 8-inch (15 to 20 cm) flour tortillas, skillet-warmed (page 15)	8
	Tropical Salsa (page 299)	

1. Coat chicken with oil and season with salt and pepper to taste.

2. Grill chicken and pineapple rings, turning once, until pineapple is slightly charred, 1 to 2 minutes per side and chicken is no longer pink inside, 6 to 8 minutes per side. Transfer pineapple to a cutting board and cut into bite-size pieces. Keep warm in preheated oven. When chicken is ready, transfer to a cutting board and let stand for 6 to 8 minutes. Cut into bite-size pieces.

3. To build tacos, place one slice of cheese on each warm tortilla. Divide chicken and pineapple equally among tortillas. Top with Tropical Salsa. Fold tortillas in half.

Pollo Monterey Tacos

A combination of peppers, bacon and cheese make this filling deliciously inviting. Folded in a warm flour tortilla, it will melt in your mouth.

Tip

When I am pressed for time I pick up a roasted chicken from the deli section of my grocery store. Typically one 4-lb (2 kg) roasted cooked chicken will yield approximately 4 cups (1 L) of cooked diced chicken.

Variation

Top each taco equally with fresh veggies such as 2 cups (500 mL) chopped romaine, 1 chopped onion or 1 tomato, seeded and diced.

- 8-inch (20 cm) square glass baking dish, greased
- Preheat oven to 350°F (180°C)

4	strips bacon, diced	4
1	green bell pepper, diced	1
1	onion, chopped	1
3 cups	diced roasted chicken (see page 32 and Tip, left)	750 mL
8	6- to 8-inch (15 to 20 cm) flour tortillas, skillet-warmed (page 15)	8
1½ cups	shredded Monterey Jack cheese	375 mL
	Fiesta Taco Sauce (page 324)	

1. In a skillet over medium heat, sauté bacon, bell pepper and onion until bacon is slightly crisp, 10 to 12 minutes. Add chicken and sauté until chicken is heated through, 4 to 6 minutes. Drain off excess fat.

2. To build tacos, divide chicken mixture equally among tortillas. Top with cheese and fold tortillas in half. Gently place each taco in a prepared baking dish side by side. Heat in preheated oven until cheese is melted, 12 to 14 minutes. Top with Fiesta Taco Sauce.

Chilled Chicken Avocado Tacos

Makes 8 tacos

This taco is colorful and full of flavor and texture. Top it with a creamy sauce and you have a small chopped chicken salad wrapped up in a warm corn tortilla.

Tip

For best results in grilling, brush the grill grate with vegetable oil or coat with a nonstick cooking spray before preheating the grill.

• **Preheat greased barbecue grill to medium-high (see Tip, left)**

1½ lbs	boneless skinless chicken breasts	750 g
2 tbsp	olive oil, divided	30 mL
	Kosher salt and freshly ground black pepper	
1	tomato, seeded and diced	1
1	green bell pepper, diced	1
½ cup	minced roasted New Mexico or Anaheim green chile peppers (2 to 3 depending on size) (see page 49)	125 mL
2 tbsp	raw sunflower seeds	30 mL
1 tbsp	red wine vinegar	15 mL
8	6-inch (15 cm) corn tortillas, skillet-warmed (page 15)	8
2	avocados	2
2 cups	chopped romaine lettuce	500 mL
	Spicy Ranch Sauce (page 326)	

1. Coat chicken with 1 tbsp (15 mL) of the oil and season with salt and pepper to taste.

2. Grill chicken, turning once, until no longer pink inside, 6 to 8 minutes per side. Transfer to a cutting board and let cool completely. Cut into bite-size pieces.

3. In a large bowl, combine tomato, bell pepper, green chiles, sunflower seeds, vinegar and remaining 1 tbsp (15 mL) of oil. Add chicken and toss to combine.

4. To build tacos, divide chicken mixture equally among tortillas. Chop avocados and place equally on top of chicken. Fold tortillas in half. Place on a platter, cover and refrigerate for at least 30 minutes or for up to 1 hour. Just before serving, remove tacos from refrigerator and stuff with lettuce and Spicy Ranch Sauce.

Oaxaca Chicken Tacos

Makes 8 tacos

This is a quick version of a classic that you will find in Mexican kitchens. Refried beans teamed with roasted chicken are among the simple flavors of Mexico.

Tips

Lard adds an authentic flavor to taco fillings and I like to use it from time to time. It actually has less cholesterol and saturated fat than butter. But you can substitute 1 tbsp (15 mL) vegetable oil or olive oil for the lard.

Serve with Pico de Gallo (page 305), Fiesta Taco Sauce (page 324) or Tomatillo Avocado Salsa (page 304).

Variation

Substitute feta cheese for the Cotija cheese.

1 tbsp	lard (see Tips, left)	15 mL
3 cups	diced roasted chicken	750 mL
4	green onions, trimmed and finely chopped	4
3	jalapeños, seeded and minced	3
1½ cups	refried beans, warmed (page 273)	375 mL
8	6-inch (15 cm) corn tortillas, skillet-warmed (page 15)	8
1 cup	crumbled Cotija cheese (see Tip, page 99)	250 mL

1. In a large skillet, heat lard over medium heat. Sauté chicken, green onions and jalapeños until vegetables are tender-crisp, 4 to 6 minutes.

2. To build tacos, spread beans equally on one side of each tortilla. Divide chicken mixture equally among tortillas. Top with cheese. Fold tortillas in half.

Buffalo Chicken Tacos with Crumbled Blue Cheese

Makes 8 tacos

Here is a taco for those that love spicy chicken wings. A little hot sauce spices up the roasted chicken. Wrap in a warm corn tortilla and top with aged blue cheese. Delicioso!

Tips

When I am pressed for time I pick up a roasted chicken from the deli section of my grocery store. Typically one 4-lb (2 kg) roasted cooked chicken will yield approximately 4 cups (1 L) of cooked diced chicken.

There are several types of sauces spiked with cayenne pepper on the market. Some are called "wing" sauce. Louisiana hot sauce is one of the originals and has a good medium flavor.

1½ tbsp	olive oil	22 mL
3 cups	shredded roasted chicken (see page 32 and Tips, left)	750 mL
¼ cup	Louisiana hot sauce (see Tips, left)	60 mL
8	6-inch (15 cm) corn tortillas, skillet-warmed (page 15)	8
2 cups	chopped romaine lettuce	500 mL
8 oz	blue cheese, crumbled	250 g

1. In a large skillet, heat oil over medium heat. Sauté chicken and hot sauce until chicken is heated through, 10 to 12 minutes.

2. To build tacos, divide chicken mixture equally among tortillas. Top with lettuce and blue cheese. Fold tortillas in half.

Buffalo Chicken Taquitos

Makes 36 taquitos

Crispy rolled corn tortillas stuffed with spicy chicken will satisfy Buffalo wing lovers and add a contemporary Mexican twist. These anojitos *or "cravings" are a perfect appetizer or late-night snack.*

Tip
Serve with Chile Cream Sauce (page 327) or Garlic Sour Cream (page 321).

Variation
For a spicier flavor, increase hot sauce by 1 tbsp (15 mL).

- Candy/deep-fry thermometer

3 cups	shredded cooked chicken (see pages 31 and 32)	750 mL
1/3 cup	Louisiana hot sauce (see Tips, page 71)	75 mL
3/4 tsp	salt	3 mL
36	6-inch (15 cm) corn tortillas, micro-warmed (page 15)	36
	Vegetable oil	

1. In a large bowl, thoroughly combine shredded chicken, hot sauce and salt.

2. To build taquitos, place about 1 heaping tbsp (15 mL) of chicken at one end of each tortilla. Gently roll tortilla tightly and secure with a toothpick. Deep-fry immediately or place rolled tacos in a resealable plastic bag to keep tacos moist. Refrigerate for up to 2 days or until ready to cook.

3. Fill a deep-fryer, deep heavy pot or deep skillet with 3 inches (7.5 cm) of oil and heat to 350°F (180°C). Using tongs, gently place 3 to 4 tacos at a time in hot oil and deep-fry, turning once, until golden brown and crispy, 2 to 3 minutes. Drain on paper towels.

Nutty Chicken Tacos

This is an unusual combination that is addictive. The cream cheese and sunflower seeds add texture and flavor to these chicken tacos.

Variation

Try a variety of salsas with this taco. Cilantro and Chile Salsa (page 305) and Pico de Gallo (page 305) are both delicious.

• **Preheat greased barbecue grill to medium-high**

2 lbs	boneless skinless chicken breasts	1 kg
1 tbsp	olive oil	15 mL
	Kosher salt and freshly ground black pepper	
4 oz	whipped cream cheese	125 g
8	6- to 8-inch (15 to 20 cm) flour tortillas, skillet-warmed (page 15)	8
¼ cup	raw sunflower seeds	60 mL
2 cups	alfalfa sprouts	500 mL
1	tomato, seeded and diced	1
	Onion Apple Salsa (page 306)	

1. Coat chicken with oil. Lightly season with salt and pepper to taste.

2. Grill chicken, turning once, until no longer pink inside, 6 to 8 minutes per side. Transfer chicken to a cutting board. Let stand for 6 to 8 minutes. Cut into thin slices.

3. To build tacos, spread a thin layer of cream cheese on one side of each tortilla. Sprinkle sunflower seeds equally over cream cheese. Divide chicken equally among tortillas. Top with sprouts, tomato and Onion Apple Salsa. Fold tortillas in half.

Parmesan Chicken Taquitos

Makes 24 rolled tacos

I love Parmesan cheese; it has intense, zesty flavor. A little goes a long way, so rolling warm tacos in a fresh grated pile of this delicious cheese adds extraordinary flavor.

Tips

You can freeze assembled tacos in an airtight container for up to 4 months. Thaw completely in the refrigerator before cooking.

For these tacos, I recommend Lemon Jalapeño Sauce (page 322) and Chipotle Ranch Sauce (page 326).

• Candy/deep-fry thermometer

3 cups	shredded cooked chicken (see pages 31 and 32)	750 mL
½ tsp	salt	2 mL
24	6-inch (15 cm) corn tortillas, micro-warmed (page 15)	24
2 cups	freshly grated Parmesan cheese	500 mL
	Vegetable oil	

1. In a large bowl, thoroughly combine chicken and salt.

2. To build tacos, place 1½ tbsp (22 mL) of chicken at one end of each tortilla. Gently roll tortilla and secure with a toothpick. Deep-fry immediately or place rolled tacos in a resealable plastic bag to keep tacos moist. Refrigerate for up to 2 days.

3. Spread cheese out on a plate or platter.

4. Fill a deep-fryer, deep heavy pot or deep skillet with 3 inches (7.5 cm) of oil and heat to 350°F (180°C). Using tongs, gently place 3 to 4 tacos at a time in the hot oil and deep-fry, turning once, until golden brown and crispy, 2 to 3 minutes. Remove from oil with tongs and quickly roll in cheese. Serve 3 or 4 per person.

Crispy Caesar Chicken Tacos with Creamy Green Chile

Makes 8 tacos

A refreshing feast in a taco shell is how I describe this taco. Lightly seasoned chicken grilled to perfection and laced with zesty, spicy sauce.

Tips

Make the dressing up to 24 hours ahead so flavors can infuse.

I prefer making my own crispy taco shells. They will be hot, crispy and delicious. Directions on taco shell "how-tos" are on page 14. However, when I am short on time I do buy high-quality prepared taco shells. Check your local grocery store and test the different brands. I tend to like the true Mexican brands because they taste more authentic to me.

• Barbecue grill

1 cup	Caesar salad dressing	250 mL
¼ cup	minced roasted New Mexico or Anaheim green chile pepper (see page 49)	60 mL
2 lbs	boneless skinless chicken breasts	1 kg
1 tbsp	olive oil	15 mL
	Kosher salt and freshly ground black pepper	
8	taco shells (see Tips, left)	8
1 tbsp	minced cilantro	15 mL
2 cups	chopped romaine lettuce	500 mL
1 cup	freshly grated Parmesan cheese	250 mL

1. In a small bowl, combine dressing and green chile. Cover and refrigerate for at least 1 hour or for up to 24 hours to meld flavors.

2. When you're ready to grill, preheat greased grill to medium-high. Coat chicken with oil. Lightly season with salt and pepper.

3. Grill chicken, turning once, until no longer pink inside, 6 to 8 minutes per side. Transfer chicken to a cutting board and let stand for 6 to 8 minutes. Cut into bite-size pieces.

4. To build tacos, divide chicken equally among taco shells. Top with dressing mixture, cilantro and lettuce. Garnish each taco with cheese.

East-West Chicken Tacos

Asian influences give a contemporary twist to this taco. Roasted nuts with a sweet glaze add texture and flavor.

Tip

The perfect size tortilla for a taco is 6 inches (15 cm). It is generally more available in corn rather than flour. Buy 8-inch (20 cm) flour tortillas and trim them with a pair of kitchen shears to 6 inches (15 cm) using a corn tortilla as a template.

1 tbsp	olive oil	15 mL
1½ lbs	boneless skinless chicken breasts, cut into ¼-inch (0.5 cm) cubes	750 g
	Spicy Asian Sauce (page 325), divided	
8	6- to 8-inch (15 to 20 cm) flour tortillas (see Tip, left), skillet-warmed (page 15)	8
1	carrot, coarsely shredded	1
½ cup	honey roasted peanuts, chopped	125 mL
4	green onions, green part only, chopped	4
2 cups	chopped butter lettuce	500 mL

1. In a large skillet, heat oil over medium-high heat. Sauté chicken until no longer pink inside and juices have evaporated, 10 to 12 minutes. Add ½ cup (125 mL) of the Spicy Asian Sauce and sauté until chicken is well coated, 4 to 6 minutes.

2. To build tacos, divide chicken mixture equally among tortillas. Top with carrot, peanuts, green onions and lettuce. Fold tortillas in half. Serve with remaining sauce.

Margarita Chicken Tacos

Tangy lime and lemon flavors come together in a marinade that speaks of Mexico. This is a fiesta of flavors wrapped in a taco!

Tip

Select a liquid margarita mix that is not too tart but evenly balanced in flavor. I like to use Jose Quervo liquid margarita mix.

• Barbecue grill

	Juice of 1 orange	
	Juice of 1 lemon	
½ cup	margarita mix (see Tip, left)	125 mL
2 tbsp	olive oil	30 mL
1 tbsp	liquid honey	15 mL
2	cloves garlic, minced	2
1½ lbs	boneless skinless chicken breasts	750 g
	Kosher salt and freshly ground black pepper	
8	6-inch (15 cm) corn tortillas, skillet-warmed (page 15)	8
2 cups	chopped romaine lettuce	500 mL
1	avocado, diced	1
2	limes, each cut into 4 wedges	2

1. In a medium bowl, combine orange and lemon juices, margarita mix, oil, honey and garlic. Mix until well blended.

2. In a large resealable plastic bag, combine marinade and chicken. Seal bag and work marinade into chicken with your fingers. Refrigerate for at least 2 hours or for up to 6 hours.

3. Preheat greased grill to medium-high. Remove chicken from marinade and discard marinade. Lightly season chicken with salt and pepper to taste. Grill chicken, turning once, until no longer pink inside, 6 to 8 minutes per side. Transfer chicken to a cutting board. Let stand for 6 to 8 minutes. Cut into thin slices.

4. To build tacos, divide chicken equally among tortillas. Top with lettuce and avocado. Fold tortillas in half. Serve lime wedges on the side.

Chipotle Chicken Tacos with Lime, Avocado and Red Onion Salsa

Chipotle chiles add an earthiness to the flavor of these tacos that is soulfully satisfying. Top it with a fresh avocado salsa and you get a fiesta of texture.

• Barbecue grill

Lime, Avocado and Red Onion Salsa

1	red onion, minced	1
	Juice of 2 limes	
1	avocado	1
	Coarse garlic salt	
	Freshly ground black pepper	
¼ cup	liquid honey	60 mL
2 tbsp	puréed chipotle chile peppers in adobo sauce	30 mL
2 tbsp	olive oil	30 mL
1½ lbs	boneless skinless chicken breasts	750 g
	Kosher salt	
8	6- to 8-inch (15 to 20 cm) corn or flour tortillas	8

1. *Lime, Avocado and Red Onion Salsa:* In a small bowl, combine red onion and lime juice. Cover and refrigerate for at least 1 hour or for up to 4 hours to allow flavors to meld. Just before serving, dice avocado and gently fold into mixture. Season salsa with garlic salt and pepper to taste.

2. In a medium bowl, combine honey, chiles and oil.

3. Preheat greased grill to medium-high. Lightly season chicken with salt and pepper. Grill chicken, turning once, until no longer pink inside, 6 to 8 minutes per side. Brush chicken all over with glaze and grill for 1 minute per side. Transfer chicken to a cutting board. Let stand for 6 to 8 minutes. Cut into bite-size pieces.

4. To build tacos, skillet warm tortillas (page 15). Divide chicken equally among tortillas. Top with salsa. Fold tortillas in half.

Sour Cream Enchilada Tacos

Makes 12 tacos

This is pure Southwest comfort food, inspired by the many casseroles I was raised on as a child. You'll find layers of flavor with the creamy sauce, chile and cheese combination.

Tip

When I am pressed for time I pick up a roasted chicken from the deli section of my grocery store. Typically one 4-lb (2 kg) roasted cooked chicken will yield approximately 4 cups (1 L) of cooked diced chicken.

- Preheat oven to 350°F (180°C)
- 8-inch (20 cm) square glass baking dish, greased

3 cups	chopped roasted chicken (see page 32 and Tip, left)	750 mL
1 cup	sour cream	250 mL
1 cup	store-bought tomato salsa or Tomato Table Salsa (page 302)	250 mL
½ cup	chopped roasted New Mexico or Anaheim green chile peppers (2 to 3 depending on size) (see page 49)	125 mL
2 cups	shredded Cheddar cheese, divided	500 mL
	Vegetable oil	
12	6-inch (15 cm) corn tortillas	12
2 cups	chopped romaine lettuce	500 mL
2	tomatoes, seeded and diced	2

1. In a large bowl, combine chicken, sour cream, salsa, green chiles and 1 cup (250 mL) of the cheese. Mix well.

2. In a medium skillet, heat 1 inch (2.5 cm) of oil over medium-high heat. It should be hot enough that a small piece of tortilla sizzles but doesn't brown. Quickly dip each tortilla in oil for 3 to 4 seconds. Stack on a plate or baking sheet.

3. To build tacos, divide chicken mixture equally among tortillas. Fold tortillas in half and place in prepared baking dish, arranging side by side. Top with remaining 1 cup (250 mL) of cheese. Bake in preheated oven until tacos are heated through and cheese is bubbling, 20 to 25 minutes. Serve on individual plates and top with lettuce and tomatoes.

Grilled Ranch Chicken Tacos

Makes 8 tacos

Zesty flavors of ranch dressing lace this grilled chicken taco. Crispy corn salsa adds a fresh sweet texture to the savory filling.

Variation
Substitute Citrus Salsa (page 301) for the Fiery Corn Relish.

• Barbecue grill

¼ cup	olive oil	60 mL
	Juice of 1 lime	
1	package (0.7 oz/19 g) dry ranch dressing mix	1
2 lbs	boneless skinless chicken breasts	1 kg
8	6- to 8-inch (15 to 20 cm) corn tortillas, skillet-warmed (page 15)	8
1	tomato, seeded and diced	1
1½ cups	shredded Cheddar cheese	375 mL
	Fiery Corn Relish (page 311)	

1. In a small bowl, whisk together oil, lime juice and dressing mix.

2. In a large resealable plastic bag, combine marinade and chicken. Seal bag and work marinade into chicken with your fingers. Refrigerate for at least 2 hours or for up to 6 hours.

3. Preheat greased grill to medium-high. Remove chicken from marinade and discard marinade. Grill chicken, turning once, until no longer pink inside, 6 to 8 minutes per side. Transfer chicken to a cutting board. Let stand for 6 to 8 minutes. Cut into bite-size pieces.

4. To build tacos, divide chicken equally among tortillas. Top with tomato, cheese and Fiery Corn Relish. Fold tortillas in half.

Roasted Garlic, Chicken and Mushroom Tacos

Makes 8 tacos

The mushrooms add a richness to this chicken filling. Top it with sun-dried tomatoes for a bright and tasty taco.

Tip

When I am pressed for time I pick up a roasted chicken from the deli section of my grocery store. Typically one 4-lb (2 kg) roasted cooked chicken will yield approximately 4 cups (1 L) of cooked diced chicken.

1 tbsp	olive oil	15 mL
4	cloves garlic, minced	4
1½ cups	sliced mushrooms	375 mL
3 cups	diced roasted chicken (see page 32 and Tip, left)	750 mL
8	6- to 8-inch (15 to 20 cm) corn or flour tortillas, skillet-warmed (page 15)	8
2 cups	chopped fresh spinach	500 mL
½ cup	freshly grated Parmesan cheese	125 mL
½ cup	oil-packed sun-dried tomatoes, drained and chopped	125 mL

1. In a large skillet, heat oil over medium-high heat. Sauté garlic and mushrooms until mushrooms are soft, about 6 minutes. Add chicken and sauté until chicken is heated through, 6 to 8 minutes.

2. To build tacos, divide chicken mixture equally among tortillas. Top with spinach, cheese and sun-dried tomatoes. Fold tortillas in half.

White Chili Chicken Tacos

From time to time I cook up a big pot of navy beans and ham. It is a family favorite that inspired these simple little tacos.

Tip

A 12-oz (340 mL) can of navy beans will give you about 1¼ cups (300 mL) once drained and rinsed. If you have a larger size can you can add the extra beans if you wish or transfer them to an airtight container and refrigerate for up to 2 days or freeze for up to 6 months.

1¼ cups	drained rinsed canned navy beans (see Tip, left)	300 mL
1 cup	shredded cooked chicken (see pages 31 and 32)	250 mL
¼ cup	chicken broth	60 mL
6 oz	cooked ham, diced	175 g
1 tsp	hot pepper flakes	5 mL
½ tsp	ground cumin	2 mL
8	6- to 8-inch (15 to 20 cm) flour tortillas (see Tip, page 76), skillet-warmed (page 15)	8
2 cups	chopped romaine lettuce	500 mL
	Pico de Gallo (page 305)	

1. In a large skillet over medium-high heat, sauté beans, chicken, broth, ham, hot pepper flakes and cumin until heated through and liquid is evaporated, 8 to 10 minutes.

2. To build tacos, divide chicken mixture equally among tortillas. Top with lettuce and Pico de Gallo. Fold tortillas in half.

Thai Chicken Tacos

Peanut flavor adds so much to this taco. Teamed with the hot peppers, chicken and veggies, it is an Asian delight.

Tip

Fried rice and steamed brown rice both make a perfect side dish for these tacos. Steamed asparagus or fresh sliced tomatoes are also a nice addition to this taco entrée.

¼ cup	peanut butter	60 mL
¼ cup	hot water	60 mL
1 tbsp	soy sauce	15 mL
1	clove garlic, minced	1
½ tsp	hot pepper flakes	2 mL
1 tbsp	peanut or vegetable oil	15 mL
3 cups	diced roasted chicken (see page 32 and Tip, page 49)	750 mL
1 cup	chopped broccoli	250 mL
8	6- to 8-inch (15 to 20 cm) flour tortillas, skillet-warmed (page 15)	8
1	carrot, coarsely grated	1

1. In a small bowl, combine peanut butter, hot water, soy sauce, garlic and hot pepper flakes.

2. In a large skillet, heat oil over medium-high heat. Sauté chicken for 3 minutes. Add peanut sauce and broccoli and sauté until broccoli is tender-crisp, about 5 minutes.

3. To build tacos, divide chicken mixture equally among tortillas. Top with carrot. Fold tortillas in half.

Chicken Cordon Bleu Tacos

This taco was inspired by the French entrée. Its crispy texture and creamy filling is tasty wrapped in a warm flour tortilla.

Tips

For a calorie saver, substitute fat-free mayonnaise for regular mayonnaise.

Serve with a drizzle of Creamy Wasabi Sauce (page 316) or Garlic Sour Cream Sauce (page 321).

Variation

Substitute Cheddar or Provolone cheese for the Swiss cheese.

- Preheat oven to 425°F (220°C)
- Rimmed baking sheet, greased
- Ovenproof platter

6 tbsp	mayonnaise	90 mL
1 tbsp	Dijon mustard	15 mL
1 cup	finely crushed corn flakes cereal	250 mL
1½ lbs	boneless skinless chicken breasts, cut into strips	750 g
8	6- to 8-inch (15 to 20 cm) flour or corn tortillas (see Tip, page 76), skillet-warmed (page 15)	8
8	thin slices Swiss cheese	8
8	thin slices deli ham	8

1. In a small bowl, combine mayonnaise and mustard. Place corn flakes on a plate. Dip chicken in mayonnaise mixture, then roll in corn flakes. Place on prepared baking sheet. Discard any excess mayonnaise mixture and crumbs.

2. Bake chicken in preheated oven until chicken is no longer pink inside and golden brown, for 10 minutes. Remove chicken from oven. Reduce oven temperature to 250°F (120°C).

3. To build tacos, top each tortilla with one slice of cheese and one slice of ham. Divide chicken equally among tortillas. Fold tortillas in half.

4. Place tacos on ovenproof platter. Bake until cheese is melted, 10 to 12 minutes.

Grilled Italian Chicken Tacos with Parmesan

Makes 8 tacos

Italian inspiration brings about a taco full of flavor. Spices and fresh herbs create an adventure in grilling and taco cuisine.

Tip

For best results in grilling, brush the grill grate with vegetable oil or coat with a nonstick cooking spray before preheating the grill.

• Preheat greased barbecue grill to medium-high (see Tip, left)

1½ lbs	boneless skinless chicken breasts	750 g
1 tbsp	olive oil	15 mL
1 tbsp	dried Italian herb seasoning	15 mL
8	6- to 8-inch (15 to 20 cm) flour tortillas (see Tip, page 76), skillet-warmed (page 15)	8
2	tomatoes, seeded and diced	2
½ cup	chopped fresh basil	125 mL
½ cup	freshly grated Parmesan cheese	125 mL

1. Coat chicken with oil, then rub with Italian seasoning.

2. Grill chicken, turning once, until no longer pink inside, 6 to 8 minutes per side. Transfer chicken to a cutting board. Let stand for 6 to 8 minutes. Cut into thin slices.

3. To build tacos, divide chicken equally among tortillas. Top with tomato, basil and cheese. Fold tortillas in half.

Chicken, Mushroom and Green Chile Tacos

Makes 8 tacos

This is a hearty sautéed taco filling. The mushroom, onion and chile combination simply wrapped is very satisfying.

Variation
Add a spoonful of Green Chile Relish (page 312) for tons of chile flavor.

2 tbsp	olive oil, divided	30 mL
1½ cups	chopped mushrooms	375 mL
1	onion, minced	1
½ cup	chopped roasted New Mexico or Anaheim green chile peppers (2 to 3 depending on size) (see page 49)	125 mL
1½ lbs	boneless skinless chicken breasts, cut into ¼-inch (0.5 cm) cubes	750 g
8	6- to 8-inch (15 to 20 cm) flour tortillas, skillet-warmed (page 15)	8
1 cup	shredded Monterey Jack cheese	250 mL

1. In a large skillet, heat 1 tbsp (15 mL) of the oil over medium-high heat. Sauté mushrooms, onion and chiles until onions are transparent, 4 to 6 minutes. Set aside.

2. In same skillet over medium-high heat, add remaining 1 tbsp (15 mL) of oil. Sauté chicken until no longer pink inside and juices have evaporated, 10 to 12 minutes. Return mushroom mixture to skillet and sauté until hot, 3 to 4 minutes.

3. To build tacos, divide chicken mixture equally among tortillas. Top with cheese. Fold tortillas in half.

Mandarin Chicken Tacos with Citrus Salsa

Contemporary flavors of orange, onion and blue cheese highlight this grilled chicken filling. It is a delicious taco to serve on a hot summer day.

• Barbecue grill

¼ cup	freshly squeezed orange juice	60 mL
2 tbsp	olive oil	30 mL
2 tbsp	liquid honey	30 mL
1 tsp	paprika	5 mL
1½ lbs	boneless skinless chicken breasts	750 g
8	6-inch (15 cm) corn tortillas	8
2 cups	chopped salad mix	500 mL
1 cup	canned drained mandarin oranges, chopped	250 mL
1	onion, minced	1
1 cup	crumbled blue cheese	250 mL
	Citrus Salsa (page 301)	

1. In a medium bowl, combine orange juice, oil, honey and paprika.

2. In a large resealable plastic bag, combine marinade and chicken. Seal bag and work marinade into chicken with your fingers. Refrigerate for at least 2 hours or for up to 6 hours.

3. Preheat greased grill to medium-high. Remove chicken from marinade and discard marinade. Grill chicken, turning once, until no longer pink inside, 6 to 8 minutes per side. Transfer chicken to a cutting board. Let stand for 6 to 8 minutes. Cut into thin slices

4. To build tacos, skillet warm tortillas (page 15). Divide chicken equally among tortillas. Top with salad mix, oranges, onion, cheese and Citrus Salsa. Fold tortillas in half.

Pollo Enchilada Tacos

Enchiladas are an everyday meal in New Mexico. You can make them in a variety of ways. Baked or stacked, they are a traditional favorite. These baked tacos are fun and innovative.

Tip

To make tacos ahead: Follow Steps 1 through 3 and refrigerate for up to 2 days. When ready to serve, remove from refrigerator and follow Step 4.

- Preheat oven to 350°F (180°C)
- 8-inch (20 cm) square glass baking dish, greased

	Vegetable oil	
12	6-inch (15 cm) corn tortillas	12
3 cups	chopped cooked chicken (see pages 31 and 32)	750 mL
2 cups	shredded Cheddar cheese, divided	500 mL
4	green onions, green parts only, minced	4
1 tsp	ground cumin	5 mL
	Kosher salt and freshly ground black pepper	
2 cups	red enchilada sauce	500 mL
3 cups	chopped romaine lettuce	750 mL
1	onion, chopped	1

1. In a medium skillet, heat 1 inch (2.5 cm) of oil over medium-high heat. It should be hot enough that a small piece of tortilla sizzles but doesn't brown. Quickly dip each tortilla in oil for 3 to 4 seconds. Stack on a plate or baking sheet.

2. In a large bowl, combine chicken, 1 cup (250 mL) of the cheese, green onions and cumin. Season with salt and pepper to taste. Mix well.

3. To build tacos, divide chicken mixture equally among tortillas. Fold tortillas in half and place in baking dish, arranging tacos side by side.

4. Pour enchilada sauce over top or inside tacos. Top with remaining 1 cup (250 mL) of cheese. Bake in preheated oven until cheese is bubbling and tortillas start to crisp, 25 to 30 minutes. Let stand for 8 to 10 minutes. Serve individually garnished with lettuce and onion.

Grilled Jerk Chicken Tacos with Hot Pineapple Sauce

Caribbean spices include sweet and savory flavors that spice up this grilled chicken filling. The hot sweet pineapple sauce is a superb finish for this taco.

Tip

There are a variety of seasoning blends on the market. Dry Caribbean spice mix is a blend of dried and minced chile peppers combined with allspice, a variety of salts and peppers. Some are very spicy; others are mild. Test a few until you find a favorite.

• Preheat greased barbecue grill to medium-high

1 tbsp	Caribbean jerk dry seasoning (see Tip, left)	15 mL
1 tsp	garlic powder	5 mL
1 tbsp	freshly squeezed lemon juice	15 mL
1½ lbs	boneless skinless chicken breasts	750 g
1 tbsp	olive oil	15 mL
8	6- to 8-inch (15 to 20 cm) flour tortillas, skillet-warmed (page 15)	8
4	green onions, green parts only, chopped	4
	Hot Pineapple Sauce (page 329)	
2 cups	chopped salad mix	500 mL

1. In a small bowl, combine seasoning, garlic powder and lemon juice.

2. Coat chicken with oil, then rub with seasoning mixture.

3. Grill chicken, turning once, until no longer pink inside, 6 to 8 minutes per side. Transfer chicken to a cutting board. Let stand for 6 to 8 minutes. Cut into thin slices.

4. To build tacos, divide chicken equally among tortillas. Top with green onions, Hot Pineapple Sauce and salad mix. Fold tortillas in half.

Black Pepper Chicken Tacos

My son created this taco, inspired by his love of spicy flavors and good healthy eating. The combination of black pepper and green chile adds a different level of spice that is terrific.

1 tbsp	olive oil	15 mL
1 lb	boneless skinless chicken breasts, cut into bite-size pieces	500 g
1	onion, chopped	1
½ cup	chopped roasted green chile peppers (2 to 3 depending on size) (see page 49)	125 mL
2 tbsp	Worcestershire sauce	30 mL
1 tbsp	freshly ground black pepper	15 mL
8	6-inch (15 cm) corn tortillas, skillet-warmed (page 15)	8
2 cups	chopped fresh spinach	500 mL
2 tbsp	chopped fresh cilantro	30 mL

1. In a large skillet, heat oil over medium-high heat. Sauté chicken until no longer pink inside, 10 to 12 minutes. Remove from skillet.

2. In same skillet, combine onion, chiles, Worcestershire sauce and pepper and sauté until vegetables are tender, 8 to 10 minutes. Stir in cooked chicken.

3. To build tacos, divide chicken mixture equally among tortillas. Top with spinach and a pinch of cilantro. Fold tortillas in half.

Chicken and Sausage Taco

Makes 8 tacos

I like cured or seasoned meats that have intense flavor and aroma. They add so much to a simple taco. Polish sausage does just that to this chicken filling.

Tip

Kielbasa comes in precooked and fresh varieties. I use a precooked sausage for this filling, resulting in a quick and easy prep time.

1 tbsp	olive oil	15 mL
8 oz	kielbasa sausage, cooked and cut into ¼-inch (0.5 cm) slices (see Tip, left)	250 g
2 cups	shredded roasted chicken (see page 32 and Tip, page 81)	500 mL
8	6- to 8-inch (15 to 20 cm) corn tortillas, skillet-warmed (page 15)	8
1½ cups	shredded sharp Cheddar cheese	375 mL
1	onion, minced	1
	Green Chile Relish (page 312)	

1. In a large skillet, heat oil over medium heat. Sauté sausage and chicken until heated through, 6 to 8 minutes.

2. To build tacos, divide chicken mixture equally among tortillas. Top with cheese, onion and Green Chile Relish. Fold tortillas in half.

Roasted Turkey, Avocado, Swiss and Sprout Tacos

Makes 8 tacos

This is truly a hand-held favorite, a sandwich-style taco. Fresh tomato, avocado and sprouts bring a familiar earthiness to the flavor of this taco.

Variation

For a little spice, add ¼ cup (60 mL) chopped pickled jalapeños, drained, to the turkey mixture.

3 cups	diced roasted turkey (see page 92 and Tip, page 93)	750 mL
½ cup	mayonnaise	125 mL
½ tsp	salt	2 mL
½ tsp	freshly ground black pepper	2 mL
8	6- to 8-inch (15 to 20 cm) flour tortillas, skillet-warmed (page 15)	8
8	thin slices Swiss cheese	8
2	avocados, cubed	2
2	tomatoes, seeded and diced	2
2 cups	alfalfa sprouts	500 mL

1. In a large bowl, combine turkey, mayonnaise, salt and pepper.

2. To build tacos, place one slice of cheese on each tortilla. Divide turkey mixture equally among tortillas. Top with avocado, tomatoes and sprouts. Fold tortillas in half.

Roasted Turkey Breast

Makes 6 to 8 cups (1.5 to 2 L) chopped or shredded cooked turkey

This is a simple recipe for moist and tender turkey breast and can be used in the turkey recipes suggested here.

Tip

Let turkey cool and place in resealable plastic bags. Refrigerate for up to 2 days or freeze for up to 4 months.

- Preheat oven to 325°F (160°C)
- 13- by 9-inch (33 by 23 cm) roasting pan, greased
- Instant-read thermometer

3 tbsp	butter, melted	45 mL
1 tbsp	olive oil	15 mL
3 to 4 lb	whole boneless turkey breast (see Tip, left)	1.5 to 2 kg
2 tbsp	kosher salt	30 mL
1 tsp	freshly ground black pepper	5 mL

1. In a small bowl, combine butter and oil. Place turkey breast in prepared roasting pan, skin side up. Rub with butter mixture. Sprinkle with salt and pepper.

2. Roast in preheated oven until an instant-read thermometer inserted into the thickest part of the breast registers 170°F (77°C), $1\frac{1}{2}$ to 2 hours. Tent with foil and let stand for 10 to 15 minutes. Transfer to a cutting board and cut into bite-size pieces or transfer to a bowl and shred with your fingers or two forks as required for your recipe, discarding skin, if desired.

Spicy BLT Turkey Tacos

Makes 8 tacos

A "takeoff" of one of my favorite sandwiches, this taco is bursting with flavor. Fresh rosemary adds an element of surprise.

Tip

For these tacos, you can use roasted whole turkey, roasted boneless or bone-in turkey pieces or grilled boneless breast cuts. Thawed, frozen precooked turkey products also work well. Look for them in the supermarket freezer section.

Variation

Substitute 2 cups (500 mL) chopped fresh spinach for the lettuce and substitute 1 cup (250 mL) shredded Monterey Jack cheese for the panela.

1 tbsp	olive oil	15 mL
½ cup	diced onion	125 mL
3 cups	diced roasted turkey (see page 92 and Tip, left)	750 mL
8	strips bacon, cooked and crumbled	8
2 tsp	fresh minced rosemary	10 mL
8	6- to 8-inch (15 to 20 cm) flour tortillas, skillet-warmed (page 15)	8
2 cups	shredded lettuce	500 mL
2	tomatoes, seeded and diced	2
1 cup	shredded panela cheese	250 mL
	Creamy Wasabi Sauce (page 316)	

1. In a skillet, heat oil over medium heat. Sauté onion and turkey until onion is transparent, 8 to 10 minutes. Reduce heat to medium-low and add cooked bacon and rosemary. Sauté until heated through, 2 to 4 minutes.

2. To build tacos, divide turkey mixture equally among tortillas. Top with lettuce, tomatoes, cheese and Creamy Wasabi Sauce. Fold tortillas in half.

Green Chile Turkey Taco Bake

This easy casserole-style taco is rich and creamy. It is a great dish to take to a potluck or serve for a busy weeknight meal.

Variation

Serve with bowls of shredded lettuce, chopped onion and tomato so each diner can garnish their own taco how they like it.

- Preheat oven to 350°F (180°C)
- 8-inch (20 cm) square glass baking dish, greased

1	can (10 oz/284 mL) condensed cream of mushroom soup	1
½ cup	roasted chopped New Mexico or Anaheim green chile peppers (2 to 3 depending on size) (see page 49)	125 mL
½ cup	milk	125 mL
½ cup	sour cream	125 mL
4 cups	diced roasted turkey (see page 92 and Tip, page 93)	1 L
Pinch	kosher salt	Pinch
12	6-inch (15 cm) corn tortillas	12
2 cups	shredded Cheddar cheese	500 mL

1. In a medium bowl, combine condensed soup, chiles, milk and sour cream. Add turkey and salt and mix well.

2. To build tacos, divide turkey filling equally among tortillas. Top with cheese. Fold tortillas in half and place in prepared baking dish, arranging side by side. Bake in preheated oven until tacos are heated through and cheese is melted and bubbling, 20 to 25 minutes.

Turkey and Jalapeño Jack Tacos with Spicy Ranch Sauce

Makes 8 tacos

This is definitely a turkey taco with a kick! Three layers of chiles add spice intensify the flavor of this taco. For the adventurous chile lovers, kick it up even more with two or three additional jalapeños!

Tip

The perfect size tortilla for a taco is 6 inches (15 cm). It is generally more available in corn rather than flour. Buy 8-inch (20 cm) flour tortillas and trim them with a pair of kitchen shears to 6 inches (15 cm) using a corn tortilla as a template.

1 tbsp	olive oil	15 mL
1	onion, cut into ¼-inch (0.5 cm) rings	1
3	jalapeños, seeded and chopped	3
3 cups	diced roasted turkey (see page 92 and Tip, page 93)	750 mL
	Salt and freshly ground black pepper	
8	6- to 8-inch (15 to 20 cm) flour tortillas, skillet-warmed (page 15)	8
	Chipotle Ranch Sauce (page 326)	
½ cup	fresh cilantro leaves	125 mL
2 cups	chopped salad mix	500 mL
1½ cups	shredded Pepper Jack cheese	375 mL

1. In a large skillet, heat oil over medium-high heat. Add onion and jalapeños. Cover and cook, stirring often, until tender, 4 to 6 minutes. Add turkey and sauté until onions are transparent, 6 to 8 minutes. Season with salt and pepper to taste.

2. To build tacos, divide turkey mixture equally among tortillas. Top with Chipotle Ranch Sauce, cilantro, salad mix and cheese. Fold tortillas in half.

Smoked Turkey Tacos with Chipotle Sauce

Lightly grilled turkey cutlets take only minutes to grill. Spicy, smoky elements come together in this sauce, accented with a twist of lime for a savory taco.

• Preheat greased barbecue grill to medium-high

1½ lbs	turkey breast, cutlets or fillets	750 g
1 tbsp	olive oil	15 mL
1½ tsp	kosher salt	7 mL
½ tsp	freshly ground black pepper	2 mL
3	chipotle chile peppers in adobo sauce, puréed	3
½ tsp	liquid smoke	2 mL
8	6-inch (15 cm) corn tortillas, skillet-warmed (page 15)	8
2 cups	shredded cabbage	500 mL
2	limes, each cut into 4 wedges	2

1. Coat turkey with oil and season with salt and pepper.

2. In a small bowl, combine chiles and liquid smoke.

3. Grill turkey, turning once, until no longer pink inside and lightly browned, 2 to 3 minutes per side. Brush both sides of turkey with chile mixture. Grill for 1 minute per side. Transfer turkey to a cutting board. Let stand for 6 to 8 minutes. Cut into bite-size pieces.

4. To build tacos, divide turkey equally among tortillas. Top with cabbage. Fold tortillas in half. Serve each with a lime wedge.

Grilled Turkey, Cayenne, Bacon and Jack Tacos

Makes 8 tacos

There is a ton of flavor in this taco with savory bacon and spicy cayenne. The charring of the turkey on the grill adds another element of texture and flavor to enjoy.

Tips

If you are short on time, skillet cooking the turkey is quick and easy. In a large skillet over medium heat, sauté cutlets until lightly browned and no longer pink inside, 2 to 3 minutes per side.

Add more flavor by drizzling each taco with a variety of sauces such as Cilantro Chile Sauce (page 325), Poblano Sauce (page 320) or Hot Pineapple Sauce (page 329).

• Preheat greased barbecue grill to medium-high

1½ lbs	turkey breast cutlets (see Tips, left)	750 g
1 tbsp	olive oil	15 mL
1 tsp	kosher salt	5 mL
½ tsp	ground cumin	2 mL
½ tsp	cayenne pepper	2 mL
½ tsp	freshly ground black pepper	2 mL
8	6-inch (15 cm) corn tortillas, skillet-warmed (page 15)	8
4	strips bacon, cooked and crumbled	4
2 cups	chopped salad mix	500 mL
1½ cups	shredded Monterey Jack cheese	375 mL

1. Coat turkey with oil and season with salt, cumin, cayenne and black pepper.

2. Grill turkey, turning once, until no longer pink inside and lightly browned, 2 to 3 minutes per side. Transfer turkey to a cutting board. Let stand for 6 to 8 minutes. Cut into bite-size pieces.

3. To build tacos, divide turkey equally among tortillas. Top with bacon, salad mix and cheese. Fold tortillas in half.

Curried Turkey Tacos

Makes 8 tacos

Infuse the flavors of India into these little wrapped bundles. Roasted turkey is glazed with curry and chutney, heightening the flavor.

Tip

A mango-based chutney tastes delicious in this recipe. However, there are a variety of flavors on the market, some less fruity and some spicy. Find your favorite and enjoy.

⅓ cup	sweet chutney (see Tip, left)	75 mL
1 tbsp	red wine vinegar	15 mL
1 tsp	curry powder	5 mL
3 cups	diced roasted turkey (see page 92 and Tip, page 93)	750 mL
8	6- to 8-inch (15 to 20 cm) flour tortillas, skillet-warmed (page 15)	8
¾ cup	cilantro leaves, stemmed	175 mL
1	red onion, thinly sliced	1

1. In a small bowl combine chutney, vinegar and curry powder.

2. In a large skillet over medium heat, sauté turkey and chutney mixture until turkey is heated through, 6 to 8 minutes.

3. To build tacos, divide turkey mixture equally among tortillas. Top with cilantro leaves and red onion. Fold tortillas in half.

Chilled Jack, Turkey and Pastrami Tacos

Makes 8 tacos

Pastrami and a spicy sauce intensify the flavor of these tacos. This is a great "pack and go" treat that everyone loves. Pack them for a picnic or take them for lunch.

1 lb	pastrami, chopped	500 g
2 cups	diced roasted turkey (see page 92 and Tip, page 93)	500 mL
8	6- to 8-inch (15 to 20 cm) flour tortillas, skillet-warmed (page 15)	8
	Creamy Wasabi Sauce (page 316)	
1 cup	shredded Monterey Jack cheese	250 mL
2 cups	shredded lettuce	500 mL

1. In a large bowl, combine pastrami and turkey.

2. To build tacos, spread one side of each tortilla with a thin layer of Creamy Wasabi Sauce. Divide turkey mixture equally among tortillas. Top with cheese and lettuce. Fold tortillas in half. Cover and refrigerate for at least 1 hour or for up to 4 hours to allow flavors to blend.

Cajun-Spiced Turkey Tacos

Red beans and the distinctive flavors and spices of Cajun country make this soft taco delicious. It is a simple sauté that is hearty and filling.

Tip

Cotija is a crumbly, sharp Mexican cheese. You could substitute freshly grated Parmesan or a milder feta or goat cheese.

Variation

Top each taco equally with fresh greens such as 1½ cups (375 mL) chopped spinach, romaine lettuce or shredded zucchini.

1 tbsp	olive oil	15 mL
2	cloves garlic, minced	2
3 cups	diced roasted turkey (see page 92 and Tip, page 93)	750 mL
1 cup	canned or cooked red beans, drained and rinsed	250 mL
1 tbsp	Cajun seasoning (page 25)	15 mL
8	6- to 8-inch (15 to 20 cm) flour tortillas, skillet-warmed (page 15)	8
½ cup	crumbled Cotija cheese (see Tip, left)	125 mL

1. In a large skillet, heat oil over medium heat. Sauté garlic, turkey, beans and Cajun seasoning until turkey is heated through and flavors are blended, 10 to 12 minutes.

2. To build tacos, divide turkey mixture equally among tortillas. Top with cheese. Fold tortillas in half.

Thanksgiving Tacos with Jalapeño Cranberry Relish

If you're not into traditional Thanksgiving day meals, try these delicious tacos. Roasted turkey topped with greens, pungent cheese and a sweet relish makes a perfect alternative.

Tip

There are a variety of salad mixes with a wide range of flavors on the market. There are red and green lettuce varieties that range in taste from intense spice to sweet and mild. "Living" lettuce and "artisan" lettuce and greens are also available. Taste and compare to find your favorite combination of greens.

• Food processor

Jalapeño Cranberry Relish

4	jalapeños, seeded and stemmed	4
12 oz	fresh or frozen cranberries, divided (3 cups/750 mL)	375 g
1 cup	canned drained mandarin oranges, divided	250 mL
½ cup	granulated sugar, divided	125 mL
3 cups	diced roasted turkey, warmed (see page 92 and Tip, page 93)	750 mL
8	6- to 8-inch (15 to 20 cm) flour tortillas, skillet-warmed (page 15)	8
2 cups	chopped salad mix (see Tip, left)	500 mL
1 cup	crumbled feta cheese	250 mL

1. *Jalapeño Cranberry Relish:* In a small saucepan, add jalapeños and enough water to cover by 1 inch (2.5 cm). Bring jalapeños to a boil over high heat. Boil until jalapeños are soft, 8 to 10 minutes. Drain. Let cool.

2. In a food processor, process half each of the cranberries, oranges, sugar and jalapeños until finely chopped. Add remaining cranberries, oranges, sugar and jalapeños and process until coarsely chopped. Transfer to an airtight container and refrigerate for least 2 hours or for up to 4 days to allow flavors to blend.

3. To build tacos, divide turkey equally among tortillas. Top with Jalapeño Cranberry Relish, salad mix and cheese. Fold tortillas in half.

Turkey Taquitos with Habanero Cream Sauce

Makes 36 rolled tacos

Little rolled turkey tacos, deep-fried and lightly salted, are the best appetizers. Top these dippable tacos with a creamy spicy sauce and you have an unforgettable appetizer.

Tip

For variety, serve with Fiesta Taco Sauce (page, 324) or Cilantro Chile Sauce (page 325) along with the Habanero Cream Sauce.

• Candy/deep-fry thermometer

3 cups	finely diced roasted turkey (see page 92 and Tip, page 93)	750 mL
	Salt	
36	4-inch (10 cm) corn tortillas, micro-warmed (page 15)	36
	Vegetable oil	
	Habanero Cream Sauce (page 323)	

1. In a large bowl, thoroughly combine shredded turkey and ¾ tsp (3 mL) salt.

2. To build tacos, place about 1 heaping tbsp (15 mL) of turkey at one end of each tortilla. Gently roll tortilla and secure with a toothpick. Deep-fry immediately or place rolled tacos in a resealable plastic bag to keep moist. Refrigerate for up to 2 days.

3. Fill a deep-fryer, deep heavy pot or deep skillet with 3 inches (7.5 cm) of oil and heat to 350°F (180°C). Using tongs, gently place 3 to 4 tacos at a time in the hot oil and deep-fry, turning once, until golden brown and crispy, 2 to 3 minutes. Drain on paper towels. Lightly season with salt. Serve with Habanero Cream Sauce.

Crispy Turkey Tacos

Makes 8 tacos

Crispy and tasty, these tacos are fun to make for a crowd. I love to serve them after Thanksgiving when we all get tired of turkey sandwiches.

Tip

For these tacos, you can use roasted whole turkey, roasted boneless or bone-in turkey pieces or grilled boneless breast cuts. Thawed, frozen precooked turkey products also work well. Look for them in the supermarket freezer section.

• Candy/deep-fry thermometer

3 cups	diced roasted turkey (see page 92 and Tip, left)	750 mL
1 cup	shredded Monterey Jack cheese	250 mL
8	6-inch (15 cm) corn tortillas, micro-warmed (page 15)	8
	Vegetable oil	
	Salsa Verde (page 300)	

1. In a large bowl, combine turkey and cheese.

2. To build tacos, divide turkey mixture equally among tortillas, placing on one half of the tortilla. Fold tortillas in half and secure the edges with toothpicks. Deep-fry immediately or place filled tortillas in a large resealable plastic bag and refrigerate until ready to cook for up to 2 days.

3. Fill a deep-fryer, deep heavy pot or deep skillet with 3 inches (7.5 cm) of oil and heat to 350°F (180°C). Using tongs, gently place 2 to 3 tacos at a time in the hot oil and deep-fry, turning once, until crispy and golden brown, 1 to 2 minutes. Drain on paper towels. Serve with Salsa Verde.

Lemon Pepper Turkey Tacos

Light and lemony, this turkey filling is quick and easy. The lemon pepper seasoning is a quick way to add intense flavor to this taco. Perfect for any weeknight meal.

1½ lbs	turkey breast, cutlets or fillets	750 g
1¼ tsp	lemon pepper	6 mL
2 tbsp	butter	30 mL
	Juice of 1 lemon	
8	6-inch (15 cm) corn tortillas, skillet-warmed (page 15)	8
2 cups	chopped salad mix	500 mL
	Tomatillo Avocado Salsa (page 304)	

1. Season turkey with lemon pepper.

2. In a large skillet, melt butter over medium heat. Add turkey and cook, turning once, until lightly browned and no longer pink inside, about 2½ minutes per side. Transfer to a cutting board. Let stand for 6 to 8 minutes. Cut into bite-size pieces.

3. In a large bowl, toss turkey with lemon juice.

4. To build tacos, divide turkey equally among tortillas. Top with salad mix and Tomatillo Avocado Salsa. Fold tortillas in half.

Sautéed Turkey and Spinach Tacos

Makes 8 tacos

This is a rich creamy turkey filling that is delicious. The accent of red bell pepper adds to the freshness and flavor of this taco.

Variation
Toss bell peppers with 1 tbsp (15 mL) minced cilantro and 1 tbsp (15 mL) chopped green onion.

2 tbsp	olive oil	30 mL
2	cloves garlic, minced	2
3 cups	chopped spinach	750 mL
3 cups	diced roasted turkey (see page 92 and Tip, page 102)	750 mL
1 cup	shredded Monterey Jack cheese	250 mL
8	6-inch (15 cm) corn tortillas, skillet-warmed (page 15)	8
2	red bell peppers, chopped	2

1. In a large skillet, heat oil over medium heat. Sauté garlic, spinach and turkey until spinach starts to wilt, 6 to 8 minutes. Add cheese and sauté until cheese is melted, about 4 minutes.

2. To build tacos, divide turkey mixture equally among tortillas. Top with bell pepper. Fold tortillas in half.

Sweet Toasted Turkey Tacos

Makes 8 tacos

Sweet and cheesy flavors lace this roasted turkey filling. Pair this contemporary taco with your favorite wine.

Variation
To add a rich buttery flavor, spread a thin layer of butter on outside of each tortilla. Then spread opposite side with apple butter and fill as in Step 1. The butter will give the outside of the taco a grilled buttery flavor.

8	6- to 8-inch (15 to 20 cm) flour tortillas, micro-warmed (page 15)	8
1/4 cup	apple butter	60 mL
8 oz	Brie cheese, thinly sliced	250 g
3 cups	diced roasted turkey (see page 92 and Tip, page 102)	750 mL
2 cups	chopped salad mix	500 mL
1	Granny Smith apple, thinly sliced	1

1. To build tacos, spread one side of each tortilla with 1 1/2 tsp (7 mL) apple butter. Top equally with cheese, turkey, salad mix and sliced apple. Fold tortillas in half.

2. In a large skillet over medium heat, in batches as necessary, grill tacos, turning once, until tortillas are crispy on both sides and cheese is melted in the middle, 4 to 6 minutes.

Layered Turkey Club Soft Tacos

Makes 8 tacos

The first time a club sandwich recipe was published in a cookbook was in 1903 in the Good Housekeeping Everyday Cook Book. *It is a true North American favorite. Here it is with a little spice and a Mexican twist!*

Tip

These tacos can also be grilled in a large skillet. Heat a large skillet over medium-high heat. Grill tacos, turning once, until tortillas are golden brown and cheese is melted, 4 to 6 minutes.

Variation

If you prefer, omit Jalapeño Cream Sauce and serve with Spicy Ranch Sauce (page 326).

- Preheat panini press (see Tip, left)

8	6- to 8-inch (15 to 20 cm) flour tortillas	8
	Butter, softened	
8	thin slices Provolone cheese	8
8	strips bacon, cooked and crumbled	8
3 cups	diced roasted turkey (see page 92 and Tip, page 102)	750 mL
1	tomato, seeded and diced	1
2 cups	chopped salad mix (see Tip, page 100)	500 mL
	Jalapeño Cream Sauce (page 323)	

1. To build tacos, butter one side of each tortilla. Gently place butter side down, and divide cheese equally among tortillas. Top with bacon. Divide turkey equally among tortillas. Top with tomato. Fold tortillas in half.

2. In batches as necessary, grill tacos on preheated panini press until cheese is melted and tortillas are golden brown. Garnish with salad mix and Jalapeño Cream Sauce.

Cinnamon Turkey Tacos

Makes 8 tacos

This tasty array of spices is delicious on grilled turkey. Cinnamon and chipotle chile are unforgettable flavors that make this taco perfect for entertaining.

• Preheat greased barbecue grill to medium-high

1½ tsp	ground cinnamon	7 mL
1 tsp	kosher salt	5 mL
½ tsp	freshly ground black pepper	2 mL
½ tsp	ground cumin	2 mL
1½ lbs	turkey breast, cutlets or fillets	750 g
1 tbsp	olive oil	15 mL
2 tbsp	liquid honey	30 mL
2 tbsp	red wine vinegar	30 mL
8	6- to 8-inch (15 to 20 cm) flour or corn tortillas, skillet-warmed (page 15)	8
2 cups	chopped salad mix	500 mL
	Chipotle Ranch Sauce (page 326)	

1. In a small bowl, combine cinnamon, salt, pepper and cumin. Coat turkey with oil and season with cinnamon mixture.

2. In another small bowl, combine honey and vinegar.

3. Grill turkey, turning once, until no longer pink inside and lightly browned, 2 to 3 minutes per side. Brush turkey with honey mixture on both sides and grill for 1 minute per side. Transfer turkey to a cutting board. Let stand for 6 to 8 minutes. Cut into bite-size pieces.

4. To build tacos, divide turkey equally among tortillas. Top with salad mix and Chipotle Ranch Sauce. Fold tortillas in half.

Beef

continued…

Classic Rolled Tacos

From time to time, my girlfriends and I get together for taco-rolling parties. We make lots of tacos for the winter months ahead. They are simple and economical. I like to pack 12 uncooked tacos in a quart-size resealable plastic bag and place it in the freezer for up to 3 months. When you are ready to eat, thaw and fry as directed.

Tips

You do not need to seal the ends. The taco looks like a small flute.

Do not overcook these tacos, crispy on the ends and soft in the middle is a perfect rolled taco.

I recommend these sauces and salsas: Fiesta Taco Sauce (page 324) and Salsa Verde (page 300).

Variation

You could substitute 2 cups (500 mL) crumbled cooked ground beef for the taco filling.

- Candy/deep-fry thermometer

2 cups	shredded cooked beef (see page 110 and Tip, page 114)	500 mL
3/4 tsp	salt	3 mL
24	6-inch (15 cm) corn tortillas, micro-warmed (page 15)	24
	Vegetable oil	

1. In a large bowl, thoroughly combine shredded beef and salt.

2. To build tacos, place about $1\frac{1}{2}$ tbsp (22 mL) of meat at one end of each tortilla. Gently roll tortilla and secure with a toothpick (see Tips, left). Deep-fry immediately or place rolled tacos in a resealable plastic bag to keep moist. Refrigerate until ready to cook for up to 2 days.

3. Fill a deep-fryer, deep heavy pot or deep skillet with 3 inches (7.5 cm) of oil and heat to 350°F (180°C). Using tongs, gently place 3 to 4 tacos at a time in the hot oil and deep-fry, turning once, until golden brown and crispy, 2 to 3 minutes. Drain on paper towels. Lightly season with salt. Serve 3 or 4 per person.

Cooking Boneless Beef

A good cut of meat, lightly seasoned and slow-cooked, creates a perfect shredded beef filling reflecting the traditional Mexican flavors of barbacoa. Customize this tender tasty meat for a variety of beef tacos.

Tip

The key to shredded beef is the meat should be falling apart and easy to shred. Measure out what you need for each recipe and freeze the remaining meat in an airtight container for up to 3 months.

2 to 3 lbs	boneless beef, chuck or sirloin roast	1 to 1.5 kg
3	cloves garlic	3
1	onion, quartered	1
¾ tsp	salt	3 mL

1. Place roast in a large pot and fill with enough water to cover the meat by 2 inches (5 cm). Add onion and garlic and bring to a gentle boil over medium-high heat. Cover, reduce heat to medium-low and simmer until meat is tender and falling apart, $1\frac{1}{2}$ to 2 hours. Remove meat. Discard broth or use in another recipe. Let meat cool for 12 to 15 minutes. Shred meat into strands with your fingers or two forks. Add salt and mix well. Let cool completely. Measure out amount needed for recipe and place remaining beef in a resealable plastic bag. Refrigerate for up to 2 days or freeze for up to 3 months.

> **Slow-Cooker Method:** Add beef, onion, garlic and 1 cup (250 mL) water to slow cooker stoneware. Slow cook on High for 4 to 5 hours. Strain, reserving broth and discarding onion and garlic. Shred meat into strands with your fingers or 2 forks. Let cool completely. Measure amount needed for taco recipe.

Beef Taquitos with Guacamole

Makes 36 mini tacos

Create a taquito, a smaller skinnier version of the classic rolled taco, by simply reducing the amount of filling. This is a popular appetizer in the Southwest. Serve three at a time topped with rich, creamy guacamole. Perfect with a margarita!

- Candy/deep-fry thermometer

2 cups	shredded cooked beef (see page 110)	500 mL
¾ tsp	salt	3 mL
36	6-inch (15 cm) corn tortillas, micro-warmed (page 15)	36
	Vegetable oil	
	Guacamole (page 316)	

1. In a large bowl, thoroughly combine shredded beef and salt.

2. To build tacos, place 1 tbsp (15 mL) of meat at one end of each tortilla. Gently roll tortilla and secure with a toothpick (see Tips, page 109). Deep-fry immediately or place rolled tacos in a resealable plastic bag to keep moist. Refrigerate until ready to cook for up to 2 days.

3. Fill a deep-fryer, deep heavy pot or deep skillet with 3 inches (7.5 cm) of oil and heat to 350°F (180°C). Using tongs, gently place 3 to 4 tacos at a time in the hot oil. and deep-fry, turning once, until golden brown and crispy, 2 to 3 minutes. Drain on paper towels. Repeat with remaining tacos. Serve on a platter with a bowl of guacamole.

Sonoran Beef Flautas

Makes 12 rolled tacos

A flour tortilla creates a lighter, flakier, crust-like shell for your "rolled" taco. The key is to find small flour tortillas, then stuff them with this tasty meat filling. This Sonoran-style taco is authentic to northern Mexico and popular in many parts of Arizona.

Tip

Small flour tortillas are hard to find. You can make your own (page 13). If you are using store-bought tortillas, look for the smallest, usually 8-inch (20 cm) and trim to a 6-inch (15 cm) size with a pair of kitchen shears.

Variation

For additional flavor add ¼ cup (60 mL) crumbled Cotija cheese to the shredded beef.

• Candy/deep-fry thermometer

2 cups	shredded cooked beef (see page 110 and Tip, page 113)	500 mL
¾ tsp	salt	3 mL
12	6-inch (15 cm) flour tortillas, micro- or skillet-warmed (page 15)	12

1. In a large bowl, thoroughly combine shredded meat and salt.

2. To build tacos, divide meat equally among tortillas and place at one end of each tortilla. Gently roll tortilla and secure with a toothpick (see Tips, page 109). Deep-fry immediately or place rolled tacos in a resealable plastic bag to keep moist. Refrigerate until ready to cook for up to 2 days.

3. Fill a deep-fryer, deep heavy pot or deep skillet with 3 inches (7.5 cm) of oil and heat to 350°F (180°C). Using tongs, gently place 4 tacos at a time in the hot oil and deep-fry, turning once, until crispy and golden brown, about 2 minutes. Drain on paper towels. Lightly season with salt.

Red Chile Flautas

Makes 24 rolled tacos

Flauta, Spanish for "flute," is a tightly rolled taco, typically made with a flour tortilla. Throughout the Southwest you will find them stuffed with a variety of fillings and served three at a time in some places. Flautas are crispy and delicious, always a finger-food delight.

Tip

Follow directions on page 110 for shredded cooked beef or use any leftover cooked roast or steak, shredded by hand or with two forks.

Variation

Create a taquito, which is a smaller version of this rolled taco, by simply reducing the meat filling to 1 tbsp (15 mL) per taco and increasing the number of tortillas to 36.

- Candy/deep-fry thermometer

2 cups	shredded cooked beef (see page 110 and Tip, left)	500 mL
1 cup	red enchilada sauce	250 mL
	Salt and freshly ground black pepper	
24	6-inch (15 cm) flour tortillas, micro-warmed (page 15)	24
	Vegetable oil	

1. In a large skillet over medium-low heat, combine beef, enchilada sauce, and salt and pepper to taste. Simmer, stirring, until meat mixture is heated through. Remove from heat and let cool to room temperature.

2. To build tacos, place about 1½ tbsp (22 mL) of meat at one end of each tortilla. Gently roll tortilla and secure with a toothpick (see Tips, page 109). Deep-fry immediately or place rolled tacos in a resealable plastic bag to keep moist. Refrigerate until ready to cook for up to 2 days.

3. Fill a deep-fryer, deep heavy pot or deep skillet with 3 inches (7.5 cm) of oil and heat to 350°F (180°C). Using tongs, gently place 4 tacos at a time in the hot oil and deep-fry, turning once, until crispy and golden brown, for 2 minutes. Drain on paper towels.

Rapido Rolled Tacos

Makes 36 rolled tacos

This is an old favorite of my sister's family. It is quick, easy and economical. The prepared beef, found in the canned meat section of your market, can be rinsed and shredded in minutes.

Tip

Select the cut of beef you like best. I have used chuck roast and sirloin roast. I prefer a stovetop method to save time. The key to shredded beef is the meat should be falling apart and easy to shred. Measure out what you need for each recipe and freeze the remaining meat in an airtight container for up to 3 months.

Variation

If you are short on time, use three 12 oz (375 g) cans roast beef in gravy, drained and rinsed.

* Candy/deep-fry thermometer

1½ cups	shredded cooked beef (see page 110 and Tip, left)	375 mL
¾ cup	shredded Cheddar cheese	175 mL
36	corn tortillas, micro-warmed (page 15)	36
	Vegetable oil	

1. In a large bowl, combine beef and cheese. Mix well.

2. To build tacos, place 1½ tbsp (22 mL) of meat mixture at one end of each tortilla. Gently roll meat and tortilla and secure with a toothpick (see Tips, page 109). Deep-fry immediately or place rolled tacos in a resealable plastic bag to keep moist. Refrigerate until ready to cook for up to 2 days.

3. Fill a deep-fryer, deep heavy pot or deep skillet with 3 inches (7.5 cm) of oil and heat to 350°F (180°C). Using tongs, gently place 4 tacos at a time in the hot oil and deep-fry, turning once, until crispy and golden brown, about 2 minutes. Drain on paper towels.

Red Hot Taco Bites

**Makes 24
mini-tacos**

*Perfect for a party! I
serve these buffet-style
so my guests can help
themselves for ease in
entertaining. Scoop up
these fun little bites
and top them with
lime-marinated onions
and a dab of sour cream
for the perfect appetizer.*

Tips

Use meat from any cooked
roast, shredded by hand
or with two forks.

I usually allow for 2 to
3 tacos per person.

2	onions, minced	2
	Juice of 2 limes	
2 cups	shredded cooked beef (see page 110 and Tips, left)	500 mL
	Salt	
1 to 2 tsp	hot pepper flakes	5 to 10 mL
1 cup	red enchilada sauce	250 mL
½ cup	minced cilantro	125 mL
	Sour cream	
24	4-inch (10 cm) corn tortillas, skillet-warmed (page 15)	4

1. In a small bowl, combine onions and lime juice. Mix well. Cover and refrigerate to allow flavors to meld for at least 20 minutes or for up to 2 hours.

2. In a large skillet over medium-low heat, sauté beef, salt to taste, hot pepper flakes to taste and enchilada sauce until meat is warmed through.

3. To serve tacos, place meat, onions, cilantro and sour cream in separate serving bowls. Serve with warm tortillas. For individual servings, place meat mixture on tortilla and top with a heaping teaspoon (5 mL) marinated onions, a pinch of cilantro and a dab of sour cream.

Shredded Beef Folded Tacos with Fiesta Taco Sauce

Makes 8 tacos

True, authentic folded tacos start with a good shredded beef filling. I slow cook a roast, season and shred it. Make ahead and freeze for convenience.

Tips

Follow directions on page 110 for shredded cooked beef or use any leftover cooked roast or steak, shredded by hand or with two forks.

If you are short on time use store-bought taco shells. There are a variety of brands to choose from. Check with your local grocer to see if they make them fresh.

2 cups	shredded cooked beef (see page 110 and Tips, left)	500 mL
	Salt and freshly ground black pepper	
8	taco shells (see Tips, left and page 14)	8
1½ cups	shredded lettuce	375 mL
1 cup	shredded Cheddar cheese	250 mL
1	onion, minced	1
1	tomato, seeded and diced	1
	Fiesta Taco Sauce (page 324)	

1. In a large bowl, toss meat with salt and pepper to taste.

2. To build tacos, divide meat equally among taco shells, gently placing meat in the shells. Top meat with lettuce, cheese and onion. Garnish with tomato chunks. Top with Fiesta Taco Sauce.

Machaca Soft Tacos

Makes 8 tacos

The word machaca *comes from the Spanish verb* machacar, *meaning to pound or crush. Culinary history tells us this meat was seasoned, cured and dried for many hours. Today, we can get the same taste by cooking in flavor and cooking out the juices. This shredded beef filling is meaty and flavorful.*

Tips

Crown this flavorful taco with a simple salsa, such as Roasted Tomato Salsa (page 299).

You can make the meat filling ahead and freeze in an airtight container for up to 3 months.

If you can't get fresh New Mexico or Anaheim chiles, you can buy canned and frozen green chiles.

Variation

Machaca and Egg Tacos are wonderful for breakfast or a late night snack. Follow Step 1. Then add 4 eggs, slightly beaten. Stir and cook until eggs are firm. Divide the egg mixture among the tortillas, and garnish with Monterey Jack cheese.

1 tbsp	vegetable oil	15 mL
2	cloves garlic, minced	2
1	onion, diced	1
½ cup	New Mexico or Anaheim roasted chopped green chiles (2 or 3 depending on size) (see page 121)	125 mL
1	tomato, seeded and chopped	1
2 cups	shredded cooked beef (see page 110)	500 mL
⅓ cup	beef broth	75 mL
	Juice of 2 limes	2
	Salt and freshly ground black pepper	
8	6- to 8-inch (15 to 20 cm) flour tortillas, skillet-warmed (page 15)	8
½ cup	shredded Monterey Jack cheese	125 mL

1. In a large skillet, heat oil over medium-low heat. Sauté garlic, onion, chiles and tomato until onion is translucent, 8 to 10 minutes. Add beef, broth and lime juice. Increase heat to medium and sauté until all juices have evaporated, 12 to 15 minutes. Season with salt and pepper to taste.

2. To build tacos, divide meat mixture equally among tortillas. Top each taco with Monterey Jack cheese. Fold tortillas in half.

Carne Seca Soft Tacos

Carne Seca, means "dried meat," which historically was done by hanging sheets of meat out in the desert air. It is often referred to as a Mexican beef jerky, which is used not only in tacos but also in stews. We can get a similar "dried" effect by skillet cooking away all the juices of the meat. Here the recipe of shredded spiced beef is sautéed to perfection with lemon juice and garlic.

Tip

The meat filling can be made ahead of time through Step 3. Let meat cool and place in a resealable plastic bag. Refrigerate until ready to serve for up to 2 days. Reheat and assemble tacos.

Variations

Slow-Cooker Method: Add beef, onions, garlic, cumin and 1 cup (250 mL) water to slow cooker stoneware. Slow cook on High for 4 to 5 hours. Strain, reserving broth and discarding onions and garlic. Shred meat.

You can replace roasted chile peppers and tomatoes with 1½ cups (375 mL) green chile salsa.

- Preheat oven to 250°F (120°C)
- Ovenproof Dutch oven

2 to 3 lbs	boneless beef chuck or blade roast	1 to 1.5 kg
2	onions, chopped	2
4	cloves garlic, minced	4
¾ tsp	ground cumin	3 mL
	Juice of 2 lemons	
4 to 6	New Mexico or Anaheim green chile peppers, roasted and chopped (see page 121)	4 to 6
2	tomatoes, seeded and chopped	2
16	6- to 8-inch (15 to 20 cm) flour or corn tortillas	16
2 cups	Monterey Jack or Mexican melting cheese	500 mL

1. In Dutch oven, combine meat, onions, garlic and cumin. Add just enough water to cover meat. Cover with foil and bake in preheated oven until meat pulls apart easily, about 6 hours. Strain, reserving broth and discarding onions and garlic. Transfer to a cutting board and shred meat using two forks.

2. In a large bowl, combine meat, lemon juice, chiles and tomatoes. Cover and refrigerate for at least 8 hours or for up to 12 hours.

3. In a large skillet over medium-high heat, sauté meat and reserved broth until all liquid has evaporated, 12 to 15 minutes.

4. To build tacos, skillet warm tortillas (page 15). Divide meat equally among tortillas. Top with cheese. Fold tortillas in half.

New Mexico Picante Roast Tacos

Makes 16 tacos

I love the simplicity of this recipe. Just throw it all in a pot and cook. You will enjoy the sweet, savory meat flavor.

Tip

The meat filling can be made ahead. Let meat cool. Place in an airtight container. Refrigerate until ready to serve for up to 2 days. Reheat, covered, in a roasting pan in a preheated 275°F (140°C) oven until heated through, about 20 minutes. Serve with warm tortillas topped with lettuce, tomato and cheese.

1	can (12 oz/341 mL) regular or light beer	1
2 cups	picante sauce or salsa	500 mL
3 tbsp	packed light brown sugar	45 mL
1 tbsp	vegetable oil	15 mL
2 lb	boneless beef, chuck or sirloin roast	1 kg
2 cups	shredded green leaf lettuce	500 mL
1 cup	shredded Cheddar cheese	250 mL
1	tomato, seeded and chopped	1
16	6- to 8-inch (15 to 20 cm) flour tortillas	16
	Jalapeño Relish (page 310), optional	

1. In a medium saucepan, combine beer, salsa and brown sugar. Bring to a boil over medium-high heat, stirring constantly. Set aside.

2. In a large pot, heat oil over medium-high heat. Brown roast on all sides. Reduce heat to medium and add beer mixture. Reduce heat to low. Cover and simmer until meat pulls apart easily, 2 to 3 hours.

3. Remove meat from pot and shred by hand or with two forks. Reserve excess sauce for dipping, if desired.

4. To build tacos, skillet warm tortillas (page 15). Divide meat, lettuce, cheese and tomato equally among tortillas. Fold tortillas in half. Serve with reserved sauce or Jalapeño Relish, if using.

Green Chile Stew Tacos

Makes 16 tacos

This rich beefy taco is a family favorite. It has an authentic Mexican taste that is saucy and delicious. On some cold winter days I make this into a brothy stew by adding the juice of the tomatoes and a cup of water.

Tip

The lard gives this taco an authentic Mexican flavor. Substitute solid vegetable shortening for the lard, if you prefer, but the taste will be different.

2 lbs	boneless beef, chuck or sirloin roast, cut into bite-size cubes	1 kg
1/4 cup	lard (see Tip, left)	60 mL
1	onion, chopped	1
1 1/2 lbs	New Mexico or Anaheim green chile peppers, roasted and chopped (see page 121)	750 g
2	cans (each 14 1/2 oz/440 mL) Mexican-style tomatoes, drained	2
4	cloves garlic, minced	4
	Kosher salt	
1 tbsp	coarsely ground black pepper	15 mL
16	6- to 8-inch (15 to 20 cm) flour tortillas	16
1/2 cup	minced onion	125 mL
1/4 cup	minced cilantro	60 mL
2 cups	chopped green or red leaf lettuce	500 mL

1. In a large pot over medium-high heat, sauté meat until browned and juices have evaporated, about 10 minutes.

2. In a large saucepan over medium heat, melt lard. Add chopped onion, chiles and tomatoes and boil gently, stirring occasionally, until onion is softened, 12 to 15 minutes.

3. Add meat cubes to tomato mixture. Reduce heat to medium-low. Add garlic, salt to taste and pepper and simmer, stirring occasionally, until thickened, 3 to 4 hours.

4. To build tacos, skillet warm tortillas (page 15). Using a slotted spoon, divide meat mixture equally among tortillas. Top each with minced onion, cilantro and lettuce. Fold tortillas in half.

Green Chile Con Carne Soft Tacos

Beefy green chile makes a tasty "sloppy" taco. Serve this family style so everyone can make their own. Double and triple it for big crowds.

1 tbsp	olive oil	15 mL
1 lb	boneless beef sirloin, cut into bite-size pieces	500 g
1 cup	beef broth	250 mL
1 cup	chopped roasted New Mexico or Anahiem green chiles (about 4 chiles) (see below)	250 mL
1½ cups	shredded Monterey Jack cheese	375 mL
8	6- to 8-inch (15 to 20 cm) flour tortillas, skillet-warmed (page 15)	8

1. In a large skillet, heat oil over medium heat. Sauté meat until browned and all juices have evaporated. Add broth and chiles and boil gently, stirring occasionally, about 10 minutes.

2. To build tacos, using a slotted spoon, divide meat mixture equally among tortillas and top with cheese. Fold tortillas in half.

Roasting Chiles

To roast chiles, such as New Mexico, Anaheim, poblano, jalapeño and habanero: Preheat greased outdoor grill to medium or preheat broiler. Place fresh chiles on outdoor grill or gas stovetop over medium heat or arrange on a baking sheet and place 2 to 3 inches (5 to 7.5 cm) away from heat under broiler. Grill or broil, turning often with tongs, until surfaces of skin are lightly charred and blistered. Immediately place peppers in a paper or plastic bag, or an airtight container and close tightly. Let peppers cool for 12 to 15 minutes. Peel off charred skin and remove stems and seeds. Tear into strips or chop as needed according to the recipe. Wash your hands thoroughly after handling chiles. Refrigerate peppers for up to 3 days or freeze in airtight container for up to 6 months.

Korean Kalbi Tacos with Asian Pear Salsa

The Asian flavors of this taco are a perfect pairing with the rustic, earthy flavor of the corn tortilla. By browning the meat and then slow cooking, you get a tender beefy filling for this Korean-style taco.

Variation

For a more savory finish, substitute Veggie Salsa (page 308) or Jicama Salsa (page 309) for the Asian Pear Salsa.

- Minimum (4-quart) slow cooker

2 tbsp	minced gingerroot	30 mL
2	cloves garlic, minced	2
2 tbsp	soy sauce	30 mL
1 tbsp	liquid honey	15 mL
2 lbs	beef short ribs, cut into sections	1 kg
2 tbsp	olive oil	30 mL
1	onion, cut into ¼-inch (0.5 cm) slices	1
8	6- to 8-inch (15 to 20 cm) flour tortillas	8
	Asian Pear Salsa (page 300)	

1. In a resealable plastic bag, combine ginger, garlic, soy sauce and honey. Add meat and seal. Work ginger marinade into meat with your hands. Seal bag and marinate in the refrigerator for at least 2 hours or for up to 24 hours.

2. Remove ribs from marinade, discarding excess marinade. In a large skillet, heat oil over medium-high heat. In batches as necessary, brown ribs on all sides until crispy, 12 to 14 minutes. Drain off fat from pan.

3. Place onion slices on bottom of slow cooker. Top with ribs. Cover and cook on Low for 6 to 8 hours or on High for 4 to 5 hours, until ribs are tender and falling off the bone.

4. Remove meat and discard liquid and onions. Gently remove meat from the bone and shred it with a fork. To build tacos, skillet warm tortillas (page 15). Divide meat equally among tortillas. Top with Asian Pear Salsa. Fold tortillas in half.

Smoky Beef Rib Tacos with Apple Chipotle Sauce

Makes 8 tacos

Apple and smoky chipotle chiles is a simply delicious crowd-pleaser. For an even smokier flavor, slow-cook the ribs in a smoker at 220°F (104°C) for 3½ hours, using hickory or mesquite wood chunks.

- 8-inch (20 cm) square glass baking dish, greased

2 lbs	boneless sliced beef short ribs	1 kg
3 tbsp	dry steak seasoning	45 mL
¾ cup	hickory-flavored barbecue sauce	175 mL
8	6-inch (15 cm) corn tortillas	8
	Apple Chipotle Sauce (page 317)	
1½ cups	chopped romaine lettuce	375 mL

1. Rub ribs thoroughly with seasoning. Place ribs into a resealable plastic bag and refrigerate for at least 1 hour or for up to 4 hours.

2. Preheat oven to 250°F (120°C). Thirty minutes before cooking, remove ribs from plastic bag and slice. Transfer to prepared baking dish, placing side by side. Bake in preheated oven for 2 hours. Remove from oven and cover each rib with barbecue sauce. Return ribs to oven for 45 minutes more. Remove from oven and carve each rib into thin slices.

3. To build tacos, skillet warm tortillas (page 15). Divide meat equally among tortillas. Top with Apple Chipotle Sauce and lettuce. Fold tortillas in half.

Beef Tenderloin Tacos with Blue Cheese and Onion Spread

Makes 16 tacos

This taco reminds me of a dish you would find in an upscale steak house. The combination of the blue cheese, fresh basil and garlic is delectably different for a taco.

Tip

I like to serve this with bowls of hot peppers. Try 6 minced jalapeños or 1 cup (250 mL) sliced pickled jalapeños.

- 13- by 9-inch (33 by 23 cm) roasting pan, greased
- Instant-read thermometer

¾ cup	sour cream	175 mL
⅓ cup	whipped cream cheese	75 mL
¼ cup	crumbled blue cheese	60 mL
2 tbsp	minced onion	30 mL
2 tbsp	milk	30 mL
Pinch	ground white pepper	Pinch
2 lbs	beef tenderloin, trimmed	1 kg
1 tbsp	olive oil	15 mL
1 tsp	kosher salt	5 mL
1 tsp	chopped basil leaves	5 mL
½ tsp	cracked black peppercorns	2 mL
1	clove garlic, minced	1
32	6- to 8-inch (15 to 20 cm) corn tortillas, skillet-steamed (page 15)	32
2 cups	chopped salad mix	500 mL
	Pico de Gallo (page 305)	

1. In a small bowl, combine sour cream, cream cheese, blue cheese, onion, milk and white pepper. Mix well, cover and refrigerate for 2 hours or for up to 24 hours.

2. Preheat oven to 425°F (220°C).

3. Coat meat evenly with oil. In a small bowl, combine salt, basil, peppercorns and garlic. Press onto all surfaces of roast.

4. Place meat in prepared pan. Roast in preheated oven for 30 to 45 minutes for medium doneness, or until an instant-read thermometer registers 150°F (70°C). Let meat stand for 8 to 10 minutes. Carve into bite-size pieces.

5. To build tacos, press 2 tortillas together for a double layer. Divide meat mixture among each double tortilla. Top with cheese mixture, salad mix and Pico de Gallo. Fold tortillas in half.

Chipotle Tenderloin Tacos

Tenderloin is an elegant yet quick-cooking cut of meat. It is tender but mild in flavor, which allows the chile flavor to come through. It is a special-occasion taco, no doubt!

Tip

Cotija is a crumbly, sharp Mexican cheese. You could substitute feta or goat cheese.

Variation

I also serve this without the chipotle chile peppers so that it will go with other salsas. Follow Step 1, but eliminate chipotles. Serve this taco with Creamy Corn Salsa (page 303) or Tomatillo Avocado Salsa (page 304).

- 13- by 9-inch (33 by 23 cm) glass baking dish, greased
- Instant-read thermometer

1 tbsp	kosher salt, or to taste	15 mL
1 tbsp	cracked black peppercorns	15 mL
2	cloves garlic, minced	2
2 lbs	beef tenderloin, trimmed	1 kg
1 tbsp	olive oil	15 mL
3	chipotle chile peppers in adobo sauce, puréed	3
2 cups	shredded lettuce or green cabbage	500 mL
3 tbsp	minced cilantro leaves	45 mL
12	6-inch (15 cm) corn tortillas	12
¾ cup	crumbled Cotija cheese (see Tip, left)	175 mL

1. In a small bowl, combine salt, peppercorns and garlic. Set aside. Place tenderloin in prepared baking dish. Coat top and sides of meat with olive oil. Press garlic mixture on top and sides of tenderloin. Then spread chiles on surface of meat. Cover and refrigerate for 2 hours.

2. Thirty minutes before baking, remove meat from refrigerator. Preheat oven to 375°F (190°C). Bake on top shelf until juices run clear or an instant-read thermometer placed in center of tenderloin reads 135°F (57°C), 20 to 25 minutes for medium-rare. Switch oven setting to broil and broil until meat is crusty, 5 to 10 minutes. Let stand about 10 minutes before carving. Cut meat across the grain into ¼-inch (0.5 cm) slices.

3. In a medium bowl, combine lettuce and cilantro.

4. To build tacos, skillet warm tortillas (page 15). Divide meat equally among tortillas. Top with cheese and lettuce mixture. Fold tortillas in half.

Spice-Rubbed Steak Tacos

Makes 8 tacos

Simple seasonings bring big flavor to this taco. I like to squeeze fresh lime juice over the meat right after I take it off the grill for a zestier steak packed with flavor. The combination of fresh lime and avocado finish it off nicely.

• Barbecue grill

1 tsp	ground cumin	5 mL
1 tsp	garlic powder	5 mL
1 tsp	kosher salt	5 mL
1 lb	boneless beef sirloin steak (1 or 2 steaks),1 inch (2.5 cm) thick	500 g
2	avocados	2
1/2 cup	tomato-based salsa	125 mL
	Juice of 1 lime	
8	6-inch (15 cm) corn tortillas	8
1 1/2 cups	chopped salad mix	375 mL

1. In a small bowl, combine cumin, garlic powder and salt. Place meat in a large, shallow dish and press spice mixture evenly onto surface of meat. Cover and refrigerate for at least 1 hour or for up to 4 hours.

2. Thirty minutes before serving, remove meat from refrigerator and let stand at room temperature. Preheat barbecue grill to medium.

3. In a small bowl, mash avocados and stir in salsa and lime juice. Cover and refrigerate until just before serving.

4. Grill steak for 5 to 8 minutes per side for medium-rare or an internal temperature of 145°F (65°C). Let stand for 10 minutes. Carve steak across the grain into 1/4-inch (0.5 cm) slices.

5. To build tacos, skillet warm tortillas (page 15). Divide meat equally among tortillas. Top with avocado mixture and salad mix. Fold tortillas in half.

Grilled Rib-Eye Tacos with Garlic and Jalapeño Relish

Makes 8 tacos

Grilling is one of America's favorite pastimes, even when making tacos! The garlic and jalapeño relish crown this taco with flavor that makes it unforgettable. Simply grilled and garnished, this rib-eye taco is hard to resist.

Tip
The meat stays more tender if cooked to medium-rare but if you prefer it more well-done, cook for 6 to 8 minutes longer.

Variation
Instead of grilling the steak, place it on a broiler pan and broil 2 to 3 inches (5 to 7.5 cm) from the heat, for 3 to 4 minutes per side.

• Preheat greased barbecue grill to medium

1 tbsp	olive oil	15 mL
5	cloves garlic, minced	5
4	green onions, thinly sliced	4
3	jalapeños, seeded and minced	3
¼ tsp	salt	1 mL
¼ tsp	freshly ground black pepper	1 mL
1½ lbs	boneless rib-eye steak, 1 inch (2.5 cm) thick	750 g
8	6- to 8-inch (15 to 20 cm) corn or flour tortillas, skillet-steamed (page 15)	8

1. In a small skillet, heat oil over medium heat. Sauté garlic, green onions, jalapeños, salt and pepper until vegetables are tender, 4 to 5 minutes. Set aside.

2. Grill steak for 5 to 8 minutes per side for medium-rare or until desired doneness (see Tip, left). Let stand for 8 to 10 minutes. Carve meat across the grain into thin strips, then dice into bite-size pieces.

3. To build tacos, divide meat equally among tortillas. Layer meat with jalapeño relish. Fold tortillas in half.

Prime Rib Tacos Pequeno

Makes 24 tacos

This is the Mexican version of little prime rib sandwiches. Stuffing warm, soft tortillas with thin slices of prime rib is an elegant treat that will melt in your mouth. The crusty seasoning gives the meat strong flavor.

Tips

Cooking your roast to medium-rare to medium works best for this recipe. You can add about 18 minutes per pound (500 g) for a medium roast after the initial 15 minutes.

The roasting time may vary slightly depending on the size and shape of your roast. It is best to use a good-quality thermometer, preferably, the digital probe-type that you leave in, to monitor the temperature of the roast while it's cooking.

I love this taco with my Creamy Wasabi Sauce (page 316), Red Onion Salsa (page 307) or Blue Cheese and Onion Relish (page 312).

- Preheat oven to 450°F (230°C)
- Large roasting pan
- Instant-read thermometer

2	cloves garlic, minced	2
3 tbsp	seasoned salt	45 mL
2 tbsp	kosher salt	30 mL
1 tbsp	cracked black peppercorns	15 mL
½ tsp	brown sugar	2 mL
2 to 3 lb	beef rib roast	1 to 1.5 kg
24	6-inch (15 cm) flour or corn tortillas	24

1. In a small bowl, combine garlic, seasoned salt, kosher salt, peppercorns and brown sugar.

2. Place meat, rib side down, in a large roasting pan and generously rub seasoning all over surface of roast. Roast in preheated oven for 15 minutes. Reduce heat to 325°F (160°C) and roast until an instant-read thermometer inserted in middle of roast registers 125 to 130°F (52 to 54°C) for medium-rare, about 20 minutes. Let roast stand for 15 to 20 minutes before slicing off the bone then across the grain into thin bite-size pieces.

3. To build tacos, skillet warm tortillas (page 15). Divide meat equally among tortillas. Fold tortillas in half.

Beef Tenderloin Tacos with
Blue Cheese and Onion Spread (page 124)

Chipotle Pork Tacos with Onion Apple Salsa (page 180)

Cuban Tacos with Chopped Pickles
and Red Onion Relish (page 173)

Fresh Baja Fish Tacos with Mexican White Sauce (page 206)

Tri-Tip Tacos with Fresh Roasted Green Chiles

Makes 16 tacos

Grilling a seasoned "quick-cooking" roast adds big flavor and little effort to this taco. Serving this "family style" allows everyone to build their own tacos just the way they like them.

Tips

This amount of salt may look like a lot, however, it is needed to season this cut of meat. About 1 tbsp (15 mL) will be lost during the grilling process.

Serve this taco with several salsas such as Pico de Gallo (page 305) or Fiesta Taco Sauce (page 324). I add a creamy sauce, such as Chile Cream Sauce, for extra flavor.

- Preheat greased barbecue grill to medium
- Instant-read thermometer

2 tbsp	garlic salt	30 mL
2 tbsp	coarsely ground black pepper	30 mL
2 tbsp	seasoned salt (see Tip, left)	30 mL
2 lb	boneless beef tri-tip or top sirloin roast	1 kg
1 lb	New Mexico or Anaheim green chile peppers, roasted and sliced into strips (see page 121)	500 g
16	6- to 8-inch (15 to 20 cm) corn or flour tortillas, skillet-warmed (page 15)	16
1½ cups	shredded Monterey Jack cheese	375 mL
	Pico de Gallo (see Tip, left)	
	Chile Cream Sauce (page 327) (see Tip, left)	

1. In a small bowl, combine garlic salt, pepper and seasoned salt. Rub seasonings generously over surface of meat.

2. Grill roast, covered, for 40 minutes, turning every 10 minutes. (The roast will start to char on the surface but will still remain rare in the center.) Remove meat from grill and double wrap in heavy foil. Return to grill for 10 to 15 minutes. Check for doneness: an instant-read thermometer inserted in the middle of the roast should register 125 to 130°F (52 to 54°C) for medium-rare or until desired doneness. Let stand for 8 to 10 minutes.

3. When ready to serve, carve meat across the grain into very thin slices. Place meat on a large serving platter and top with the chile strips. Serve with warmed tortillas, cheese, Pico de Gallo and Chile Cream Sauce.

Roasted Rib-Eye Tacos with Ancho Bourbon Sauce

Rib-eye, or cowboy steak as some call it, makes a delicious taco filling. Seared to perfection, then topped off with this zesty sauce, this steak taco is quick and easy.

Tip

This steak can also be grilled over medium heat for 4 to 5 minutes per side for medium-rare. Let meat stand for 8 to 10 minutes. Carve meat into thin strips, then dice into bite-size pieces.

Variations

Mexican Queso Fresco cheese, with a slightly different yet distinctive taste, is a good substitute for the Monterey Jack cheese.

5 tbsp	butter, divided	75 mL
2 tbsp	beef broth	30 mL
2 tbsp	bourbon	30 mL
1 tbsp	ancho chile powder	15 mL
1½ tsp	ground cumin	7 mL
1	clove garlic, minced	1
1 lb	boneless rib-eye steak, about 1 inch (2.5 cm) thick	500 g
	Salt and freshly ground black pepper	
2 tbsp	olive oil	30 mL
8	6- to 8-inch (15 to 20 cm) corn tortillas, skillet-warmed (page 15)	8
2 cups	chopped salad mix	500 mL
1 cup	shredded Monterey Jack cheese	250 mL

1. In a small saucepan over medium heat, combine 3 tbsp (45 mL) of the butter, broth, bourbon, chile powder, cumin and garlic. Bring to a gentle boil and boil for 3 to 5 minutes. Remove from heat and let sauce cool slightly.

2. Season steak with salt and pepper. In a large heavy skillet over high heat, add oil and remaining 2 tbsp (30 mL) of butter, swirling around bottom of pan until mixture is bubbling. Add steak and sear on both sides until it has reached the desired degree of doneness: 4 to 5 minutes per side for medium-rare, 6 to 7 minutes for medium. Carve steak into thin slices and transfer to a bowl.

3. Spoon sauce over meat, making sure that the meat is well coated.

4. To build tacos, divide meat equally among tortillas. Top meat mixture with salad mix and cheese. Fold tortillas in half.

Kobe Beef Tacos

Kobe beef, renowned for its tenderness, has an intense marbling that gives the meat a buttery, rich flavor. The "flat iron" cut is a best value when selecting a cut of Kobe beef, especially for this taco. A special occasion calls for a special cut of meat. Enjoy a taco that is a cut above the rest!

Tips

Grill Kobe beef to a medium-rare doneness for the best flavor. Overcooking will result in loss of flavor.

These tacos are delicious with Chile Cream Sauce (page 327) or, for a fresh, zesty flavor, add Chimichurri Sauce (page 328).

• Preheat greased barbecue grill to medium

1½ lbs	Kobe beef flat-iron steak	750 g
2 tbsp	olive oil	30 mL
	Salt and freshly ground black pepper	
8	6- to 8-inch (15 to 20 cm) flour tortillas, skillet-warmed (page 15)	8
½ cup	freshly grated Parmesan cheese	125 mL
1 to 2 cups	chopped salad mix	250 to 500 mL
1	tomato, seeded and chopped	1

1. Coat steak with olive oil. Sprinkle with salt and pepper.

2. Grill steak over medium heat for 4 to 5 minutes per side for medium-rare or until desired doneness. Let stand for 8 to 10 minutes. Carve steaks into thin strips.

3. To build tacos, divide meat equally among tortillas. Top meat with cheese, salad mix and tomato. Fold tortillas in half.

Sirloin Tacos with Caramelized Onions

Caramelized onions top this taco with perfection. Little hints of sweet savory flavors in the marinade add another dimension you will love.

Tip

This steak can also be pan-seared in a large heavy skillet over high heat. Add oil and remaining 2 tbsp (30 mL) of butter, swirling around bottom of pan until mixture is bubbling. Add steak and sear on both sides until it has reached the desired degree of doneness: 4 to 5 minutes per side for medium-rare, 6 to 7 minutes for medium.

• Instant-read thermometer

1/4 cup	freshly squeezed lime juice	60 mL
2 tbsp	vegetable oil	30 mL
2 tbsp	brown sugar, light or dark	30 mL
1 lb	boneless beef sirloin steak, 1 inch (2.5 cm) thick	500 g
2 tbsp	olive oil	30 mL
2	large onions, cut into 1/4-inch (0.5 cm) wedges	2
1 tbsp	balsamic vinegar	15 mL
2 tsp	Worcestershire sauce	10 mL
1/4 tsp	kosher salt	1 mL
1/4 tsp	freshly ground black pepper	1 mL
8	6- to 8-inch (15 to 20 cm) corn or flour tortillas	8
	Pico de Gallo (page 305)	

1. In a resealable plastic bag, combine lime juice, vegetable oil and brown sugar. Add steak, seal bag and refrigerate for at least 1 hour or for up to 4 hours.

2. Preheat broiler. Place steak on rack in a broiler pan so surface of beef is 2 to 3 inches (5 to 7.5 cm) from heat. Broil, turning once, for 4 to 6 minutes per side, until an instant-read thermometer registers 145°F (65°C) for medium-rare or 160°F (71°C) for medium. Let stand for 8 to 10 minutes. Slice meat into 1/4-inch (0.5 cm) thick slices.

3. In a large skillet, heat olive oil over medium heat. Add onions, vinegar, Worcestershire sauce, salt and pepper. Cover and cook, stirring occasionally, until onions are a deep golden brown, 16 to 18 minutes.

4. To build tacos, skillet warm tortillas (page 15). Divide meat equally among tortillas. Top with onions. Top each taco with Pico de Gallo. Fold tortillas in half.

New York Strip Tacos with Green Chile and Jack Cheese

Makes 8 tacos

You will find this steak and queso entrée in many steakhouses across the Southwest. It is a favorite. This juicy beef dripping with a cheesy topping will have your guests coming back for seconds.

Tip

The perfect size tortilla for a taco is 6 inches (15 cm). It is generally more available in corn rather than flour. Buy 8-inch (20 cm) flour tortillas and trim them with a pair of kitchen shears to 6 inches (15 cm) using a corn tortilla as a template.

Variation

Serve with additional toppings, such as 1 large tomato, seeded and diced, or 1 red onion, diced.

• Preheat greased barbecue grill to medium

1 lb	boneless beef top loin or strip steaks, each ½ inch (1 cm) thick	500 g
2 tbsp	olive oil	30 mL
2 tsp	kosher salt	10 mL
1 tsp	cracked black peppercorns	5 mL
½ cup	chopped roasted New Mexico or Anaheim green chile peppers (see page 121)	125 mL
1 cup	shredded Monterey Jack cheese	250 mL
1 tbsp	chicken broth	15 mL
8	6- to 8-inch (15 to 20 cm) corn or flour tortillas (see Tip, left), skillet-steamed (page 15)	8
2 cups	chopped salad mix	500 mL

1. Coat steaks with olive oil. Sprinkle with salt and peppercorns.

2. Grill steaks for 4 to 5 minutes per side for medium-rare or until desired doneness. Let stand for 8 to 10 minutes. Carve steaks into bite-size pieces.

3. In a small microwave-safe bowl, combine chiles, cheese and chicken broth. Microwave for 30 seconds and stir. Continue to microwave and stir until cheese is completely melted.

4. To build tacos, divide meat equally among tortillas. Top meat with chile cheese mixture and salad mix. Fold tortillas in half.

Steak and Egg Breakfast Tacos

What a glorious breakfast taco to wake up to! When I was in college, we used to drop by a local diner for a cheap but delicious plate of steak and eggs, usually after a late Saturday night. This meaty egg taco is delicious and inexpensive to make.

Tip

Serve with Fiesta Taco Sauce (page 324), New Mexico Green Chile Sauce (page 320) or Green Chile Relish (page 312).

Variation

For a heartier taco, add ½ cup (125 mL) refried beans. Spread 1 tbsp (15 mL) warmed refried beans on each tortilla, then layer a portion of the meat and top with egg mixture.

2 tbsp	olive oil, divided	30 mL
12 oz	boneless beef sirloin steak, ½ inch (1 cm) thick, cut into bite-size pieces	375 g
	Salt and freshly ground black pepper	
1 tbsp	olive oil	15 mL
8	eggs, slightly beaten	8
8	6- to 8-inch (15 to 20 cm) corn or flour tortillas, skillet-warmed (page 15)	8
1 cup	shredded sharp Cheddar cheese	250 mL

1. In a large skillet, heat 1 tbsp (15 mL) of the oil over medium heat. Sauté meat until all juices have evaporated and meat is slightly charred. Add salt and pepper to taste. Remove steak from skillet. Keep warm.

2. In same skillet, heat remaining 1 tbsp (15 mL) of oil over medium-low heat. Add eggs and cook, stirring, until scrambled and set.

3. To build tacos, divide meat and eggs equally among tortillas. Top with cheese and fold tortillas in half.

Sirloin Mulita Tacos

Mulita is Spanish for "little mule," which is slang for "Mexican sandwich." The bacon gives this taco a salty flavor and added texture.

Tip

Fresh Pico de Gallo (page 305) is delicious with this taco.

1 tbsp	olive oil	15 mL
1 lb	boneless beef sirloin steak, cut into bite-size pieces	500 g
½ cup	minced green bell pepper	125 mL
8	strips bacon, cooked and crumbled	8
8	6- to 8-inch (15 to 20 cm) flour tortillas, skillet-warmed (page 15)	8

1. In large skillet, heat oil over medium heat. Sauté meat and bell pepper until all juices have evaporated and the meat is slightly charred. Reduce heat to low. Add bacon pieces and sauté until bacon is heated and flavors blend.

2. To build tacos, divide meat mixture equally among tortillas. Fold tortillas in half.

Sirloin Carnitas

Tender, seared meats are a Mexican favorite when it comes to beefy tacos. Simple flavors topped with fresh Guacamole and Pico de Gallo make a celebration favorite.

Variation

You can serve this taco with bowls of a variety of additional fresh toppings, such as diced tomato, minced green onion, shredded lettuce and fresh cilantro.

1 tbsp	olive oil	15 mL
1½ lbs	boneless beef sirloin steak, cut into bite-size pieces	750 g
1½ tsp	seasoned salt	7 mL
½ tsp	garlic powder	2 mL
12	6- to 8-inch (15 to 20 cm) corn or flour tortillas, skillet-warmed (page 15)	12
2	limes, each cut into 6 wedges	2
	Guacamole (page 316)	
	Pico de Gallo (page 305)	

1. In a large skillet, heat oil over medium heat. Sauté meat, seasoned salt and garlic powder until all juices have evaporated and meat is slightly charred.

2. To build tacos, divide meat equally among tortillas. Top with guacamole and Pico de Gallo. Fold tortillas in half. Serve with a wedge of lime.

Salpicon Tacos with Tangy Chipotle Sauce

Makes 24 tacos

"Salpicon" is actually a term borrowed from the French, meaning a dish prepared with many diced and minced ingredients bound by a sauce. My tangy orange sauce does just that along with adding flavor to this delicious beefy taco platter. I love to serve it in the warmest months of the year.

Tip

Follow directions on page 110 for shredded cooked beef or use any leftover cooked roast or steak, shredded by hand or with two forks.

	Juice of 1 orange	
½ cup	Italian dressing	125 mL
3	chipotle chile peppers in adobo sauce, puréed	3
2 tbsp	minced cilantro leaves	30 mL
2 cups	shredded cooked beef (see Tip, left)	500 mL
12 oz	Monterey Jack cheese, cubed	375 g
3	avocados	3
24	4-inch (10 cm) corn tortillas	24
	Salsa Verde (page 300)	
	Spicy Ranch Sauce (page 326)	

1. In a large bowl, whisk together orange juice, dressing, chile purée and cilantro until well blended.

2. Add meat and cheese to the dressing mixture, and coat well. Place on a large serving platter and cover. Refrigerate for at least 2 hours to allow flavors to mingle.

3. Just before serving, remove meat mixture from refrigerator. Skillet warm tortillas (page 15). Slice avocados lengthwise. Arrange slices on top of meat. Serve with warmed tortillas, Salsa Verde and Spicy Ranch Sauce.

Grilled Carne Asada Tacos with Pico de Gallo

Makes 12 tacos

Carne Asada is an intensely flavored meat that is very popular in Mexico. It is quick to marinate and easy to grill.

Tip

There are several different cuts of meat you can use for this recipe. Skirt steak or minute steak are best due to the thin cut and quick cooking time.

- Barbecue grill

Marinade

	Juice of 3 lemons	
3	cloves garlic, minced	3
½ cup	drained sliced pickled jalapeños	125 mL
½ cup	teriyaki sauce	125 mL
1 tbsp	minced red bell pepper	15 mL
1 tbsp	granulated sugar	15 mL
2 tsp	kosher salt	10 mL
1½ lbs	beef skirt or minute steak (see Tip, left)	750 g
12	6- to 8-inch (15 to 20 cm) flour or corn tortillas	12
	Pico de Gallo (page 305)	
2	limes, each cut into 6 wedges	2

1. *Marinade:* In a medium bowl, combine lemon juice, garlic, jalapeños, teriyaki sauce, bell pepper, sugar and salt until sugar and salt have dissolved.

2. In a large resealable plastic bag, add marinade and meat and seal. Work marinade through meat with your fingers. Refrigerate meat for at least 2 hours or for up to 6 hours.

3. Preheat greased barbecue grill to medium. Remove meat from marinade, discarding marinade. Grill meat for 4 to 5 minutes per side for medium-rare. When meat is just barely pink inside, remove from grill. Let stand for 8 to 10 minutes. Carve meat across the grain into thin slices, then cut into bite-size pieces.

4. To build tacos, skillet warm tortillas (page 15). Divide meat equally among tortillas and top with Pico de Gallo. Fold tortillas in half. Serve with a wedge of lime.

Grilled Carne Asada and Bean Tacos

Makes 12 tacos

The refried beans make this a hearty, meaty taco. I like to serve it with fresh produce such as chopped romaine lettuce, onions, and tomato for a crisp fresh finish.

Tips

If you are short on time consider the canned or dried versions of refried beans found in the Mexican food section of your grocery store.

Serve with any of the following: Roasted Tomato Salsa (page 299), Tomatillo Avocado Salsa (page 304) or Chipotle Ranch Sauce (page 326).

1	recipe Carne Asada (page 137)	1
12	6- to 8-inch (15 to 20 cm) corn or flour tortillas	12
1 cup	refried beans (page 273), warmed (see Tip, left)	250 mL
1	tomato, diced	1
1	onion, diced	1
2 cups	chopped salad mix	500 mL

1. Prepare Carne Asada as directed in Steps 1 through 3.

2. To build tacos, skillet warm tortillas (page 15). Spread an equal amount of beans on one side of each tortilla. Divide Carne Asada among tortillas. Top with tomato, onion and salad mix. Fold tortillas in half.

Fajita Jalapeño Steak Tacos

Makes 12 tacos

This taco is for those who dare to eat spicy hot peppers. The jalapeño pepper blends well with grilled meats and onions, but it does have a bite!

Tip

Instead of grilling the steak, place it on a broiler pan and broil 2 to 3 inches (5 to 7.5 cm) away from heat for 3 to 4 minutes per side.

- Barbecue grill

2 tbsp	olive oil, divided	30 mL
4	limes, divided	4
1½ lbs	beef skirt steak	750 g
1 tsp	salt	5 mL
½ tsp	freshly ground black pepper	2 mL
1	onion, sliced into ¼-inch (0.5 cm) thick rings	1
3	jalapeños, seeded and chopped	3
12	6- to 8-inch (15 to 20 cm) corn or flour tortillas	12

1. In a small bowl, whisk together 1 tbsp (15 mL) of the olive oil and juice of 2 limes. In a resealable bag, add lime mixture and steak and seal. Refrigerate for at least 2 hours or for up to 6 hours.

2. Preheat greased barbecue grill to medium-high. Remove meat from marinade and discard marinade. Season both sides with salt and pepper. Grill steak for 4 to 5 minutes per side for medium-rare, depending on thickness of steak. Let steak stand for 6 to 8 minutes. Thinly slice meat across the grain, then into bite-size pieces.

3. In a large skillet, heat remaining 1 tbsp (15 mL) of oil over medium heat. Sauté onion rings and jalapeños until tender and skin is charred, about 10 minutes.

4. Cut remaining 2 limes into 6 wedges each. To build tacos, skillet warm tortillas (page 15). Divide meat, onion and jalapeños equally among tortillas. Fold tortillas in half. Serve with lime wedges.

Grilled Fajita Steak and Shrimp Tacos

Makes 12 tacos

This is my favorite surf 'n' turf taco. Tender shrimp sautéed with sweet peppers and onions complement the grilled beefy taste of this taco. Cooked shrimp speeds up the prep time.

Variation

Instead of grilling the steak, place it on a broiler pan and broil 2 to 3 inches (5 to 7.5 cm) away from the heat or sear in a large cast-iron skillet over medium-high heat for 3 to 4 minutes per side.

- Preheat greased barbecue grill to medium-high (see Variation, left)

1 lb	beef skirt steak	500 g
2 tbsp	olive oil, divided	30 mL
	Kosher salt	
12	medium shrimp, cooked, peeled, deveined and coarsely chopped	12
1	onion, sliced into ¼-inch (0.5 cm) thick rings	1
1	red bell pepper, julienned	1
1	orange bell pepper, julienned	1
	Salt and freshly ground black pepper	
8	6- to 8-inch (15 to 20 cm) corn or flour tortillas	8
2	limes, cut into 6 wedges	2

1. Brush meat with 1 tbsp (15 mL) of the oil. Season with salt to taste. Grill for 3 to 4 minutes per side, depending on the thickness of the steak, until medium-rare and well browned on surface. Let stand for 5 minutes. Thinly slice meat across the grain.

2. In a large skillet, heat remaining 1 tbsp (15 mL) of oil over medium heat. Sauté shrimp, onion, red and orange bell peppers and salt and pepper to taste until peppers are tender-crisp, vegetables are slightly charred and shrimp is heated through, 10 to 12 minutes.

3. To build tacos, skillet warm tortillas (page 15). Divide meat and shrimp mixture equally among tortillas and fold tortillas in half. Serve with lime wedges.

Sirloin and Chorizo Frijole Tacos

Chorizo, a spicy Mexican sausage, blends well with frijoles (refried beans) and sirloin. I tried this combination years ago and since then it has become a family favorite.

1 tbsp	olive oil	15 mL
1 lb	boneless beef sirloin steak, cut into bite-size pieces	500 g
4 oz	fresh chorizo sausage, removed from casings	125 g
1 cup	refried beans (page 273), warmed	250 mL
8	6- to 8-inch (15 to 20 cm) corn or flour tortillas, skillet-warmed (page 15)	8
1 cup	shredded Monterey Jack cheese	250 mL
1 cup	shredded lettuce	250 mL

1. In a large skillet, heat oil over medium-high heat. Sauté steak until well browned and all juices have evaporated, 6 to 8 minutes. Add chorizo and sauté until sirloin is slightly charred and chorizo is slightly browned. Drain excess grease.

2. To build taco, spread refried beans equally on one side of each tortilla. Top with meat mixture, cheese and lettuce. Fold tortillas in half.

Strip Steak Tacos with Spicy Mushroom Sauce

This is an American steak classic. The sautéed mushrooms add a subtle richness to the tacos.

Tip

The perfect size tortilla for a taco is 6 inches (15 cm). It is generally more available in corn rather than flour. Buy 8-inch (20 cm) flour tortillas and trim them with a pair of kitchen shears to 6 inches (15 cm) using a corn tortilla as a template.

2 tbsp	butter	30 mL
2 tbsp	olive oil, divided	30 mL
10 to 12	mushrooms, sliced	10 to 12
2 tbsp	steak sauce	30 mL
½ tsp	cracked black peppercorns	2 mL
½ tsp	hot pepper flakes	2 mL
1 lb	boneless beef top loin or strip loin steak, ½ inch (1 cm) thick	500 g
8	6- to 8-inch (15 to 20 cm) flour tortillas (see Tip, left)	8
1½ cups	salad mix, chopped	375 mL

1. In a large skillet, melt butter and 1 tbsp (15 mL) of the oil over medium heat. Sauté mushrooms, steak sauce, peppercorns and hot pepper flakes until mushrooms are soft and well coated with sauce, 10 to 12 minutes. Set aside.

2. In same skillet, heat remaining 1 tbsp (15 mL) of oil over high heat. Add steak and sear for 3 to 4 minutes per side for medium doneness. Let steaks stand for 8 to 10 minutes. Thinly slice across the grain.

3. To build tacos, skillet warm tortillas (page 15). Divide meat and mushroom sauce equally among tortillas. Top with salad mix. Fold tortillas in half.

Orange Chipotle Skirt Steak Tacos

Makes 12 tacos

A chipotle chile pepper is a smoked jalapeño. I use it in this recipe to get a sweet, smoky barbecue flavor.

Tip

I like the orange chile flavor combination with a zesty relish like Red Onion Relish (page 315).

Variation

Apple jelly can be substituted for orange marmalade for a another hint of sweetness.

- Barbecue grill
- Instant-read thermometer

2 tbsp	olive oil	30 mL
	Juice of 1 lime	
1½ lbs	beef skirt steak	750 g
½ cup	orange marmalade	125 mL
3	chipotle chile peppers in adobo sauce, puréed	3
12	6- to 8-inch (15 to 20 cm) flour tortillas	12
1½ cups	chopped salad mix	375 mL

1. In a small bowl, whisk together olive oil and lime juice. In a resealable bag, add lime marinade and steak and seal. Refrigerate for at least 2 hours or for up to 24 hours.

2. Preheat greased barbecue grill to medium. Meanwhile, in a small saucepan over medium heat, combine marmalade and chiles and heat, stirring often, until bubbling and well blended.

3. Remove steak from marinade and discard marinade. Grill steak until an instant-read thermometer registers 145°F (65°C) for medium-rare, 5 to 8 minutes per side.

4. Immediately spread steak with warm marmalade mixture on both sides. Let stand for 10 minutes. Carve steaks across the grain into bite-size pieces.

5. To build tacos, skillet warm tortillas (page 15). Divide meat equally among tortillas. Top with salad mixture. Fold tortillas in half.

Bistro Beef Tacos with Blue Cheese and Onion Relish

These beefy tacos have a light, saucy flavor accented with the blue cheese relish. It is a memorable combination.

Variation

To grill steaks, place on a grill over medium-high heat and grill, covered, until an internal temperature registers 145°F (65°C) for medium-rare, 5 to 8 minutes per side. Let stand for 10 minutes before carving into thin slices.

1 lb	boneless beef top loin or strip loin steaks, each ½ inch (1 cm) thick	500 g
1 tsp	salt	5 mL
¾ tsp	freshly ground black pepper	3 mL
2 tbsp	butter, divided	30 mL
½ cup	balsamic vinegar	125 mL
2	shallots, minced	2
8	6- to 8-inch (15 to 20 cm) flour tortillas, skillet-warmed (page 15)	8
	Blue Cheese and Onion Relish (page 312)	
2 cups	shredded lettuce	500 mL

1. Season steak on both sides with salt and pepper.

2. In a large heavy skillet, melt 1 tbsp (15 mL) of the butter over high heat, coating bottom of skillet. Sear steak on each side until desired doneness; 3 to 4 minutes per side for a medium-rare pink center, 6 to 7 minutes for medium-well. Let steak stand for 8 to 10 minutes.

3. Reduce heat to medium and add remaining 1 tbsp (15 mL) of butter, vinegar and shallots to skillet. Bring to a gentle boil, stirring constantly. Boil sauce until reduced by half, about 12 minutes.

4. Cut steak across the grain into thin slices and transfer to a bowl. Pour sauce over meat, coating well. Drain and discard any excess sauce.

5. To build tacos, divide meat equally among tortillas. Top with Blue Cheese and Onion Relish and lettuce. Fold tortillas in half.

Sonoma Steak Tacos

I learned long ago that fresh herbs heighten the taste of any dish. Rosemary has an earthy, fresh flavor that goes well with beef.

Tip
Citrusy flavors really accent this taco. Try Lemon Jalapeno Sauce (page 322) or Citrusy Lime Salsa (page 307).

- Preheat greased barbecue grill to medium
- Instant-read thermometer

1 tbsp	finely chopped fresh rosemary	15 mL
1 tbsp	kosher salt	15 mL
1 tsp	freshly grated lemon zest	5 mL
2	cloves garlic, minced	2
1 lb	boneless beef sirloin steak, 1 inch (2.5 cm) thick	500 g
1 tbsp	olive oil	15 mL
1/4 tsp	freshly ground black pepper	1 mL
8	6- to 8-inch (15 to 20 cm) flour or corn tortillas, skillet-warmed (page 15)	8
2 cups	chopped salad mix	500 mL
1/2 cup	crumbled Cotija or freshly grated Parmesan cheese	125 mL

1. In a small bowl, combine rosemary, salt, lemon zest and garlic and mix well.

2. Brush steak thoroughly with olive oil. Rub steak with rosemary mixture.

3. Grill steak until an internal temperature registers 145°F (65°C) for medium-rare, 5 to 8 minutes per side. Let stand for 10 minutes. Carve into bite-size pieces.

4. To build tacos, divide meat equally among tortillas. Top with salad mix and cheese. Fold tortillas in half.

Cajun Beef Tacos

Create a Cajun feast with tacos full of spices. I save time by using a prepared Cajun spice mix.

- Barbecue or indoor grill
- Instant-read thermometer

1 lb	boneless beef sirloin steak, 1 inch (2.5 cm) thick	500 g
1 tbsp	olive oil	15 mL
3 tbsp	Cajun seasoning	45 mL
8	6- to 8-inch (15 to 20 cm) flour or corn tortillas	8
1	red onion, chopped	1
2 tbsp	balsamic vinegar	30 mL
1½ cups	shredded lettuce	375 mL
½ cup	grated Romano cheese	125 mL

1. Brush meat with olive oil, then rub with Cajun seasoning on all sides and place in a glass baking dish. Cover and refrigerate for at least 1 hour or for up to 4 hours.

2. Preheat greased grill to medium. Grill steaks, covered, until an internal temperature registers 145°F (65°C) for medium-rare, 5 to 8 minutes per side. Let stand for 10 minutes before carving into bite size pieces.

3. In a small bowl, toss together red onion, lettuce and vinegar.

4. To build tacos, divide meat equally among tortillas. Top meat with lettuce mixture and cheese. Fold tortillas in half.

Beefy Adobo Tacos

Makes 8 tacos

Grilling up this smoky, spicy taco with a marinated onion garnish is sure to catch the BBQ lover's attention.

- Barbecue grill
- Instant-read thermometer

1	red onion, chopped	1
	Juice of 1 lemon	
3	chipotle chile peppers in adobo sauce, puréed	3
¼ cup	hickory barbecue sauce	60 mL
1 lb	boneless beef shoulder, top blade or flat-iron steak	500 g
1 tsp	salt	5 mL
1 tsp	freshly ground black pepper	5 mL
8	6-inch (15 cm) corn tortilla	8
1 cup	shredded lettuce	250 mL

1. In a small bowl, combine red onion and lemon juice. Mix well and refrigerate for at least 30 minutes or for up to 2 hours.

2. Preheat greased grill to medium. Meanwhile, in a small saucepan over low heat, combine chiles and barbecue sauce, stirring, until well blended.

3. Season steak with salt and pepper. Grill steak until an instant-read thermometer registers 145°F (65°C) for medium-rare, 5 to 8 minutes per side, brushing both sides of steak with barbecue sauce in the last 2 minutes. Let stand for 10 minutes. Carve into bite size pieces.

4. To build tacos, skillet warm tortillas (page 15). Divide meat equally among tortillas. Top with red onion mixture and lettuce. Fold tortillas in half.

Classic Folded Beef Tacos

This is an early Americanized version of a Mexican beef taco. As simple as this taco is, the combination of ground beef, crispy corn tortillas, fresh lettuce, onion, tomato and Cheddar cheese is delicioso!

Tips

When I am in a rush I do buy high-quality prepared taco shells. But I prefer making my own. For directions on taco shell "how-to's" see page 14.

I like this taco with most tomato-based salsas. I even like it with good old ketchup!

Variation

For a spicier taco, season beef with 1 tsp (5 mL) hot pepper flakes along with salt and pepper.

1 lb	ground sirloin	500 g
	Salt and freshly ground black pepper	
8	taco shells (see Tips, left)	8
1½ cups	shredded lettuce	375 mL
1 cup	shredded Cheddar cheese	250 mL
1	onion, minced	1
1	tomato, seeded and diced	1
	Tomato Table Salsa (page 302)	

1. In a large skillet over medium heat, sauté beef, breaking up meat with a spoon, until meat is browned and no longer pink, about 12 minutes. Drain off excess fat. Add salt and pepper to taste.

2. To build tacos, divide meat equally among taco shells. Top with lettuce, cheese, onion, tomato and Tomato Table Salsa.

Red Chile Con Carne Soft Tacos

Fun Tex-Mex tacos get everyone's attention. Good old-fashioned chile and beans layered with flavor is a crowd pleaser.

Tips

There are a variety of beans on the market. Beans in chili sauce or red beans are the best selection.

Serve chile con carne, family style, in a large bowl with warmed flour tortillas. Offer bowls of lettuce, cheese, onions and tomatoes.

1 lb	lean ground beef	500 g
1 tsp	garlic powder	5 mL
1 tsp	ground cumin	5 mL
3 tbsp	chili powder	45 mL
1	can (15 oz/425 mL) chili beans (see Tip, left)	1
12	6- to 8-inch (15 to 20 cm) flour tortillas, skillet-warmed (page 15)	12
2 to 3 cups	shredded lettuce	500 to 750 mL
1½ cups	shredded Cheddar cheese	375 mL
1 to 2	onions, minced	1 to 2
1 to 2	tomatoes, chopped	1 to 2

1. In a large skillet over medium heat, sauté beef, garlic powder and cumin, breaking up meat with a spoon, until meat is browned and no longer pink, 10 to 12 minutes. Drain off excess fat. Reduce heat to medium-low. Add chili powder, ½ cup (125 mL) water and beans and boil gently, stirring often, until well blended and heated through.

2. To build taco, place 2 heaping tbsp (30 mL) of chile mixture in a tortilla. Top with lettuce, cheese, onion and tomato.

Beef and Green Chile Rolled Tacos

This is one of my favorite little tacos. BGs (Beef and Green Chile) are quick and inexpensive to make. I always keep a batch or two in the freezer for a last-minute dinner or for snacks.

Tips

These tacos are smaller in size. I make two to three tacos per person and find that people will eat at least two of these little tacos.

I recommend these sauces and salsas: Fiesta Taco Sauce (page 324), Garlic Sour Cream (page 321), Cilantro Chile Sauce (page 325) and Salsa Verde (page 300).

From time to time, my girlfriends and I get together for taco-rolling parties. We make lots of tacos to freeze for the winter months ahead. I like to pack 12 tacos in a quart (1 L) size resealable plastic bag and freeze for up to 6 months. When you are ready to cook, thaw completely in the refrigerator and cook as directed.

Do not overcook these tacos, crispy on the ends and soft in the middle is a perfect rolled taco.

- Candy/deep-fry thermometer

1 lb	lean ground beef	500 g
¼ cup	roasted chopped New Mexico or Anaheim green chile (see page 121)	60 mL
¾ tsp	salt	3 mL
12	6-inch (15 cm) corn tortillas, micro-warmed (page 15)	12
	Vegetable oil	

1. In a large skillet over medium heat, sauté beef and green chile, breaking up meat with a spoon, until meat is browned and no longer pink, 12 to 14 minutes. Drain off excess fat. Stir in salt.

2. To build tacos, place about 1½ tbsp (22 mL) of meat across one end of each tortilla. Gently roll tortilla and secure with a toothpick. Deep-fry immediately or place rolled tacos in a resealable plastic bag to keep moist. Refrigerate until ready to cook for up to 2 days.

3. Fill a deep-fryer, deep heavy pot or deep skillet with 3 inches (7.5 cm) of oil and heat to 350°F (180°C). Using tongs, gently place 3 to 4 tacos at a time in the hot oil and deep-fry, turning once, until golden brown and crispy, about 2 minutes. Drain on paper towels. Serve 3 or 4 per person.

Variation

When I am pressed for time and have lots of mouths to feed I make this quick beefy rolled taco. Start with 1 lb (500 g) lean ground beef and twelve 6-inch (15 cm) micro-warmed corn tortillas. To build tacos, place about 1½ tbsp (22 mL) of raw meat across one end of each tortilla. Gently roll tortilla and secure with a toothpick. Fill a deep-fryer, deep heavy pot or deep skillet with 3 inches (7.5 cm) of oil and heat to 350°F (180°C). Using tongs, gently place 3 to 4 tacos at a time in the hot oil and deep-fry, turning once, until golden brown and crispy, 3 to 4 minutes. Drain on paper towels.

Spicy Beef and Queso Tacos

The smoky flavor of a smoked jalapeño in adobo sauce adds a richness to this meaty filling. In this taco, the accent of the cheesy chile queso adds another layer of flavor that you will love.

Tip

Queso can be made in the microwave. In a medium microwave-safe bowl, combine cheese, chicken broth and chile. Microwave on Medium (50%) for 45 seconds and stir. Repeat for 45 seconds more or until cheese is completely melted.

• Preheat oven to 200°F (100°C)

1 lb	lean ground beef	500 g
2	chipotle chile peppers in adobo sauce, puréed	2
	Salt and freshly ground black pepper	
1 lb	pasteurized prepared cheese product, such as Velveeta, cubed	500 g
2 tbsp	chicken broth	30 mL
¼ cup	chopped roasted New Mexico or Anaheim green chile (see page 121)	60 mL
8	taco shells (see Tips, page 148)	8
1 cup	shredded lettuce	250 mL
1	tomato, seeded and diced	1

1. In a large skillet over medium heat, sauté beef and chipotle peppers, breaking up meat with a spoon, until meat is browned and no longer pink, about 12 minutes. Drain off excess fat. Season with salt and pepper to taste. Cover and keep warm in preheated oven.

2. In a medium pot over medium-low heat, combine cheese, broth and chiles (see Tip, left). Heat, stirring, until cheese is completely melted and mixture is well blended. Reduce heat to low and keep warm.

3. To build tacos, divide meat equally among taco shells. Top with cheese mixture. Garnish each taco with lettuce and tomato.

Crispy Beef Party Tacos

This is an inexpensive appetizer for feeding a hungry crowd. Kids can't get enough of these and my friends say the same. I like to serve a platter of these with a variety of salsas, sour cream and guacamole.

Tips

Make Ahead: Complete Steps 1 and 2. Refrigerate for up to 2 days or freeze for up to 3 months. When you are ready to complete the recipe, bring tacos to room temperature then continue with Step 3.

I like to serve these party tacos with Roasted Tomato Salsa (page 299), Fiesta Taco Sauce (page 324) and Cilantro and Chile Salsa (page 305).

Variations

Add 2 tsp (10 mL) hot pepper flakes along with salt for a spicier meat filling.

Substitute 1 lb (500 g) ground turkey or 2 cups (500 mL) roasted and shredded chicken or beef for the ground beef.

• Candy/deep-fry thermometer

1 lb	lean ground beef	500 g
3	cloves garlic, minced	3
¾ tsp	salt	3 mL
36	4-inch (10 cm) corn tortillas, micro-warmed (page 15)	36
	Vegetable oil	

1. In a large skillet over medium heat, sauté beef, garlic and salt, breaking up meat with a spoon, until meat is browned and no longer pink, 8 to 10 minutes. Drain off excess fat.

2. To build tacos, place about 1 tbsp (15 mL) of the meat mixture on one half of each tortilla, fold over and secure with a toothpick. Deep-fry immediately or place folded tacos in a resealable plastic bag to keep moist. Refrigerate until ready to cook for up to 2 days.

3. Fill deep-fryer, deep heavy pot or deep skillet with 3 inches (7.5 cm) of oil and heat to 350°F (180°C). Using tongs, gently place 4 tacos at a time in the hot oil and deep-fry, turning once, until tacos are crispy and golden brown, 1 to 2 minutes. Drain on paper towels.

Big Beefy Tacos

This is a flavor loved by millions! Anything can be made into a taco, even a fast-food hamburger.

Variations

To create a little heat in this taco with jalapeño, add 1 tbsp (15 mL) drained minced pickled jalapeños to the dressing mixture.

For a different chile flavor, add 1 tsp (5 mL) puréed chipotle chile in adobo sauce to dressing mix.

1½ lbs	ground sirloin	750 g
	Salt and freshly ground black pepper	
½ cup	Thousand Island dressing	125 mL
½ cup	mayonnaise	125 mL
8	6- to 8-inch (15 to 20 cm) flour tortillas, skillet-warmed (page 15)	8
24	pickle slices, chilled	24
8	slices American or Cheddar cheese	8
½ cup	minced onion	125 mL
2 cups	shredded lettuce	500 mL

1. In a large skillet over medium heat, sauté beef, breaking up meat with a spoon, until browned and no longer pink, about 12 minutes. Season with salt and pepper to taste.

2. In a small bowl, combine dressing and mayonnaise.

3. To build tacos, spread one side of each tortilla with dressing mixture. Place one piece of cheese on top of dressing mixture in the center of each tortilla. Divide beef equally among tortillas. Top each taco with 4 pickles, onion and lettuce. Fold tortillas in half.

Beefy Guacamole Cheese Tacos

Makes 8 tacos

Here crispy corn tortilla shells are stuffed with ground beef and topped with guacamole, adding a smooth layer of flavor to this taco.

Tip

This is best served with a tomato-based salsa such as Tomato Table Salsa (page 302) or Fiesta Taco Sauce (page 324).

Variation

I love lots of produce on my tacos! You can get creative and include all of your favorites. Try adding chopped tomato, minced onion, shredded zucchini, minced jicama, chopped fresh or pickled jalapeños.

1 lb	ground sirloin	500 g
¾ tsp	seasoned salt	3 mL
8	taco shells (see Tip, page 148)	8
	Guacamole (page 316)	
1 cup	shredded sharp Cheddar cheese	250 mL
1 to 2 cups	shredded lettuce	250 to 500 mL

1. In a large skillet over medium heat, sauté beef and salt, breaking up meat with a spoon, until meat is browned and no longer pink, about 12 minutes. Drain off excess fat.

2. To build tacos, divide meat equally among taco shells. Top with guacamole, cheese and lettuce.

Mexican Hash Tacos

I like to put a little heat in my tacos. Mexican hash is a combination of two comfort foods — potatoes and beef — blended with the taste of cayenne pepper.

Tip

I like this taco without any fresh produce. However, a taste of minced onion or fresh tomato would add a nice flavor and texture.

2	potatoes, cut into ½-inch (1 cm) cubes	2
2 tbsp	olive oil, divided	30 mL
1 tsp	seasoned salt	5 mL
Pinch	cayenne pepper	Pinch
1 lb	ground sirloin	500 g
8	6-inch (15 cm) corn tortillas, skillet-warmed (page 15)	8
	Tomato Table Salsa (page 302)	
1 cup	shredded Monterey Jack cheese	250 mL

1. In a large bowl, gently toss potatoes with 1 tbsp (15 mL) of the olive oil, salt and cayenne until potatoes are well coated.

2. In a large skillet, heat remaining 1 tbsp (15 mL) of oil over medium-high heat. Sauté potatoes until soft and golden brown, 12 to 14 minutes. Remove from skillet. Reduce heat to medium and add beef. Sauté, breaking up meat with a spoon, until meat is browned and no longer pink, about 12 minutes. Drain off excess fat.

3. Return potatoes to meat mixture and stir well.

4. To build tacos, divide meat mixture equally among each tortilla. Top with salsa and cheese. Fold tortillas in half.

Baked Beefy Tacos

Makes 12 tacos

This is pure Southwest comfort food, inspired by the many casseroles I was raised on as a child. You'll find layers of flavor with the creamy sauce, chile and cheese combination.

Variation

Serve with bowls of shredded lettuce, chopped onion and tomato.

- Preheat oven to 350°F (180°C)
- 8-inch (20 cm) square glass baking dish, greased

1 lb	ground beef	500 g
2	cloves garlic, minced	2
Pinch	kosher salt	Pinch
1	can (10 oz/284 mL) condensed creamy mushroom soup	1
½ cup	chopped roasted New Mexico or Anaheim green chiles (2 to 3 chiles) (see page 121)	125 mL
1 cup	milk	250 mL
12	6-inch (15 cm) corn tortillas, skillet-warmed (page 15)	12
2 cups	shredded Cheddar cheese, divided	500 mL

1. In a large skillet over medium heat, sauté beef, garlic and salt, breaking up meat with a spoon, until meat is browned and no longer pink, about 12 minutes. Drain off excess fat.

2. In a medium bowl, combine soup, chiles and milk, mixing well. Stir into meat mixture in skillet.

3. Fill each tortilla with a heaping tbsp (15 mL) of the meat mixture. Reserve ½ cup (125 mL) cheese for garnish. Top with 1½ cups (375 mL) cheese, divided among each tortilla. Fold tortillas in half and place in prepared baking dish, arranging side by side. Spread any remaining meat mixture over the top or inside of tacos. Top with reserved cheese. Bake in preheated oven until tacos are heated through and cheese is melted and bubbling, 20 to 25 minutes.

Bacon Cheddar Beef Tacos

Makes 8 tacos

I love this combination of flavors! This is a takeoff on one of my favorite burgers. Here, quality equals flavor. A sharp Cheddar and good-quality bacon makes this taco memorable.

Variation

I love lots of produce on my tacos. Add any or all of the following for a big fresh flavor: chopped tomato, minced onion, shredded zucchini, minced jicama or chopped fresh or pickled jalapeños.

1 lb	ground sirloin	500 g
¾ tsp	seasoned salt	3 mL
8	6- to 8-inch (15 to 20 cm) flour tortillas, skillet-warmed (page 15)	8
1 cup	shredded sharp Cheddar cheese	250 mL
8	strips bacon, cooked until crisp and diced	8
1 to 2 cups	shredded lettuce	250 to 500 mL
½ cup	ranch dressing	125 mL

1. In a large skillet over medium heat, sauté beef and salt, breaking up meat with a spoon, until meat is browned and no longer pink, about 12 minutes. Drain off excess fat.

2. To build tacos, divide meat filling equally among tortillas. Top with cheese, bacon and lettuce. Drizzle ranch dressing over lettuce on each tortilla. Fold tortillas in half.

Texas Chile Tacos

I like using black-eyed peas for this Texas-style taco. They are smaller, have a good texture and a subtle taste. Serve them on New Year's Day and you're guaranteed good luck.

Tip

The perfect size tortilla for a taco is 6 inches (15 cm). It is generally more available in corn rather than flour. Buy 8-inch (20 cm) flour tortillas and trim them with a pair of kitchen shears to 6 inches (15 cm) using a corn tortilla as a template.

1 lb	ground sirloin	500 g
	Salt and freshly ground black pepper	
½ cup	cooked or canned black-eyed peas, drained and rinsed	125 mL
1	package (1.5 oz/45 g) taco seasoning	1
1 cup	tomato sauce	250 mL
8	6- to 8-inch (15 to 20 cm) corn or flour tortillas (see Tip, left), skillet-warmed (page 15)	8
1	onion, minced	1
1 cup	shredded jalapeño Jack cheese	250 mL
2 cups	shredded lettuce	500 mL

1. In a large skillet over medium heat, sauté beef, breaking up meat with a spoon, until meat is browned and no longer pink, about 12 minutes. Season with salt and pepper to taste. Drain off excess fat.

2. Add peas, taco seasoning and tomato sauce to the meat mixture and mix well. Reduce heat to low and simmer, stirring, until well blended.

3. To build tacos, divide meat mixture equally among tortillas. Top with onion, cheese and lettuce. Fold tortillas in half.

Blue Cheese Burger Tacos

The simple combination of ground beef and blue cheese is amazing. This taco is upscale and delicious!

Variation

Replace Red Onion Salsa with caramelized onions, which add a rich flavor to this taco. To make them, slice a large onion crosswise and separate into rings. Season with salt and a pinch of sugar. In a large skillet, heat 1 tbsp (15 mL) olive oil over medium-high heat. Add onions and sauté until onions are transparent and caramelized, 12 to 15 minutes.

1 lb	extra-lean ground sirloin	500 g
1 tsp	seasoned salt	5 mL
Pinch	freshly ground black pepper	Pinch
8	6- to 8-inch (15 to 20 cm) flour tortillas, skillet-warmed (page 15)	8
½ cup	crumbled blue cheese	125 mL
	Red Onion Salsa (page 307)	
2 cups	shredded lettuce	500 mL

1. In a large skillet over medium heat, sauté meat, breaking up meat with a spoon, until meat is browned and no longer pink, about 12 minutes. Season with salt and pepper to taste. Drain off excess fat.

2. To build tacos, divide meat equally among tortillas. Top with blue cheese, Red Onion Salsa and lettuce. Fold tortillas in half.

Sonoran Taco Dogs

Makes 8 hot dogs

Natives of Sonora, Mexico, are big fans of Mexican-style hot dogs, bacon-wrapped dogs that became popular in the 1950s. This is my version of our favorite "dog," refashioned with a little Mexican flavor.

Tip

Top these hot dogs with any or all of the following: fresh Guacamole (page 316), Garlic Sour Cream (page 321) or shredded Monterey Jack or Cheddar cheeses.

- Preheat oven to 250°F (120°C)

8	beef wieners	8
8	strips bacon	8
1 tbsp	olive oil	15 mL
2	onions, sliced into rings	2
8	6- to 8-inch (15 to 20 cm) flour tortillas, skillet-warmed (page 15)	8
1 cup	refried beans (page 273), warmed	250 mL
1 cup	chopped drained dill pickles	250 mL
¼ cup	chopped drained pickled jalapeño peppers	60 mL

1. Wrap each wiener in 1 strip of bacon, securing each end with a toothpick. In a large skillet over medium-high heat, brown wieners, turning often, until bacon is crispy and wieners are cooked through, 4 to 6 minutes. Remove from skillet and keep warm in preheated oven.

2. In same skillet, heat oil over medium heat. Sauté onions until translucent and softened, 10 to 12 minutes.

3. To build tacos, spread refried beans on one side of each flour tortilla. Place a wiener in the center of each tortilla. Garnish with sautéed onions, pickles and jalapeños. Fold tortillas in half.

Rancher's Breakfast Taco

*Simple but hearty —
breakfast for a king.
The beef and green chile
combination lends itself
to both corn and flour
tortillas.*

Variations

Crumbled pork sausage
can be substituted for the
ground beef.

Additional condiments can
be served as well. Top with
minced onions, chopped
tomatoes or cilantro.

8 oz	ground sirloin	250 g
1	clove garlic, minced	1
	Salt	
6	eggs, slightly beaten	6
¼ cup	chopped roasted New Mexico or Anahiem green chile (see page 121)	60 mL
8	6- to 8-inch (15 to 20 cm) corn or flour tortillas, skillet-warmed (page 15)	8

1. In a large skillet over medium heat, sauté beef and garlic, breaking up meat with a spoon, until meat is browned and no longer pink, about 12 minutes. Drain off excess fat. Season with salt to taste.

2. Reduce heat to medium-low. Add eggs and chile to meat mixture. Sauté until eggs are scrambled and set.

3. To build tacos, divide meat mixture equally among each tortilla. Fold tortillas in half.

Hickory Brisket Tex-Mex Tacos with Cabbage Relish

Makes 8 tacos

This is a Texas-style taco — slow-cooked brisket and a coleslaw-style relish give it an authentic Tex-Mex flavor.

1½ cups	shredded red cabbage	375 mL
1 tbsp	minced red onion	15 mL
2 tbsp	balsamic vinaigrette	30 mL
2 cups	cooked beef brisket (see below), thinly sliced and cut into bite-size pieces	500 mL
½ cup	barbecue sauce	125 mL
	Salt and freshly ground black pepper	
8	6- to 8-inch (15 to 20 cm) flour tortillas	8

1. In a small bowl, combine cabbage, red onion and vinaigrette, mixing well. Cover and refrigerate, stirring once, for at least 20 minutes or for up to 2 hours.

2. In a large skillet over medium-low heat, combine beef pieces and barbecue sauce. Season with salt and pepper to taste. Sauté until meat is heated completely, 4 to 6 minutes.

3. To build tacos, divide meat equally among tortillas. Top with cabbage relish. Fold tortillas in half.

Oven-Roasted Beef Brisket

This is a simple brisket recipe that is perfect for tacos.

- Preheat oven to 300°F (150°C)
- Roasting pan, greased

1	onion, sliced	1
4 lb	piece beef brisket, trimmed	2 kg
2 tbsp	seasoned salt	30 mL
2 tbsp	liquid smoke	30 mL

1. Place onion slices on the bottom of roasting pan. Rub brisket on both sides with salt. Place meat on top of onion slices and sprinkle with liquid smoke. Cover with foil and seal edges. Bake in preheated oven for 4 hours or until beef is fork tender. Let stand for 20 to 30 minutes. Discard onions. Slice brisket thinly across the grain. Chop brisket slices into smaller bite-size pieces for taco filling.

Smoked Brisket Tacos with Chipotle Cream Sauce

Makes 8 tacos

Some people can't get enough of a smoky meaty flavor. In this taco you can get that smoky flavor right in your kitchen. The brisket filling and spicy cream sauce make a perfect match.

Variation

For a milder smoke flavor, reduce liquid smoke to 1 tbsp (15 mL).

¾ cup	ranch dressing	175 mL
1	chipotle chile pepper in adobo sauce, puréed	1
2 tbsp	sour cream	30 mL
1 tbsp	olive oil	15 mL
2 cups	cooked beef brisket (see page 162), thinly sliced and cut into bite-size pieces	500 mL
2 tbsp	liquid smoke	30 mL
	Salt and freshly ground black pepper	
8	6-inch (15 cm) corn tortillas, skillet-steamed (page 15)	8
1½ cups	shredded green cabbage	375 mL

1. In a small bowl, combine dressing, chile and sour cream. Cover and refrigerate, stirring once, for at least 20 minutes or for up to 2 hours.

2. In a large skillet, heat oil over medium heat. Sauté beef and liquid smoke until meat is heated completely, 4 to 6 minutes. Season with salt and pepper to taste.

3. To build tacos, divide meat equally among tortillas. Top with cabbage and cream sauce. Fold tortillas in half.

Salpicon Summer Tacos

A combination of shredded beef, cheese and vegetables makes this version of salpicon (minced vegetables combined in a sauce) a hearty and refreshing summer salad taco. Lots of flavors bound together by a delicious sauce is irresistible. Garnish with fresh avocado slices and radishes to make an impressive presentation.

Variation

Adjust the heat by reducing or increasing the chipotle chiles.

1 cup	Italian dressing	250 mL
3	chipotle chile peppers in adobo sauce, puréed	3
1 tbsp	finely chopped cilantro	15 mL
	Juice of 2 limes	
3 cups	shredded cooked beef brisket (see page 162), at room temperature	750 mL
1 cup	shredded Monterey Jack cheese	250 mL
4	tomatoes, seeded and chopped	4
1 cup	chopped roasted New Mexico or Anaheim green chiles (4 to 6 chiles depending on size) (see page 121)	250 mL
4	avocados	4
8	radishes, thinly sliced	8
24	4-inch (10 cm) corn tortillas	24
	Cilantro and Chile Salsa (page 305) and/or Roasted Tomato Salsa (page 299)	

1. In a large bowl, whisk together dressing, chipotle chiles, cilantro and lime juice until well blended. Add meat and mix well.

2. Add cheese, tomatoes and green chiles to meat mixture and toss until well coated.

3. Transfer to a large serving bowl. Cover and refrigerate for at least 2 hours or for up to 6 hours to allow flavors to mingle.

4. Before serving, seed and peel avocados. Slice lengthwise and arrange on top of meat. Place radish slices on top of meat around edge of bowl. Serve with skillet-warmed tortillas, Cilantro and Chile Salsa and/or Roasted Tomato Salsa.

Corn Beef and Potato Tacos

Makes 8 tacos

This is a St. Patrick's Day favorite in our house! The combination of corned beef and green chile is delightful. It is a Mexican way to toast the Irish!

Variation

For a more traditional Irish flavor, combine cabbage, oil, vinegar, salt and pepper in a small saucepan. Sauté over medium heat until cabbage is tender. Drain excess liquid. Continue with Steps 2 and 3.

• Preheat oven to 250°F (120°C)

2 cups	shredded green cabbage	500 mL
2 tbsp	olive oil	30 mL
2 tbsp	vinegar	30 mL
1/2 tsp	salt	2 mL
Pinch	freshly ground black pepper	Pinch
1 lb	corned beef, cooked and cut into bite-size pieces	500 g
1 cup	chopped roasted New Mexico or Anaheim green chiles (4 to 6 chiles depending on size) (see page 121)	250 mL
1	baking potato, cooked and diced	1
8	6- to 8-inch (15 to 20 cm) corn tortillas, skillet-warmed (page 15)	8
1/4 cup	Dijon mustard	60 mL
1 cup	shredded Monterey Jack cheese	250 mL
1/2 cup	minced red onion	125 mL

1. In a small bowl, combine cabbage, oil, vinegar, salt and pepper and refrigerate for 30 minutes or for up to 4 hours.

2. In a large skillet over medium heat, sauté corned beef, green chiles and potato until heated through, 4 to 6 minutes.

3. To build tacos, spread one side of each tortilla with mustard. Divide corned beef mixture among tortillas. Top with cabbage mixture, cheese and red onion. Fold tortillas in half.

Mexican Rueben Tacos

Makes 8 tacos

Here's a Rueben with a kick! My New Mexico version boasts a hint of green chile and smoky chipotle chile flavor.

• **Preheat oven to 250°F (120°C)**

1/2 cup	Thousand Island dressing	125 mL
1	chipotle chile pepper in adobo sauce, puréed	1
2 tbsp	sour cream	30 mL
8 oz	corned beef, cooked, sliced and diced	250 g
1/4 cup	chopped roasted New Mexico or Anaheim green chiles (see page 121)	60 mL
1/4 cup	diced red onion	60 mL
1/4 cup	drained sauerkraut	60 mL
8	6- to 8-inch (15 to 20 cm) flour tortillas	8
8	thin slices Swiss cheese	8

1. In a medium bowl, combine dressing, chipotle chile and sour cream. Refrigerate until ready to use or for up to 6 hours.

2. In a large skillet over medium heat, sauté corned beef until heated through, 4 to 6 minutes. Remove from skillet. Cover and keep warm in preheated oven.

3. In the same skillet, sauté green chiles, red onion and sauerkraut until onion is soft and translucent, 10 minutes.

4. To build tacos, skillet warm tortillas (page 15). Spread 1 tbsp (15 mL) of the dressing on one side of each tortilla. Place one slice of cheese on top of dressing. Divide corned beef equally among tortillas. Divide sautéed chile mixture equally over meat on each tortilla. Fold tortillas in half.

Pork and Lamb

Pork

Sausage

continued…

Lamb

Tacos el Pastor

These pineapple and pork tacos are the original fusion food — a cross between Middle Eastern shawarma and Mexican chile-rubbed grilled pork. This is my version of Mexico's favorite taco.

Tips

Serve with bowls of fresh cilantro leaves, chopped radishes, crumbled Cotija cheese or queso fresco cheese, chopped onions and jalapeños.

Poblano Sauce (page 320) and Jalapeño Cream Sauce (page 323) are also good with these tacos.

- Blender or food processor

½ cup	canned pineapple chunks, juice reserved	125 mL
1	onion, chopped	1
2 tbsp	minced cilantro	30 mL
5	chipotle chile peppers in adobo sauce	5
1 lb	pork tenderloin, cut into ½-inch (1 cm) cubes	500 g
1 tbsp	olive oil	15 mL
16	6-inch (15 cm) corn tortillas	16
	Pico de Gallo (page 305)	
4	limes, cut into wedges	4

1. In blender or food processor, purée pineapple, onion, cilantro and chiles until smooth. Add a bit of pineapple juice if the purée is too thick.

2. In a resealable plastic bag, combine pork and pineapple marinade and seal bag. Refrigerate for at least 4 hours or for up to 24 hours.

3. Remove pork from marinade and discard marinade. In a large skillet, heat oil over medium-high heat. Sauté pork until browned and just a hint of pink remains inside, about 10 minutes.

4. To build tacos, skillet warm tortillas (page 15). Stack 2 tortillas per taco, divide pork among tortillas. Top with Pico de Gallo. Fold tortillas in half. Serve each with a lime wedge.

Southern Pulled Pork Tacos with Honey Mustard Glaze

Makes 16 tacos

Tacos infused with some Southern flavors will liven up any meal. The slow roasting infuses flavor and tenderness.

Variation

To bake in oven: Preheat oven to 300°F (150°C). Line a roasting pan with foil, leaving enough on the ends to fold up and seal; place pork in the center of the foil. Pour chicken broth and garlic cloves over pork. Bring the edges of foil together and fold to seal. Bake in preheated oven until pork is falling apart and easy to shred, about 5 hours.

- Minimum 3½-quart slow cooker (see Variation, left)

Honey Mustard Glaze

2 tbsp	apple cider vinegar	30 mL
2 tbsp	granulated sugar	30 mL
3 tbsp	liquid honey	45 mL
2 tbsp	Dijon mustard	30 mL
2 lb	boneless pork shoulder blade (butt) roast	1 kg
1 tbsp	kosher salt	15 mL
1 tsp	freshly ground black pepper	5 mL
½ cup	chicken broth	125 mL
4	cloves garlic, minced	4
16	6-inch (15 cm) corn tortillas	16
2 cups	shredded cabbage	500 mL

1. *Honey Mustard Glaze:* In a small saucepan over medium heat, combine vinegar and sugar. Bring to a boil, stirring, until sugar dissolves.

2. Reduce heat to low. Whisk in honey and mustard and cook, stirring, until well blended and heated through. Let cool to room temperature.

3. Rub pork all over with salt and pepper. Transfer to slow cooker. Add chicken broth and garlic. Cover and cook on Low for 8 to 10 hours or High for 4 to 6 hours, until pork is very tender and easy to shred.

4. Transfer pork to a cutting board and discard juices in slow cooker. Cut off strings and shred pork using two forks, discarding excess fat.

5. To build tacos, skillet warm tortillas (page 15). Divide pork equally among tortillas. Drizzle with Honey Mustard Glaze and top with cabbage. Fold tortillas in half.

Grilled Pork Loin Tacos with Apple, Onion and Garlic Relish

The charred flavor of the pork accents the unexpected flavors in this sweet relish. This is a grilling favorite that can also be cooked in the oven.

Tip

Use a reduced-sodium soy sauce for a less salty tasting pork.

Variation

To bake in oven: Preheat oven to 375°F (190°C). Place pork in a 13- by 9-inch (33 by 23 cm) glass baking dish and bake until internal temperature reaches 160°F (71°C) and juices run clear, 20 to 25 minutes.

- Barbecue grill (see Variation, left)
- Instant-read thermometer

1½ lbs	pork tenderloin (about 3 small)	750 g
½ cup	soy sauce (see Tip, left)	125 mL
8	6- to 8-inch (15 to 20 cm) flour tortillas	8
	Apple, Onion and Garlic Relish (page 313)	
2 cups	chopped salad mix	500 mL

1. In a large resealable bag, combine pork and soy sauce. Seal and refrigerate. Marinate for at least 3 hours or for up to 6 hours.

2. Preheat greased grill to medium-high. Remove pork from marinade and discard marinade. Grill pork, covered, turning to brown all sides, until an instant-read temperature registers 160°F (71°C) and a hint of pink remains in pork, 15 to 18 minutes. Let pork stand for 8 to 10 minutes. Carve into bite-size pieces.

3. To build tacos, skillet warm tortillas (page 15). Divide pork equally among tortillas. Top with Apple, Onion and Garlic Relish and salad mix. Fold tortillas in half.

Pork Fajita Tacos with Peach and Red Onion Salsa

Fajitas are always a hit and the unexpected is even more inviting. The sweet and tangy flavors of peaches and onion crown this taco.

Tip

The perfect size tortilla for a taco is 6 inches (15 cm). It is generally more available in corn rather than flour. Buy 8-inch (20 cm) flour tortillas and trim them with a pair of kitchen shears to 6 inches (15 cm) using a corn tortilla as a template.

1 tbsp	olive oil	15 mL
1 tbsp	soy sauce	15 mL
1½ lbs	pork tenderloin, cut crosswise into thin slices	750 g
1	onion, julienned	1
1	red bell pepper, julienned	1
1	green bell pepper, julienned	1
	Kosher salt and cracked black peppercorns	
8	6- to 8-inch (15 to 20 cm) corn or flour tortillas (see Tip, left), skillet-warmed (page 15)	8
	Peach and Red Onion Salsa (page 302)	

1. In a large skillet, heat, oil and soy sauce over medium-high heat. Add pork and stir-fry until pork is browned and just a hint of pink remains inside, 4 to 6 minutes. Add onion and red and green bell peppers and stir-fry until vegetables are tender, 3 to 4 minutes. Season with salt and pepper to taste.

2. To build tacos, divide pork mixture equally among tortillas. Top with Peach and Red Onion Salsa. Fold tortillas in half.

Cuban Tacos with Chopped Pickles and Red Onion Relish

Makes 8 tacos

This is my version of a Cuban sandwich that became a favorite for workers in Cuban cigar factories. It makes a good layered taco that is mouthwatering!

- Preheat oven to 325°F (160°C)
- 8-inch (20 cm) square glass baking dish, greased

24	dill pickles, minced	24
1	red onion, minced	1
8	6- to 8-inch (15 to 20 cm) flour tortillas, skillet-warmed (page 15)	8
2 to 3 tbsp	prepared mustard	30 to 45 mL
8	thin slices Swiss cheese	8
1 lb	grilled or roasted pork loin (see page 174), chopped	500 g
8	thin slices baked ham	8

1. In a small bowl, combine pickles and red onion.

2. To build tacos, spread one side of each tortilla with a thin layer of mustard and top with one slice of cheese. Divide pork and ham equally among tortillas and place on top of cheese. Top with pickle mixture. Fold tortillas in half.

3. Transfer tacos to prepared baking dish and arrange side by side. Cover with foil and bake in preheated oven until cheese is melted and tacos are heated through, 15 to 20 minutes.

Roasted Pork Tacos with Chimichurri Sauce

Lightly seasoned pork is accented with a sauce loaded with fresh herbs and intense flavor. This is a simple roasted taco crowned with flavor that anyone can create.

- Preheat oven to 350°F (180°C)
- 13- by 9-inch (33 by 23 cm) glass baking dish
- Instant-read thermometer

2 lbs	pork tenderloin (about 2 large)	1 kg
1 tbsp	kosher salt	15 mL
2 tsp	cracked black peppercorns	10 mL
1 tsp	dried Italian seasoning	5 mL
16	6-inch (15 cm) corn tortillas, skillet-warmed (page 15)	16
	Chimichurri Sauce (page 328)	

1. Rub pork all over with salt, peppercorns and Italian seasoning. Transfer to baking dish and bake in preheated oven until an instant-read thermometer registers 160°F (71°C), 20 to 30 minutes. Let stand for 8 to 10 minutes. Carve crosswise into thin slices.

2. To build tacos, divide pork equally among tortillas. Top with Chimichurri Sauce and fold tortillas in half.

Chile Verde Tacos

Makes 8 tacos

On most cool winter days I am craving comfort food. Tender pork folded into a zesty green chile sauce makes a delicious taco that hits the spot. The secret of this recipe is the sauce, which can be made ahead.

1 lb	boneless pork shoulder blade (butt), cut into ½-inch (1 cm) pieces	500 g
1 cup	New Mexico Green Chile Sauce (page 320)	250 mL
8	6- to 8-inch (15 to 20 cm) corn or flour tortillas	8

1. Place pork in a large pot. Add just enough water to cover. Bring to a boil over medium-high heat. Reduce heat and boil gently, stirring occasionally, until water and juices evaporate, 25 to 35 minutes. Reduce heat to low. Add chile sauce and simmer, stirring, until flavors are blended, 8 to 10 minutes.

2. To build tacos, skillet warm tortillas (page 15). Divide pork mixture equally among tortillas. Fold tortillas in half.

Classic Carnita Tacos with Fresh Lime

Makes 16 tacos

This shredded pork taco is a timeless classic in Mexico. My recipe ties together the distinctive flavors of Mexico — chile, pork and lime. Tacos make great party food and these are no exception.

Tip

Serve with bowls of fresh cilantro leaves, chopped radishes, crumbled Cotija cheese or queso fresco cheese, chopped onions and jalapeños.

Variations

Red Chile Carnitas: Add 1½ cups (375 mL) New Mexico Red Chile Sauce (page 319) or prepared red enchilada sauce, in Step 2 after juices have evaporated. Sauté over medium heat until heated through, 6 to 8 minutes.

Red Chile Carnitas with Hominy: Increase tortillas to 24. Add 1½ cups (375 mL) New Mexico Red Chile Sauce (page 319) or prepared red enchilada sauce and 1 cup (250 mL) drained minced hominy in Step 2 after juices have evaporated. Sauté over medium heat until heated through, 6 to 8 minutes.

2 lb	boneless pork shoulder blade (butt) roast, cubed	1 kg
1	onion, sliced	1
2	cloves garlic, chopped	2
2 tbsp	kosher salt	30 mL
1 tbsp	olive oil	15 mL
2	onions, diced	2
4	serrano chile peppers or jalapeños, seeded and chopped	4
16	6- to 8-inch (15 to 20 cm) corn tortillas	16
4	fresh limes, cut into quarter wedges	4

1. Place pork in a large pot. Add just enough water to cover. Add sliced onion, garlic and salt and bring to a boil over medium-high heat. Reduce heat to medium-low, cover and boil gently until pork is tender, 2 to 3 hours. Remove pork from pot, reserving 1 cup (250 mL) of liquid. Let pork cool slightly, then shred or chop into tiny pieces, discarding excess fat.

2. In a large skillet, heat oil over medium heat. Sauté onions and chiles until tender, 4 to 6 minutes. Add pork and reserved liquid. Cook over medium-high heat, stirring, until all juices have evaporated, about 15 minutes.

3. To build tacos, skillet warm tortillas (page 15). Divide pork mixture equally among tortillas. Fold tortillas in half. Serve each with a fresh lime wedge.

Marinated Pork Chop Tacos

Makes 8 tacos

This recipe includes a delicious marinade that adds zing to this pork taco. A sweet corn salsa lends another dimension all its own.

Variation

To oven bake: Preheat oven to 350°F (180°C). Place chops in a lightly greased 13- by 9-inch (33 by 23 cm) glass baking dish and bake until a hint of pink remains inside, 20 to 25 minutes. Thinly slice.

- Barbecue grill
- Instant-read thermometer

4	boneless pork loin chops (each 4 oz/125 g)	4
½ cup	beer	125 mL
⅓ cup	soy sauce	75 mL
2 tbsp	brown sugar	30 mL
2	jalapeños, seeded and minced	2
1 cup	cooked corn kernels	250 mL
1	avocado, diced	1
1 tbsp	minced fresh cilantro	15 mL
2 tsp	balsamic vinegar	10 mL
	Salt and freshly ground black pepper	
8	6- to 8-inch (15 to 20 cm) flour tortillas	8
1 cup	shredded Monterey Jack cheese	250 mL

1. In a resealable plastic bag, combine pork chops, beer, soy sauce, brown sugar and jalapeños. Seal and gently massage bag to evenly distribute marinade. Refrigerate for at least 2 hours or for up to 24 hours.

2. In a small bowl, combine corn, avocado, cilantro and vinegar. Season with salt and pepper to taste.

3. Preheat greased grill to medium-high. Grill chops, covered, turning once, until a hint of pink remains inside or an instant-read thermometer registers 160°F (71°C), 3 to 5 minutes per side. Let stand for 8 to 10 minutes. Dice into bite-size pieces.

4. To build tacos, skillet-warm tortillas (page 15). Divide pork equally among tortillas. Top with corn mixture and cheese. Fold tortillas in half.

Sweet-and-Sour Pork Tacos

Makes 8 tacos

My kids love Asian food, so this taco is a favorite. Serve with a big bowl of rice and green salad and you will please the crowd.

2 tbsp	vegetable oil, divided	30 mL
1 cup	snow peas, trimmed	250 mL
1	red bell pepper, chopped	1
1	onion, chopped	1
1 lb	boneless pork loin, cut into bite-size pieces	500 g
¾ cup	sweet-and-sour sauce	175 mL
8	6- or 8-inch (15 to 20 cm) corn or flour tortillas, skillet-warmed (page 15)	8
1½ cups	shredded cabbage	375 mL

1. In a large skillet, heat 1 tbsp (15 mL) of the oil over medium-high heat. Sauté snow peas, bell pepper and onion until tender crisp, 2 to 3 minutes. Set aside.

2. Add remaining 1 tbsp (15 mL) of oil to skillet. Add pork and stir-fry until browned and just a hint of pink remains inside, 10 to 12 minutes.

3. Reduce heat to medium-low. Add sweet-and-sour sauce and return vegetables to pan. Cook, stirring, until sauce is bubbling and vegetables are heated through.

4. To build tacos, divide pork mixture equally among tortillas. Top with cabbage. Fold tortillas in half.

Garlic and Rosemary Pork Loin Tacos

Makes 8 tacos

This simple rub is full of fresh herbs grown all around the U.S. Southwest. It adds a flavorful crust to this cut of meat, making a taco elegant enough for entertaining.

Tip
Serve with Chile Basil Sauce (page 328), Veggie Salsa (page 308) or Jicama Salsa (page 309).

- Roasting pan
- Instant-read thermometer

2 tsp	minced rosemary	10 mL
1 tsp	kosher salt	5 mL
½ tsp	cracked black peppercorns	2 mL
1	clove garlic, minced	1
1½ lbs	pork tenderloin (about 2)	750 g
2 tbsp	olive oil	30 mL
8	6-inch (15 cm) corn tortillas	8
2 cups	chopped salad mix	500 mL
1	red bell pepper, chopped	1

1. In a small bowl, combine rosemary, salt, peppercorns and garlic until well blended. Coat pork all over with oil. Rub top and sides with rosemary mixture, forming a light crust. Wrap in foil and refrigerate for at least 2 hours or for up to 24 hours.

2. Preheat oven to 375°F (190°C). Unwrap pork and place in roasting pan. Bake until an instant-read thermometer registers 160°F (71°C), 20 to 25 minutes. Let stand for 8 to 10 minutes. Carve crosswise into thin slices.

3. To build tacos, skillet warm tortillas (page 15). Divide pork equally among tortillas. Top with salad mix and bell pepper. Fold tortillas in half.

Carne Adovada Soft Tacos with Fresh Lime

Makes 16 tacos

This is my variation of a traditional marinated pork that is legendary in Mexico. It is soaked in a rich red chile sauce and spices for a tender succulent filling.

2 lbs	boneless pork shoulder blade (butt), cut into bite-size pieces	1 kg
2 cups	New Mexico Red Chile Sauce (page 319)	500 mL
1 tsp	hot pepper flakes	5 mL
1 tsp	dried oregano	5 mL
1 tsp	ground cumin	5 mL
1 tsp	garlic powder	5 mL
1 tsp	onion powder	5 mL
16	6-inch (15 cm) corn tortillas, skillet-warmed (page 15)	16
1	onion, minced	1
4	limes, cut into quarter wedges	4

1. Place pork in a large pot. Add just enough water to cover. Bring to a boil over medium-high heat. Reduce heat and boil gently, stirring occasionally, until water and juices have evaporated, 15 to 20 minutes. Reduce heat to low. Add red chile sauce, hot pepper flakes, oregano, cumin, garlic powder and onion powder. Mix well until all spices are well blended and sauce is heated through.

2. To build tacos, divide pork mixture equally among tortillas. Top with minced onion. Fold tortillas in half. Serve each with a lime wedge.

Chipotle Pork Tacos with Onion Apple Salsa

There are a wide range of flavors in this taco. The smoky rich flavor of the pork teamed with the sweet savory salsa is a winning combination.

Tip

For best results in grilling, brush the grill grate with vegetable oil or coat with a nonstick cooking spray before preheating the grill.

Variation

Pork Pesto Tacos: Substitute ¼ cup (60 mL) prepared basil pesto for the chile and honey mixture.

- Preheat greased barbecue or indoor grill to medium (see Tip, left)
- Instant-read thermometer

¼ cup	liquid honey	60 mL
1 tbsp	olive oil	30 mL
3	chipotle chile peppers in adobo sauce, puréed	3
4	boneless pork loin chops	4
1 tsp	kosher salt	5 mL
½ tsp	freshly ground black pepper	2 mL
½ cup	minced red cabbage	125 mL
½ cup	minced green cabbage	125 mL
8	6-inch (15 cm) corn tortillas, skillet-warmed (page 15)	8
	Onion Apple Salsa (page 306)	

1. In a small bowl, combine honey, oil and chiles. Set aside.

2. Rub pork all over with salt and pepper. Grill pork, turning once, until just a hint of pink remains inside or an instant-read thermometer registers 160°F (71°C), 3 to 5 minutes per side. Just before removing from grill, brush with honey mixture, turning once. Let stand for 8 to 10 minutes. Cut into bite-size pieces.

3. In a small bowl, toss together red and green cabbage.

4. To build tacos, divide pork equally among tortillas. Top with cabbage and Onion Apple Salsa. Fold tortillas in half.

Slow-Cooked BBQ Pork Tacos

Makes 16 tacos

This is my version of a spicy Southern-style pork taco. Enjoy the smoky, spicy flavor that the South has come to love.

Tip
Heat levels vary in slow cookers. Check your meat toward the end of the cooking time for tenderness and doneness so not to overcook.

Variation
For added flavor, top this taco with your favorite coleslaw.

• 3 to 6-quart slow cooker

2	cloves garlic, minced	2
2 tbsp	cracked black peppercorns	30 mL
2 tsp	seasoned salt	10 mL
2 tsp	brown sugar	10 mL
2½ lbs	boneless pork shoulder blade (butt) roast, trimmed	1.25 kg
1 cup	barbecue sauce	250 mL
½ cup	red enchilada sauce	125 mL
½ cup	tomato-based chili sauce	125 mL
1½ tsp	hot smoked paprika	7 mL
16	6- to 8-inch (15 to 20 cm) flour tortillas	16
2 cups	shredded cabbage	500 mL
1	onion, minced	1

1. In a small bowl, combine garlic, peppercorns, salt and brown sugar. Rub all over pork shoulder. Transfer to a large bowl and cover and refrigerate overnight.

2. Transfer seasoned pork to slow cooker. Add barbecue, enchilada and chili sauces. Cover and cook on Low for 8 to 10 hours or on High for 4 to 6 hours. Add paprika. Cover and cook on Low for 1 hour more so flavors blend. Transfer pork to a cutting board. Skim off any excess fat from sauce. Cut off strings and shred pork with two forks, discarding excess fat. Return pork to sauce.

3. Transfer shredded pork to a large serving bowl. Let guests build their own tacos with warmed tortillas (page 15), cabbage and onion.

Char Siu Tacos

Makes 8 tacos

This is a simple taco that brings together Latin culinary techniques and Korean flavors. The roasted pork is lightly seasoned and glazed with honey. Another level of flavor is added by using a savory Korean sauce.

Variation

Substitute ½ cup (125 mL) unsweetened pineapple juice for the hoisin sauce.

- Preheat oven to 350°F (180°C)
- 13- by 9-inch (33 by 23 cm) glass baking dish
- Instant-read thermometer

¾ cup	hoisin sauce	175 mL
½ cup	soy sauce	125 mL
½ cup	rice wine, such as sake	125 mL
1 tbsp	granulated sugar	15 mL
⅓ cup	liquid honey	75 mL
2 lbs	pork tenderloin (about 2 large)	1 kg
1 tbsp	kosher salt	15 mL
1 tsp	cracked black peppercorns	5 mL
2 tbsp	liquid honey	30 mL
16	6-inch (15 cm) corn tortillas, skillet-warmed (page 15)	16
½ cup	chopped onion	125 mL
1 tbsp	minced fresh cilantro	15 mL
2 cups	shredded cabbage	500 mL

1. In a medium bowl, combine hoisin sauce, soy sauce, wine and sugar, stirring until sugar dissolves. Stir in ⅓ cup (75 mL) honey until well blended. Set aside.

2. Rub pork all over with salt and peppercorns. Transfer to baking dish, tucking thin end underneath, and bake in preheated oven for 15 minutes. Remove and spread pork with 2 tbsp (30 mL) honey. Return to oven and roast until an instant-read thermometer inserted in the thickest part registers 160°F (71°C), 5 to 10 minutes. Let stand for 8 to 10 minutes. Carve crosswise into thin slices.

3. In a small bowl, combine onion and cilantro.

4. To build tacos, divide pork equally among tortillas. Top with hoisin sauce mixture, onion mixture and cabbage. Fold tortillas in half.

Bacon and Avocado Breakfast Tacos

Makes 8 tacos

Crisp salty bacon and smooth luscious avocado make this egg taco come alive. It's a breakfast favorite in southern New Mexico.

Tip
Serve with Fiesta Taco Sauce (page 324) or Cilantro and Chile Salsa (page 305).

1 tbsp	olive oil	15 mL
8	eggs, slightly beaten	8
8	6- to 8-inch (15 to 20 cm) corn tortillas, skillet-warmed (page 15)	8
8	strips bacon, cooked and crumbled	8
2	avocados, diced	2
1	tomato, seeded and diced	1

1. In a large skillet, heat oil over medium heat. Add eggs and scramble, stirring, until set.

2. To build tacos, divide eggs equally among tortillas. Top with bacon, avocados and tomato. Fold tortillas in half.

Potato and Bacon Crispy Tacos

Makes 8 tacos

We call these tacos "Dorados," Spanish for the word golden. It describes this crispy golden corn shell stuffed with potato and bacon perfectly.

- Candy/deep-fry thermometer

2	baking potatoes, baked and diced	2
4	strips bacon, cooked and crumbled	4
8	6- to 8-inch (15 to 20 cm) corn tortillas, micro-warmed (page 15)	8
	Vegetable oil	

1. In a large bowl, combine potatoes and bacon.

2. To build tacos, divide potato mixture equally among tortillas, placing mixture on one half of tortilla. Fold over and secure with a toothpick. Deep-fry immediately or place folded tacos in a resealable plastic bag to keep moist. Refrigerate until ready to cook for up to 2 days.

3. Fill a deep-fryer, deep heavy pot or deep skillet with 3 inches (7.5 cm) of oil and heat to 350°F (180°C). Using tongs, gently place 2 to 3 tacos at a time into the hot oil and deep-fry, turning once, until golden brown and crispy, 2 to 3 minutes. Drain on paper towels.

BLT Tacos
with Spicy Cream Salsa

This taco is full of texture and packed with flavor. It starts with crispy bacon then it's layered with a fresh corn salad. It is cool and refreshing.

Tips

For the corn, you can use drained canned, frozen, thawed or roasted.

In order to blend all of the textures in the taco do not overcook bacon.

2	green onions, green part only, minced	2
2	jalapeños, seeded and chopped	2
1	tomato, chopped	1
1 cup	cooked corn kernels (see Tips, left)	250 mL
½ cup	ranch dressing	125 mL
Pinch	cayenne pepper	Pinch
8	6- to 8-inch (15 to 20 cm) flour tortillas, skillet-warmed (page 15)	8
16	strips bacon, cooked and crumbled	16
1 cup	shredded jalapeño Jack cheese	250 mL
2 cups	shredded lettuce	500 mL

1. In a medium bowl, combine green onions, jalapeños, tomato and corn. Add ranch dressing and cayenne and stir until well blended. Cover and refrigerate for at least 2 hours or for up to 6 hours.

2. To build tacos, divide bacon equally among tortillas. Top with spicy creamy salsa, cheese and lettuce. Fold tortillas in half.

Grilled Onion and Pork Crispy Tacos

Makes 8 tacos

This is a simple weeknight dish. It is quick, easy and loaded with flavor. The cumin heightens the taste of the pork filling.

Tip

If you are short on time, use store-bought taco shells. There are a variety of brands to choose from. Check with your local grocer to see if they make them fresh.

Variation

Top with additional fresh produce such as fresh chopped spinach, sliced radishes and chopped jalapeños.

2 tbsp	olive oil, divided	30 mL
1 lb	boneless pork loin, diced	500 g
1 tsp	ground cumin	5 mL
	Kosher salt	
2	onions, sliced	2
8	taco shells (page 14) (See Tip, left)	8
2 cups	chopped salad mix	500 mL
1	red bell pepper, chopped	1
	Salsa Verde (page 300)	

1. In a large skillet, heat 1 tbsp (15 mL) of the oil over medium-high heat. Sauté meat, cumin, and salt to taste until all juices have evaporated and pork is a bit crispy, 12 to 14 minutes. Transfer to a bowl and set aside.

2. Reduce heat to medium. Add remaining 1 tbsp (15 mL) of oil to skillet. Sauté onions until softened and transparent, 12 to 14 minutes.

3. To build tacos, divide pork equally among taco shells. Top with onions, salad mix and bell pepper. Top with Salsa Verde.

Zesty Orange Pork Tacos

Makes 8 tacos

I love the combination of citrus flavor teamed with a tender pork filling. Crowned with a citrus salsa, this is the perfect dish for entertaining.

- Barbecue grill
- Instant-read thermometer

1 cup	diced mandarin oranges (10 to 12)	250 mL
1/4 cup	minced red onion	60 mL
2 tbsp	minced fresh cilantro	30 mL
	Juice of 2 limes	
1/2 cup	orange juice	125 mL
2 tbsp	liquid honey	30 mL
1 tbsp	olive oil	15 mL
4	boneless pork loin chops, diced	4
8	6-inch (15 cm) corn tortillas	8
2 cups	chopped salad mix	500 mL

1. In a small bowl, combine oranges, red onion and cilantro. Cover and refrigerate for 2 to 3 hours to allow flavors to blend.

2. In a large resealable plastic bag, combine lime and orange juices, honey and oil. Add pork, seal and gently massage bag to evenly distribute marinade. Refrigerate for at least 2 hours or for up to 24 hours.

3. Preheat greased grill to medium-high heat. Remove pork chops from marinade, discarding marinade. Grill chops, covered, turning once, until just a hint of pink remains inside or an instant-read thermometer registers 160°F (71°C), 3 to 5 minutes per side. Let stand for 8 to 10 minutes. Dice into bite-size pieces.

4. To build tacos, skillet warm tortillas (page 15). Divide pork equally among tortillas. Top with salad mix and orange salsa mixture. Fold tortillas in half.

Luau Pork Panini Tacos

These tacos are stuffed with a sweet and savory filling. Lightly grilling the tortillas creates a crisp buttery crust.

Tip

These tacos can also be grilled in a large skillet. Heat a large skillet over medium-high heat. Grill tacos on each side until tortillas are golden brown and cheese is melted, 4 to 6 minutes.

Variation

If you prefer, omit pineapple and serve with Tropical Salsa (page 299).

* Panini press (see Tip, left)

1 tbsp	olive oil	15 mL
1 lb	boneless pork loin or pork chops, diced	500 g
2	cloves garlic, minced	2
1/2 tsp	ground cumin	2 mL
Pinch	seasoned salt	Pinch
	Butter, softened	
8	6- to 8-inch (15 to 20 cm) flour tortillas	8
8	thin slices Provolone cheese	8
8	thin slices deli ham	8
1 cup	drained canned pineapple tidbits	250 mL

1. In a large skillet, heat oil over medium-high heat. Sauté diced pork, garlic, cumin and salt until all juices have evaporated and meat is a bit crispy, 10 to 12 minutes.

2. Meanwhile, preheat panini press.

3. To build tacos, butter one side of each tortilla. Gently place, buttered side down, on a work surface and divide cheese equally among tortillas. Top with ham. Divide pork equally among tortillas. Top with pineapple pieces. Fold tortillas in half. Grill each taco on a panini press until golden brown.

Asparagus and Prosciutto Taquitos

Makes 8 tacos

Fun, easy and gourmet cheesy is how I describe this appetizer. It is so simple but the fresh and flavorful ingredients will have a big impact on your guests.

- Candy/deep-fry thermometer

8	thin slices prosciutto	8
8	6-inch (15 cm) corn tortillas, micro-warmed (page 15)	8
8	asparagus spears, trimmed	8
½ cup	freshly grated Parmesan cheese	125 mL
	Spicy Asian Sauce (page 325)	

1. To build tacos, place 1 slice of prosciutto across one end of each tortilla. Top with 1 asparagus spear. Gently roll asparagus in tortilla and secure with a toothpick. Place rolled tacos in resealable plastic bag to keep moist. Use immediately or refrigerate for up to 6 hours.

2. Fill deep-fryer, deep heavy pot or deep skillet with 3 inches (7.5 cm) of oil and heat to 350°F (180°C). Using tongs, gently place 3 to 4 tacos at a time in the hot oil and deep-fry, turning once, until golden brown and crispy on the ends and a bit soft in the middle, 2 to 3 minutes. Drain on paper towels. Lightly sprinkle tacos with cheese and serve with Spicy Asian Sauce for dipping.

Chorizo and Potato Tacos

Spicy Mexican sausage and spuds are staple breakfast favorites among Mexican food lovers, although this taco can be served any time of the day.

Tips

Some chorizo sausages are stronger than others. Try a variety and find your favorite. For a spicier taco, add 2 oz (60 g) more fresh chorizo.

Serve with Tomato Table Salsa (page 302) or Garlic Sour Cream (page 321).

3 tbsp	olive oil	45 mL
2 cups	diced potatoes	500 mL
4 oz	fresh chorizo sausage, removed from casing	125 g
8	6-inch (15 cm) corn tortillas, skillet-warmed (page 15)	8

1. In a large skillet, heat oil over medium-high heat. Sauté potatoes until soft and golden brown, 10 to 12 minutes. Remove skillet from heat.

2. In a small skillet over medium heat, sauté sausage, breaking up with a spoon, until lightly browned, about 8 minutes. Drain excess grease.

3. Add sausage to potatoes and sauté over medium-low heat, stirring until well blended and heated through, 4 to 6 minutes.

4. To build tacos, divide potato mixture equally among tortillas. Fold tortillas in half.

Grilled Bratwurst and Beer Fajita Tacos with Jalapeño Mustard

Makes 8 tacos

I love this taco! Typically, "fajitas" are marinated ahead of time. But I created this quick skillet version that has lots of flavor and is perfect for a weeknight meal.

Tip

Use different colored peppers for a more attractive dish. Orange, red and yellow bell peppers will lend a sweeter flavor to this taco.

Variations

Add more fresh produce, such as shredded lettuce or diced tomato on top of the meat mixture.

I also like to serve this with ½ cup (125 mL) drained sauerkraut, divided equally among the tacos.

• Preheat greased barbecue grill to medium

4	bratwurst sausage	4
2 tbsp	olive oil, divided	30 mL
⅓ cup	beer	75 mL
1	onion, julienned	1
2	bell peppers, any colors, julienned (see Tip, left)	2
2 tbsp	minced drained pickled jalapeños	30 mL
½ cup	prepared mustard	125 mL
8	6- to 8-inch (15 to 20 cm) corn or flour tortillas, skillet-warmed (page 15)	8

1. Pierce sausages a few times with a fork. Grill, covered, turning once, until juices run clear, for about 15 minutes or according to package directions. Let cool slightly and cut into bite-size pieces.

2. In a large skillet, heat 1 tbsp (15 mL) of the oil over medium heat. Sauté sausage, beer, onion and bell peppers until peppers are tender-crisp and liquid has evaporated, 10 to 12 minutes.

3. In a small saucepan over low heat, combine remaining 1 tbsp (15 mL) of olive oil and jalapeños, mashing jalapeños well. Stir in mustard.

4. To build tacos, divide sausage mixture equally among tortillas. Drizzle with mustard mixture. Fold tortillas in half.

Spicy Chorizo Tacos

Highly spiced and flavored meats have always been popular in the Mexican culture. I add a bit more heat to this Mexican-style chorizo taco with hot pepper flakes.

Variations

For a spicier taco, add 2 to 4 oz (60 to 125 g) more chorizo to the filling or add another 1 tsp (5 mL) hot pepper flakes, or add both.

For a savory-sweet version, add ½ cup (125 mL) minced raisins when cooking the meat in Step 1.

1 lb	ground beef	500 g
4 oz	fresh chorizo sausage, removed from casings	125 g
1 tsp	hot pepper flakes	5 mL
Pinch	kosher salt	Pinch
8	6-inch (15 cm) corn tortillas, skillet-warmed (page 15)	8
2 cups	shredded lettuce	500 mL
1 cup	shredded Cheddar cheese	250 mL
1	tomato, seeded and chopped	1

1. In a large skillet over medium heat, sauté beef, sausage, hot pepper flakes and salt, breaking up sausage with a spoon, until beef is no longer pink, 10 to 12 minutes. Drain off excess fat.

2. To build tacos, divide beef mixture equally among tortillas. Top with lettuce, cheese and tomato. Fold tortillas in half.

Monterey, Mushroom and Sausage Tacos

This taco can be served at breakfast, lunch or dinner. The creamy, meaty filling blends the mushroom and spices in a delicious way.

Tip

I like using a pre-seasoned sausage. There are many varieties available at your local market, such as hot, spicy or sage.

Variation

Create an appetizer by replacing the 6-inch (15 cm) tortillas with twenty-four 4-inch (10 cm) corn tortillas.

1 lb	seasoned pork sausage (bulk or removed from casings) (see Tip, left)	500 g
10	mushrooms, finely chopped	10
1 tsp	hot pepper flakes	5 mL
4 oz	cream cheese, at room temperature	125 g
12	6-inch (15 cm) corn tortillas, skillet-warmed (page 15)	12
1½ cups	chopped salad mix	375 mL
½ cup	shredded Monterey Jack cheese	125 mL
1	tomato, seeded and diced	1

1. In a large skillet over medium heat, sauté sausage until brown, 10 to 12 minutes. Drain off excess fat. Add mushrooms and hot pepper flakes and sauté until mushrooms are browned, 6 to 8 minutes. Stir in cream cheese until melted.

2. To build tacos, divide sausage mixture equally among tortillas. Top with salad mix, cheese and tomato. Fold tortillas in half.

Chorizo and Egg Tacos

This breakfast combination is an all-time favorite in the Southwest. The chorizo, a spicy Mexican sausage, and crispy potato are perfect together, nestled among the fluffy scrambled eggs.

Tips

I like this breakfast taco because it takes very little time to prepare and all 8 tacos can be made ahead and kept warm, covered, in a preheated 200°F (100°C) oven for up to 1 hour.

Top this taco with Roasted Tomato Salsa (page 299) or Salsa Verde (page 300).

1 tbsp	olive oil	15 mL
1	potato, cut into ¼-inch (1 cm) dice	1
	Salt	
4 oz	fresh chorizo sausage, removed from casings	125 g
4	eggs, lightly beaten	4
8	6-inch (15 cm) corn or flour tortillas, skillet-warmed (page 15)	8
1 cup	shredded Cheddar cheese	250 mL

1. In a medium skillet, heat oil over medium heat. Add potato and cook, covered, about 10 minutes. Remove lid, and cook, stirring, until potato is soft, lightly browned and crispy, 8 to 10 minutes more. Season with salt to taste.

2. Reduce heat to medium-low. Add chorizo to potato in skillet. Sauté chorizo, breaking up with a spoon until chorizo is well browned, 8 to 10 minutes. Drain excess grease. Add eggs and cook, stirring, until set.

3. To build tacos, divide egg mixture equally among tortillas. Top with cheese. Fold tortillas in half.

Italian Sausage and Pepper Tacos

Italian flavors blend well in this international favorite. It's like a bite of pizza in a tortilla! Add a spoonful of Chile Basil Sauce (page 328) for even more flavor.

Tip

Serve this Italian-style taco with Chile Cream Sauce (page 327) or Chile Basil Sauce (page 328). Occasionally, I also serve it with 1½ cups (375 mL) marinara sauce, warmed, for dipping.

• Preheat greased barbecue grill to medium

4	Italian sausages	4
1 tbsp	olive oil	15 mL
2	red bell peppers, julienned	2
2	cloves garlic, minced	2
1	onion, julienned	1
	Salt	
8	6- to 8-inch (15 to 20 cm) flour tortillas, skillet-warmed (page 15)	8
1 cup	shredded mozzarella cheese	250 mL

1. Pierce sausages a few times with a fork. Grill, covered, turning once, until juices run clear, for about 15 minutes or according to package directions. Let cool slightly and cut into bite-size pieces.

2. In a large skillet, heat oil over medium heat. Sauté sausage, bell peppers, garlic and onion until onion and peppers are slightly charred and sausage is heated through, 10 to 12 minutes. Season with salt to taste.

3. To build tacos, divide sausage mixture equally among tortillas. Top with cheese. Fold tortillas in half.

Creole Sausage and Red Bean Tacos

Makes 8 tacos

I call this "Infused Bayou Cooking." The combination of Cajun spices and red beans wrapped in a corn tortilla is delicious.

Tips

You shouldn't think of lard as a four-letter word, nor should you shy away from bacon drippings. They both add flavor and are used in many authentic Mexican dishes. However, you can substitute 2 tsp (10 mL) vegetable oil for the lard. There will be a slight change in flavor.

Top this taco with Jalapeño Relish (page 310) or Veggie Salsa (page 308).

• **Preheat greased barbecue grill to medium**

4	Cajun sausages	4
2 tsp	lard or bacon drippings (see Tips, left)	10 mL
1 cup	cooked or canned red beans, drained and rinsed	250 mL
	Salt	
8	6- to 8-inch (15 to 20 cm) corn tortillas, skillet-warmed (page 15)	8
1 cup	shredded lettuce	250 mL
1	red onion, minced	1
1	tomato, seeded and diced	1
1 cup	shredded Monterey Jack cheese	250 mL

1. Pierce sausages a few times with a fork. Grill, covered, turning once, until juices run clear, for about 15 minutes or according to package directions. Let cool slightly and cut into bite-size pieces.

2. In large skillet, heat lard over medium heat. Add beans and mash to a chunky consistency. Add 1 tbsp (15 mL) water and cook, stirring, until beans are heated through, 6 to 8 minutes. Beans should be easy to stir but not runny. If they are too thick add an additional 1 tbsp (15 mL) of water. Season with salt to taste.

3. To build tacos, spread an equal amount of beans on one side of each tortilla. Divide sausage equally among tortillas. Top with lettuce, red onion, tomato and cheese. Fold tortillas in half.

Black Bean and Sausage Tacos

Makes 8 tacos

A hint of basil complements the black beans and pork flavor in this hearty taco.

Tip

There are a variety of salad mixes with a wide range of flavors on the market. There are red and green lettuce varieties that range in taste from intense spice to sweet and mild. "Living" lettuce and "artisan" lettuce and greens are also available. Taste and compare to find your favorite combination of greens.

1 lb	mild pork sausage, crumbled	500 g
1	clove garlic, minced	1
2 tsp	minced basil	10 mL
	Salt	
1 cup	cooked or canned black beans, drained and rinsed	250 mL
8	6- to 8-inch (15 to 20 cm) corn tortillas, skillet-warmed (page 15)	8
2 cups	chopped salad mix (see Tip, left)	500 mL
½ cup	freshly grated Parmesan cheese	125 mL
1	tomato, seeded and diced	1
	Poblano Sauce (page 320)	

1. In a large skillet over medium heat, sauté sausage, garlic and basil until well browned, 10 to 12 minutes. Drain off excess fat. Season with salt to taste.

2. Reduce heat to medium-low. Stir in beans and cook, stirring, until heated through.

3. To build tacos, divide sausage mixture equally among tortillas. Top with salad mix, cheese and tomato. Drizzle with Poblano Sauce. Fold tortillas in half.

Sunrise Fiesta Tacos

Makes 8 tacos

As a rule, breakfast tacos are easy to make and these little gems will leave a lasting impression. The double corn tortilla wrap on each taco along with the double meat add extra flavor. Whip them up in minutes.

Tips

I like to use Jimmy Dean sausage. But any breakfast sausage will work. You can choose from a variety of different seasoned sausages.

I like to top this taco with a rich tomato flavor. Try Roasted Tomato Salsa (page 299) or Veggie Salsa (page 308) for a healthier breakfast taco.

8 oz	mild pork sausage (bulk or removed from casings) (see Tips, left)	250 g
1	green or red bell pepper, diced	1
1	onion, diced	1
6	eggs, slightly beaten	6
6	New Mexico chile peppers, roasted and diced (about ¾ cup/175 mL) (see page 121)	6
4 oz	cooked ham, diced	125 g
16	6-inch (15 cm) corn tortillas, skillet-warmed (page 15)	16
¾ cup	shredded Cheddar cheese	175 mL

1. In a large skillet over medium heat, sauté sausage, bell pepper and onion, breaking up meat with the back of a spoon, until sausage is well browned, 10 to 12 minutes. Drain off excess fat.

2. Reduce heat to medium-low. Add eggs, chiles and ham to the meat mixture. Cook, stirring, until eggs are set.

3. To build tacos, stack 2 tortillas together for each taco. Divide sausage mixture equally among each double tortilla. Top with cheese. Fold tortillas in half.

Hangover Tacos

If spicy hot chile is just the cure for a hangover, this taco is perfect for the day after a good time. It's spicy and flavorful, and the double wrapped tortilla makes it very filling. I like serving these tacos with a warm spicy sauce.

Variation

Substitute New Mexico Red or Green Chile Sauce with Tomato Table Salsa (page 302) or Cilantro and Chile Salsa (page 305).

8	strips bacon, diced	8
6 oz	fresh chorizo sausage, removed from casings	175 g
8	eggs, lightly beaten	8
1/4 cup	diced roasted New Mexico green chiles (see page 121)	60 mL
16	6-inch (15 cm) corn tortillas, skillet-warmed (page 15)	16
3/4 cup	shredded Cheddar cheese	175 mL
2	jalapeños, seeded and chopped	2
	New Mexico Red Chile Sauce (page 319) or New Mexico Green Chile Sauce (page 320)	

1. In a large skillet over medium-high heat, sauté bacon until crisp, 12 to 14 minutes. Transfer to a plate lined with paper towel and let cool.

2. Reduce heat to medium. Add sausage to skillet and sauté, breaking up with a spoon, until well browned, 4 to 6 minutes. Add eggs and green chiles and cook, stirring, until eggs are set.

3. To build tacos, stack 2 tortillas together for each taco. Divide sausage mixture equally among each double tortilla. Top with bacon, cheese and jalapeños. Fold tortillas in half. Spoon a little New Mexico Red or Green Chile Sauce on top of each taco or use as a dipping sauce.

Scrambled Sausage Tacos with New Mexico Green Chile Sauce

We start eating chile early in the morning at my house. This is comfort food to wake up to! The green chile sauce adds a depth of flavor that complements the chorizo and sausage.

4	eggs	4
2 tbsp	milk	30 mL
8 oz	mild pork sausage (bulk or removed from casings)	250 g
4 oz	fresh chorizo sausage, removed from casings (see Tips, page 189)	125 g
	Salt and freshly ground black pepper	
8	6- to 8-inch (15 to 20 cm) corn tortillas, skillet-warmed (page 15)	8
¾ cup	shredded Monterey Jack cheese	175 mL
	New Mexico Green Chile Sauce (page 320)	

1. In a small bowl, whisk together eggs and milk.

2. In a large skillet over medium heat, sauté pork and chorizo sausages, breaking up meat with back of a spoon, until sausages are well browned, 10 to 12 minutes. Drain off excess fat. Add eggs and cook, stirring, until set. Season with salt and pepper to taste.

3. To build tacos, divide sausage mixture equally among tortillas. Top with cheese and chile sauce. Fold tortillas in half.

Smothered New Mexico Breakfast Tacos

This taco casserole is scrumptious. Enjoy spicy Mexican sausage and eggs smothered in a rich green chile sauce.

Variation

For a meatier version, add 4 oz (125 g) ground beef and follow Step 1.

- Preheat oven to 350°F (180°C)
- 8-inch (20 cm) square glass baking dish, greased

4 oz	fresh chorizo sausage, removed from casings	125 g
10	eggs, lightly beaten	10
12	6-inch (15 cm) corn tortillas, skillet-warmed (page 15)	12
2 cups	shredded Cheddar cheese, divided	500 mL
2 cups	green enchilada sauce or New Mexico Green Chile Sauce (page 320)	500 mL
1 cup	shredded iceberg lettuce	250 mL
1	tomato, seeded and minced	1

1. In a large skillet, sauté chorizo until well browned, 6 to 8 minutes. Add eggs and cook, stirring, until scrambled and set.

2. To build tacos, divide egg mixture equally among tortillas. Divide 1 cup (250 mL) of the cheese equally among tortillas. Spoon 1 tbsp (15 mL) of sauce on each taco. Fold tortillas in half and place in prepared baking dish, arranging side by side. Drizzle remaining sauce on top of tacos. Sprinkle remaining 1 cup (250 mL) of cheese over all of the tacos.

3. Bake in preheated oven until cheese is bubbling and tortillas start to crisp, 18 to 20 minutes. Let stand for 8 to 10 minutes. Serve individually garnished with lettuce and tomato.

Grilled Lamb Tacos with Salsa Verde

If lamb is one of your favorite meats then this taco is for you. Grilled to perfection with a touch of cumin then crowned with a fresh Salsa Verde, this taco is simple and tasty.

Tips

For best results in grilling, brush the grill grate with vegetable oil or coat with a nonstick cooking spray before preheating the grill.

For a creamy sweet flavor, try these tacos with Creamy Corn Salsa (page 303) or Veggie Salsa (page 308).

• Preheat greased barbecue grill to medium-high (see Tips, left)

2 tsp	salt	10 mL
2 tsp	freshly ground black pepper	10 mL
1 tsp	ground cumin	5 mL
4	lamb chops (about 1 lb/500 g)	4
2 tbsp	olive oil	30 mL
8	6-inch (15 cm) flour tortillas, skillet-warmed (page 15)	8
	Salsa Verde (page 300)	

1. In a small bowl, combine salt, pepper and cumin. Brush chops with oil and sprinkle all over with spice mixture.

2. Grill chops, covered, turning once, for 5 to 8 minutes per side for medium. Let stand for 6 to 10 minutes. Carve meat from bone and cut into bite-size pieces.

3. To build tacos, divide lamb equally among tortillas. Top with Salsa Verde. Fold tortillas in half.

Spicy Lamb Soft Tacos

Hot pepper flakes add a kick to this skillet taco. The creamy cucumber salsa is refreshing and simple, making it perfect for last-minute dinner guests.

Tip

Serve with Jalapeño Cream Sauce (page 323) or Tomato Table Salsa (page 302).

1 lb	ground lamb	500 g
1 tsp	hot pepper flakes	5 mL
1 tsp	garlic powder	5 mL
	Salt	
1	English cucumber, shredded	1
½ cup	Greek yogurt	125 mL
2 tsp	minced garlic	10 mL
1 tbsp	freshly squeezed lemon juice	15 mL
3 tbsp	finely chopped fresh mint	45 mL
½ tsp	kosher salt	2 mL
Pinch	freshly ground black pepper	Pinch
8	6- to 8-inch (15 to 20 cm) corn tortillas	8
1	tomato, seeded and diced	1

1. In a large skillet over medium heat, sauté lamb, hot pepper flakes and garlic powder until meat is no longer pink inside, 10 to 12 minutes. Season with salt to taste.

2. In a small bowl, combine cucumber, yogurt, garlic, lemon juice, mint, kosher salt and pepper. Mix well.

3. To build tacos, divide lamb equally among tortillas. Top with cucumber salsa and tomato. Fold tortillas in half.

Crispy Chile-Rubbed Lamb Tacos

This skillet taco is a weeknight delight. The chile flavor works well with the sharpness of the Cotija cheese.

Variation
Crumbled feta cheese can be substituted for Cotija cheese.

2 tbsp	all-purpose flour	30 mL
1 tsp	cayenne pepper	5 mL
1 tsp	kosher salt	5 mL
½ tsp	freshly ground black pepper	2 mL
2 tbsp	olive oil, divided	30 mL
1 lb	boneless lamb loin, diced (about 4 chops)	500 g
8	6-inch (15 cm) corn tortillas, skillet-steamed (page 15)	8
	Lemon Jalapeño Sauce (page 322)	
2 cups	shredded lettuce	500 mL
1½ cups	crumbled Cotija cheese	375 mL

1. In a small bowl, combine flour, cayenne, salt and pepper. In a large bowl, combine 1 tbsp (15 mL) of the oil and lamb and toss until meat is well coated. Sprinkle seasoning mixture over lamb and gently toss.

2. In a large skillet, add heat remaining 1 tbsp (15 mL) of oil over medium-high heat. Add lamb and sauté until golden brown and crispy on edges, 12 to 14 minutes.

3. To build tacos, divide lamb equally among tacos. Top with Lemon Jalapeño Sauce, lettuce and cheese. Fold tortillas in half.

Gyro Tacos

Makes 8 tacos

Grilled or roasted lamb, thinly sliced and wrapped in a soft bread or pita, became a hit in New York in the 70s. It was the American Greek Sandwich. This is my Mexican-style American Greek version.

Tip

Serve with Creamy Wasabi Sauce (page 316), Chimichurri Sauce (page 328) or Creamy Garlic Spread (page 321).

- Barbecue grill
- Instant-read thermometer

	Juice of 2 lemons	
3 tbsp	olive oil	45 mL
5	cloves garlic, minced	5
1 tbsp	kosher salt	15 mL
1 tsp	freshly ground black pepper	5 mL
2 lb	boneless lamb top round or leg roast	1 kg
16	6- to 8-inch (15 to 20 cm) flour tortillas	16
	Red Onion Relish (page 315)	
	Basic Taco Cream Sauce (page 322)	

1. In a small bowl, combine lemon juice, oil, garlic, salt and pepper. Butterfly lamb horizontally through the middle of the roast (without cutting all the way through, so the top piece opens out like a book). Transfer lamb to a large, shallow dish. Pierce with a sharp knife in several places so marinade will penetrate the meat. Pour marinade over roast. Cover and refrigerate for at least 2 hours or for up to 6 hours.

2. Preheat greased grill to medium-high heat. Remove lamb from marinade and discard marinade. Grill lamb, covered, for 3 to 4 minutes on each side, then reduce heat to medium and grill for 6 to 8 minutes more on each side or until an instant-read thermometer inserted into the thickest part registers 145°F (65°C) for medium. Remove from heat. Let stand for 10 minutes. Thinly slice meat across the grain.

3. To build tacos, skillet warm tortillas (page 15). Divide lamb equally among tortillas. Top with Red Onion Relish. Fold tortillas in half. Serve Basic Taco Cream Sauce on the side.

Fish and Seafood

Fresh Baja Fish Tacos with Mexican White Sauce

Makes 8 tacos

Baja, the peninsula of Mexico located south of California, is famous for its fish tacos. Gaining popularity around the globe, these lightly fried fish delights are addictive, layered with cabbage, cream sauce and Pico de Gallo.

Tip
There are concerns about the sustainability of some fish and seafood so we recommend you check reliable sites such as www.seachoice.org for the latest information.

Variations
For added flavor, add a pinch each of ground cumin, dried oregano and ground white pepper to the Mexican White Sauce.

Substitute the Mexican White Sauce with Spicy Ranch Sauce (page 326).

• Candy/deep-fry thermometer

Mexican White Sauce

¾ cup	mayonnaise	175 mL
½ cup	plain yogurt	125 mL
	Juice of 1 lime	
1 cup	all-purpose flour	250 mL
¾ cup	light beer	175 mL
1 tsp	kosher salt	5 mL
1½ lbs	skinless cod or tilapia fillets (see Tip, left)	750 g
	Vegetable oil	
8	6- to 8-inch (15 to 20 cm) corn or flour tortillas	8
1 cup	thinly shredded red cabbage	250 mL
1 cup	thinly shredded green cabbage	250 mL
	Pico de Gallo (page 305)	

1. *Mexican White Sauce:* In a small bowl, combine mayonnaise, yogurt and lime juice. Cover and refrigerate for at least 2 hours or for up to 24 hours.

2. In a large bowl, combine flour, beer and salt. Mix well to a thick consistency.

3. Rinse fish and pat dry with paper towel. Cut crosswise into 1-inch (2.5 cm) wide strips.

4. Fill a deep-fryer, deep heavy pot or deep skillet with 1 inch (2.5 cm) of oil and heat to 350°F (180°C). Using tongs, dredge fish pieces in batter and gently place in oil. Deep-fry 3 to 4 pieces at a time, turning once, until golden brown, about 1 minute per side. Drain on paper towels. Discard any excess batter.

5. To build tacos, skillet warm tortillas (page 15). Divide fish equally among each tortilla. Top with cabbage, Mexican White Sauce and Pico de Gallo. Fold tortillas in half.

Crusted Halibut and Jalapeño Tacos

Makes 8 tacos

This fish taco has a baked, crusty tartar sauce topping. Pickled jalapeño adds a bit of spice with the taco sauce, adding balance.

Tips

Panko bread crumbs are Japanese bread crumbs that are toasted, giving them a crispy texture. Look for them in grocery stores where the bread crumbs are sold.

The perfect size tortilla for a taco is 6 inches (15 cm). It is generally more available in corn rather than flour. Buy 8-inch (20 cm) flour tortillas and trim them with a pair of kitchen shears to 6 inches (15 cm) using a corn tortilla as a template.

- Preheat oven to 450°F (230°C)
- 8-inch (20 cm) square glass baking dish, greased

¼ cup	light mayonnaise	60 mL
¼ cup	sour cream	60 mL
1 tbsp	minced pickled jalapeño	15 mL
1½ lbs	halibut steaks	750 g
2 tbsp	panko bread crumbs (see Tip, left)	30 mL
8	6- to 8-inch (15 to 20 cm) flour or corn tortillas (see Tips, left), skillet-warmed (page 15)	8
2 cups	chopped salad mix	500 mL
	Fiesta Taco Sauce (page 324)	

1. In a small bowl, combine mayonnaise, sour cream and jalapeño. Set aside.

2. Rinse halibut and pat dry with paper towel. Arrange in prepared baking dish. Bake in preheated oven until fish flakes easily when tested with a fork, 8 to 10 minutes. Drain off any liquid and pat top of each steak with a paper towel, getting rid of excess moisture. Preheat broiler.

3. Spoon mayonnaise mixture on top of each steak spreading it to the edges. Sprinkle with panko. Broil halibut until crust is golden brown and bubbling, 2 to 3 minutes.

4. To build tacos, gently divide fish equally among tortillas. Top with salad mix and Fiesta Taco Sauce. Fold tortillas in half.

Spicy Crab Tacos

Delicate crabmeat sautéed with jalapeño and bathed in a light butter sauce is the perfect filling for tacos. Top this taco with fresh avocado and lime for a contemporary taste.

Tip

You can find lump crab in the frozen seafood section or canned on shelves in most markets. If frozen, thaw and drain, and if canned, drain. There are also good fish retail resources online.

1 tbsp	butter	15 mL
1 tbsp	olive oil	15 mL
1	clove garlic, minced	1
1	jalapeño, seeded and minced	1
1	tomato, seeded and diced	1
1 lb	lump crabmeat	500 g
8	6-inch (15 cm) corn tortillas, skillet-warmed (page 15)	8
4	green onions, green parts only, minced	4
1 cup	shredded Monterey Jack cheese	250 mL
2	avocados, thinly sliced	2
	Pico de Gallo (page 305)	
2	limes, each cut into 4 wedges	2

1. In a large skillet, heat butter and oil over medium-high heat. Sauté garlic, jalapeño and tomato until tender, 1 to 2 minutes. Add crab and sauté until opaque, 6 to 8 minutes.

2. To build tacos, divide crab mixture equally among tortillas. Top with green onions, cheese, avocados and Pico de Gallo. Fold tortillas in half. Serve with a wedge of lime.

Crispy Coconut Shrimp Tacos with Orange Salsa

Makes 8 tacos

Sweet coconut surrounds each piece of shrimp in these tacos. Hand-battered and lightly fried then crowned with a tangy orange sauce, the shrimp in these tacos are overflowing with flavor.

Tips

A dry tempura batter mix can be found in the seafood section of most grocery stores. The batter should coat the shrimp but not be too thick. If tempura mixture seems too thick, add up to 1/4 cup (60 mL) more beer to reach desired consistency.

Shrimp are labeled by size according to how many are in an average pound (454 g). There are 31 to 35 medium shrimp in one pound (454 g). About 3 shrimp will fit in 6-inch (15 cm) tortillas and about 4 in 8-inch (20 cm) tortillas. Purchase the number you need based on the size of tortillas you have.

- Candy/deep-fry thermometer

1 cup	dry tempura batter mix (see Tips, left)	250 mL
3/4 cup	light beer (see Tips, left)	175 mL
2 cups	sweetened flaked coconut	500 mL
	Vegetable oil	
24 to 32	medium shrimp, peeled and deveined (see Tips, left)	24 to 32
8	6- to 8-inch (15 to 20 cm) corn or flour tortillas, skillet-warmed (page 15)	8
1 cup	shredded red cabbage	250 mL
1 cup	shredded green cabbage	250 mL
	Orange Salsa (page 301)	

1. In a medium bowl, place tempura mix and slowly add beer and whisk to a thick consistency.

2. Place coconut in a shallow dish.

3. Fill a deep-fryer, deep heavy pot or deep skillet with 2 inches (5 cm) of oil and heat to 350°F (180°C). Using tongs, dip shrimp, one at a time, in batter. Roll in coconut. Gently place 4 to 6 shrimp at a time in the hot oil and deep-fry, turning once, until coconut is golden brown and shrimp is opaque, 2 to 3 minutes. Drain on paper towels.

4. To build tacos, divide shrimp equally among tortillas. Top with red and green cabbage and Orange Salsa. Fold tortillas in half.

Cajun Shrimp Tacos

Delicate shrimp simmered in a tangy sauce boosts the flavor of these tacos. With fresh flour tortillas and topped with a spicy cream sauce, Cajun-style, these tacos are sure to be a hit.

Tip

Cajun seasoning is usually a blend of garlic, pungent chile spices, peppers, sea salt, onion, and paprika. Look for spice blends in your market or online.

2 tbsp	freshly squeezed lemon juice	30 mL
1 tbsp	Worcestershire sauce	15 mL
1 tbsp	butter	15 mL
1	clove garlic, minced	1
24 to 32	medium shrimp, peeled and deveined (see Tips, page 209)	24 to 32
1 tbsp	Cajun seasoning (see Tip, left)	15 mL
8	6- to 8-inch (15 to 20 cm) flour tortillas, skillet-warmed (page 15)	8
2 cups	shredded green cabbage	500 mL
	Cajun Sauce (page 327)	

1. In a large skillet over medium-high heat, sauté lemon juice, Worcestershire, butter and garlic for 2 minutes. Stir in shrimp and Cajun seasoning. Cover, reduce heat to medium-low and simmer until shrimp is pink and opaque, 3 to 5 minutes.

2. To build tacos, using a slotted spoon, divide shrimp equally among tortillas. Be careful not to add excess liquid to tacos. Top with cabbage and Cajun Sauce. Fold tortillas in half.

Spice-Rubbed Shrimp Tacos

Stress-free entertaining is what you get with this shrimp taco. Toss and broil with ease to serve up a spicy mouthwatering taco.

Tip

Creole seasoning, unlike Cajun, is a milder more traditional flavor from the South. It is usually a blend of cayenne pepper, garlic powder, black pepper, salt and paprika.

- Preheat broiler
- Rimmed baking sheet

1 tbsp	Creole seasoning (see Tip, left)	15 mL
2	cloves garlic, minced	2
1 tbsp	minced fresh cilantro	15 mL
1 tsp	kosher salt	5 mL
	Juice of 1 lime	
2 tbsp	olive oil	30 mL
24 to 32	medium shrimp, peeled and deveined (see Tips, page 209)	24 to 32
8	6- to 8-inch (15 to 20 cm) corn tortillas, skillet-warmed (page 15)	8
½ cup	chopped fresh cilantro	125 mL
2 cups	chopped salad mix	500 mL
	Citrus Salsa (page 301)	

1. In a large bowl, whisk together Creole seasoning, garlic, 1 tbsp (15 mL) cilantro, salt, lime juice and oil. Add shrimp and gently toss until well coated.

2. Spread shrimp out on baking sheet. Broil shrimp 3 to 4 inches (7.5 to 10 cm) from heat until bright pink, 2 to 3 minutes. Using tongs, turn each shrimp over and broil until pink and opaque, 2 to 3 minutes.

3. To build tacos, divide shrimp equally among tortillas. Top with ½ cup (125 mL) cilantro, salad mix and Citrus Salsa. Fold tortillas in half.

Ceviche Fresco Tacos

This is a fun and refreshing fish taco! The combination of chiles, fish and lime offers the authentic flavors of Mexico. Flavor is added by marinating the fish in a citrus bath. Miraculously, the citric acid of the lime naturally poaches the fish without heat.

Tip

Salt can make fish tough so season ceviche with salt and pepper just before serving.

1 lb	halibut steak	500 g
	Juice of 10 limes	
1	onion, finely chopped	1
5	tomatoes, seeded and finely chopped	5
2	jalapeños, seeded and minced	2
1	yellow chile pepper, seeded and minced	1
1	clove garlic, minced	1
	Kosher salt and freshly ground black pepper	
8	6-inch (15 cm) corn tortillas	8
1 tbsp	minced fresh cilantro	15 mL
2	avocados, diced	2

1. Rinse halibut and pat dry with paper towel. Cut into $\frac{1}{4}$-inch (0.5 cm) cubes. In a large bowl, combine fish and lime juice. Add onion, tomatoes, jalapeños, chile pepper and garlic. Cover and refrigerate, stirring occasionally, for 2 hours. Just before serving, season with salt and pepper to taste.

2. To build tacos, skillet warm tortillas (page 15). Using a slotted spoon, divide fish mixture equally among tortillas. Top with cilantro and avocados. Fold tortillas in half.

Surfin' Seafood Taco Steamers

This taco is like a mini shrimp cocktail. Fresh seafood is swimming in a spicy tomato sauce with chunky veggies throughout. Wrap it up in a double corn tortilla for added flavor. These little steamers carry the taste of "happy hour" all over them.

Tips

Use a medium-heat store-bought salsa or Roasted Tomato Salsa (page 299), Tomato Table Salsa (page 302) or Tomato Relish (page 311).

Panela cheese is a semisoft Mexican cheese that can be grated and sprinkled easily for a flavorful topping or garnish.

Variation

Substitute Monterey Jack cheese for the panela cheese.

½ cup	chopped celery	125 mL
3	green onions, green parts only, chopped	3
1	tomato, seeded and chopped	1
½ cup	chunky tomato salsa (see Tips, left)	125 mL
½ cup	cocktail sauce	125 mL
	Juice of 1 lime	
1 lb	cooked shrimp, chopped	500 g
16	6-inch (15 cm) corn tortillas	16
2 cups	chopped romaine lettuce	500 mL
1 cup	shredded panela cheese (see Tips, left)	250 mL

1. In a large bowl, combine celery, green onions, tomato, salsa, cocktail sauce and lime juice. Fold in shrimp until well coated. Cover and refrigerate for at least 1 hour or for up to 4 hours.

2. To build tacos, micro warm tortillas (page 15). Press 2 tortillas together for a double layer. Divide shrimp equally among tortillas. Top with lettuce and cheese.

Lobster Tacos with Tropical Salsa

A contemporary and fresh twist on this fish taco makes it a favorite for entertaining. The sautéed lobster is piled high with the fresh, sweet flavor of tropical fruits.

Tips

Look for frozen cooked lobster in the frozen seafood section of most grocery stores or order from an online supplier.

Typically it takes 4½ to 6 lbs (2.25 to 3 kg) of raw whole lobsters in the shell to yield 1 lb (500 g) of lobster meat.

1 tbsp	olive oil	15 mL
1 lb	cooked lobster meat, chopped (see Tips, left)	500 g
2 tbsp	freshly squeezed lemon juice	30 mL
1 tbsp	butter	15 mL
8	6- to 8-inch (15 to 20 cm) flour tortillas, skillet-warmed (page 15)	8
2 cups	chopped salad mix	500 mL
	Tropical Salsa (page 299)	
1	lemon, cut into 8 wedges	1

1. In a large skillet, heat oil over medium heat. Sauté lobster and lemon juice until lobster is heated throughout, 8 to 10 minutes. Add butter, stirring until melted and lobster is coated, 1 to 2 minutes.

2. To build tacos, with a slotted spoon, divide lobster mixture equally among tortillas. Top with salad mix and Tropical Salsa. Fold tortillas in half. Serve with lemon wedges.

Butter Garlic Lobster Tacos

Makes 8 tacos

If you love lobster with a buttery garlic flavor, you will enjoy these tacos. Wrapped in warm tortillas, the lobster filling is topped with simple flavors of fresh romaine and Parmesan cheese.

2 tbsp	butter	30 mL
1 tbsp	olive oil	15 mL
1 lb	cooked lobster meat, chopped (see Tips, page 214)	500 g
2	cloves garlic, minced	2
1 tbsp	minced fresh cilantro	15 mL
8	6-inch (15 cm) corn tortillas, skillet-warmed (page 15)	8
2 cups	shredded Romaine lettuce	500 mL
1 cup	freshly grated Parmesan cheese	250 mL
	Chile Basil Sauce (page 328)	

1. In a large skillet, heat butter and oil over medium heat. Sauté lobster, garlic and cilantro until lobster is heated through, 8 to 10 minutes.

2. To build tacos, with a slotted spoon, divide lobster mixture equally among tortillas. Top with lettuce and cheese. Fold tortillas in half. Serve Chile Basil Sauce on the side.

Tequila Shrimp Tacos

Makes 8 tacos

Gold tequila has a sweet distinctive flavor that lights up this taco. Shrimp sautéed in a buttery, velvety sauce and spiked with tequila and pepper delights the senses.

¼ cup	butter	60 mL
1 tbsp	olive oil	15 mL
3	cloves garlic, minced	3
3 oz	gold tequila	90 mL
12 oz	cooked shrimp, chopped	375 g
1 tbsp	chopped fresh cilantro	15 mL
1 tsp	hot pepper flakes	5 mL
8	6-inch (15 cm) corn tortillas, skillet-warmed (page 15)	8
2 cups	chopped salad mix	500 mL

1. In a large skillet, heat butter and oil over medium-high heat. Sauté garlic, tequila and shrimp until shrimp is heated through, 6 to 8 minutes. Remove from heat and stir in cilantro and hot pepper flakes.

2. To build tacos, using a slotted spoon, divide shrimp mixture equally among tortillas. Be careful not to add excess liquid. Top with salad mix. Fold tortillas in half.

Mahi Mahi Tacos with Citrus Salsa

This lightly seasoned fillet is crowned with fresh taste. Layering cream sauce and salsa boosts the texture and flavor.

Variations

Serve each taco with 1 tbsp (15 mL) Guacamole (page 316).

Divide ¼ cup (60 mL) minced pickled jalapeños equally among tacos.

* Preheat greased barbecue grill to medium-high heat

1½ lbs	mahi mahi fillets	750 g
2 tbsp	olive oil	30 mL
¾ tsp	salt	3 mL
½ tsp	freshly ground black pepper	2 mL
8	6-inch (15 cm) corn tortillas, skillet-warmed (page 15)	8
	Chile Cream Sauce (page 327)	
2 cups	shredded cabbage	500 mL
	Citrus Salsa (page 301)	

1. Rinse mahi mahi and pat dry with paper towel. Brush fillets with oil on both sides. Season with salt and pepper. Grill fillets, turning once, until opaque in center, 3 to 4 minutes per side. Transfer to a cutting board and cut into bite-size pieces.

2. To build tacos, divide fish equally among tortillas. Top with Chile Cream Sauce, cabbage and Citrus Salsa. Fold tortillas in half.

Grilled Halibut Steak and Avocado Tacos

Makes 8 tacos

Simply grilled halibut defines this taco. Cool fresh flavors are added with avocado, tomato and lime.

Variation

Add 8 oz (250 g) spicy Cajun sausage to the halibut in Step 1. Grill sausage over medium heat, turning often, until lightly browned and juices run clear, 6 to 8 minutes per side. Transfer sausage to cutting board and cut into bite-size pieces. Divide equally among tortillas.

• Preheat greased barbecue grill to medium-high heat

1½ lbs	halibut steaks	750 g
2 tbsp	olive oil	30 mL
1 tsp	salt	5 mL
½ tsp	freshly ground black pepper	2 mL
8	6- to 8-inch (15 to 20 cm) flour tortillas, skillet-warmed (page 15)	8
1	tomato, seeded and diced	1
2	avocados, diced	2
2	limes, each cut into 4 wedges	2

1. Rinse halibut and pat dry with paper towel. Brush steaks with oil on both sides. Season with salt and pepper. Grill halibut, turning once, until firm and opaque in the center, about 4 minutes per side. Transfer fish to cutting board and cut into bite-size pieces.

2. To build tacos, divide fish equally among tortillas. Top with tomato and avocados. Fold tortillas in half. Serve with a wedge of lime.

Cod and Pepper Tacos with Lemon-Jalapeño Sauce

Makes 8 tacos

This fish taco is tangy and spicy. The lemony flavor complements the peppers and light, flaky fish.

Tip

There are concerns about the sustainability of some fish and seafood so we recommend you check reliable sites such as www.seachoice.org for the latest information.

Variation

Instead of cod, substitute flounder, a mild and delicate fish like cod.

* Preheat oven to 200°F (100°C)
* Ovenproof dish

1 tbsp	olive oil	15 mL
½ cup	chopped green bell pepper	125 mL
½ cup	chopped red bell pepper	125 mL
1 lb	skinless cod fillets (see Tip, left)	500 g
2 tsp	lemon pepper	10 mL
	Salt	
2 tbsp	butter	30 mL
2	cloves garlic, minced	2
8	6-inch (15 cm) corn tortillas, skillet-warmed (page 15)	8
2 cups	chopped romaine lettuce	500 mL
	Lemon Jalapeño Sauce (page 322)	
1	lemon, cut into 8 wedges	1

1. In a large skillet, heat oil over medium-high heat. Sauté green and red peppers until tender-crisp, 6 to 8 minutes. Transfer to an ovenproof dish and keep warm in preheated oven.

2. Rinse cod and pat dry with paper towel. Season fillets on both sides with lemon pepper and 1 tsp (5 mL) salt.

3. In same skillet, melt butter over medium-high heat. Add garlic and fillets and fry, turning once, until fish flakes with a fork, 4 to 5 minutes per side. Transfer to a cutting board and cut into bite-size pieces. Season with salt to taste.

4. To build tacos, divide fish equally among tortillas. Top with peppers, lettuce and Lemon Jalapeño Sauce. Fold tortillas in half. Serve with a lemon wedge.

Beer-Battered Fish Taco Steamers

Makes 8 tacos

Golden crispy-crusted fish wrapped in two steamed tortillas carry the taste of sunny California beaches and good times. Top them with a fresh Pico de Gallo and you have an unforgettable taco.

Tip

For a thinner crust, add ¼ cup (60 mL) more beer, 1 tbsp (15 mL) at a time, to the batter.

• Candy/deep-fry thermometer

1 cup	all-purpose flour	250 mL
	Salt	
½ tsp	freshly ground black pepper	2 mL
¼ tsp	ground cumin	1 mL
Pinch	cayenne pepper	Pinch
¾ cup	beer (see Tip, left)	175 mL
1½ lbs	skinless firm white fish fillets	750 g
	Vegetable oil	
16	6-inch (15 cm) corn tortillas, micro-warmed (page 15)	16
2 cups	chopped cabbage	500 mL
1	avocado, sliced	1
	Pico de Gallo (page 305)	
2	limes, each cut into 4 wedges	2

1. In a small bowl, combine flour, 1 tsp (5 mL) salt, pepper, cumin and cayenne. Add beer and whisk until smooth.

2. Rinse fish and pat dry with paper towel. Cut into 1-inch (2.5 cm) cubes.

3. Fill a deep-fryer, deep heavy pot or deep skillet with 2 inches (5 cm) of oil and heat to 350°F (180°C). Working with 2 to 3 pieces at a time, using a slotted spoon, gently coat fish with batter. Place in the hot oil and deep-fry, turning once, until crispy and golden brown, 2 to 3 minutes. Drain on paper towels. Season lightly with salt. Discard any excess batter.

4. To build tacos, divide fish equally among tortillas. Top with avocado, cabbage and Pico de Gallo. Fold tortillas in half. Serve with a wedge of lime.

Catfish Tacos
with Chile Cream Sauce

This quick, pan-seared fish is full of flavor. Sauté, dice and create a great-tasting taco in minutes.

1 tsp	ground allspice	5 mL
1 tsp	hot pepper flakes	5 mL
1 tsp	garlic and herb seasoning blend	5 mL
1 lb	skinless catfish fillets	500 g
1 tbsp	butter	15 mL
8	6-inch (15 cm) corn tortillas, skillet-warmed (page 15)	8
2 cups	chopped salad mix	500 mL
	Chile Cream Sauce (page 327)	

1. Rinse catfish and pat dry with paper towel. In a small bowl, combine allspice, hot pepper flakes and garlic and herb seasoning. Season one side of each fillet with spice mixture.

2. In a large skillet, melt butter over medium-high heat. Add fillets, seasoned side down and fry, turning once, until fish flakes easily with a fork, about 3 minutes per side.

3. To build tacos, divide fish equally among tortillas. Top with salad mix and Chile Cream Sauce. Fold tortillas in half.

Tempura-Fried Fish Tacos with Salsa Verde

Lightly breaded fish nestled in a fresh tortilla is a mouthwatering treat. Fresh cabbage and green chile sauce accent this simple fish taco.

Tip

A dry tempura batter mix can be found in the seafood section of most grocery stores. The batter should coat the shrimp but not be too thick. If tempura mixture seems too thick, add up to ¼ cup (60 mL) more beer to reach desired consistency.

• Candy/deep-fry thermometer

1 cup	dry tempura batter mix (see Tip, left)	250 mL
¾ cup	light beer	175 mL
1 tsp	salt	5 mL
½ tsp	freshly ground black pepper	2 mL
8 oz	skinless tilapia fillets	250 g
	Vegetable oil	
12 to 16	medium shrimp, peeled and deveined	12 to 16
8	6- to 8-inch (15 to 20 cm) corn or flour tortillas, skillet-warmed (page 15)	8
2 cups	shredded cabbage	500 mL
1	tomato, seeded and diced	1
1	avocado, cubed	1
	Salsa Verde (page 300)	

1. In a medium bowl, whisk together tempura, beer, salt and pepper until smooth.

2. Rinse tilapia and pat dry with paper towel. Cut into 1-inch (2.5 cm) pieces.

3. Fill a deep-fryer, deep heavy pot or deep skillet with 3 inches (7.5 cm) of oil and heat to 350°F (180°C). Using tongs, dip shrimp and fish pieces, one by one, in batter. Gently place 4 to 6 shrimp at a time in the hot oil and deep-fry until crust is golden brown and shrimp is opaque, 2 to 3 minutes. Drain on paper towels. Repeat with tilapia. Discard any excess batter.

4. To build tacos, divide shrimp and tilapia equally among tortillas. Top with cabbage, tomato, avocado and Salsa Verde. Fold tortillas in half.

Grilled Prosciutto-Wrapped Shrimp Tacos

Cured ham wrapped around delicate pieces of shrimp add immense flavor to this taco. Lightly basted with an Asian sauce, these tacos are a savory, sizzling treat.

Tips

Shrimp are labeled by size according to how many are in an average pound (454 g). There are 31 to 35 medium shrimp in one pound (454 g). About 3 shrimp will fit in 6-inch (15 cm) tortillas and about 4 in 8-inch (20 cm) tortillas. Purchase the number you need based on the size of tortillas you have.

Garnish with a mild cheese such as 1 cup (250 mL) shredded Monterey Jack cheese, divided equally among tacos.

- Preheat greased barbecue grill to medium-high
- Vegetable grill grate, greased
- Toothpicks, soaked in water for 30 minutes

8 to 9 oz	thinly sliced prosciutto	250 to 275 g
24 to 32	medium shrimp, peeled and deveined (see Tip, left)	500 g
	Spicy Asian Sauce (page 325), divided	
8	6- to 8-inch (15 to 20 cm) flour tortillas, skillet-warmed (page 15)	8
2 cups	chopped salad mix	500 mL

1. Cut enough prosciutto into 3- by 1-inch (7.5 by 2.5 cm) strips so you have 1 strip for each shrimp. Wrap 1 piece of prosciutto around each shrimp and secure with a toothpick. Set about $1/2$ cup (125 mL) Spicy Asian Sauce aside for topping.

2. Place shrimp on prepared vegetable grate and grill until shrimp is pink and opaque, about 3 minutes. Baste with some of the remaining sauce. Using tongs, turn shrimp and continue to grill until pink and opaque throughout, 3 to 4 minutes more. Baste with sauce and transfer to a platter.

3. To build tacos, divide shrimp equally among tortillas. Top with salad mix and remaining sauce.

Lemon Pepper Shrimp Tacos

This is a palate-pleasing combination that I have found is universally liked. A trio of shrimp, lemon juice and lemon pepper accent the seafood filling for this taco.

Tip

Lemon pepper is a spice blend made of lemon zest and peppercorns. It can be found in the spice section of your supermarket. It can also be found through retail resources online.

2 tbsp	olive oil	30 mL
1	clove garlic, minced	1
2 tbsp	freshly squeezed lemon juice	30 mL
2 tsp	lemon pepper (see Tip, left)	10 mL
24 to 32	medium shrimp, peeled and deveined (see Tips, left)	24 to 32
1 tbsp	butter	15 mL
	Salt	
8	6- to 8-inch (15 to 20 cm) corn or flour tortillas, skillet-warmed (page 15)	8
2 cups	chopped romaine lettuce	500 mL
1	lemon, cut into 8 wedges	1

1. In a large skillet, heat oil over medium heat. Sauté garlic, lemon juice, lemon pepper and shrimp until shrimp is pink and opaque throughout, 6 to 8 minutes. Add butter and stir until melted and shrimp is coated. Season with salt to taste.

2. To build tacos, with a slotted spoon, divide shrimp equally among tortillas. Top with lettuce. Fold tortillas in half. Serve with lemon wedges.

Mediterranean Fish Tacos

Makes 8 tacos

I love the fresh flavors of the Mediterranean. This taco is stuffed full of fresh fish and topped with creamy dill sauce accented with capers. Halibut picks up a good smoky aroma from the grill, adding to the flavor of these tacos.

- Preheat greased barbecue grill to medium-high
- Food processor

Tzatziki Sauce

1½ cups	Greek yogurt or drained plain yogurt	375 mL
3 tbsp	freshly squeezed lemon juice	45 mL
½	English cucumber, peeled, seeded and chopped	½
2	cloves garlic minced	2
1 tbsp	extra virgin olive oil	15 mL
1 tbsp	chopped fresh dill	15 mL
1 tbsp	capers, drained	15 mL
Pinch	salt	Pinch
Pinch	freshly ground black pepper	Pinch

Halibut

1 lb	halibut steak	500 g
2 tbsp	olive oil	30 mL
1 tsp	salt	5 mL
½ tsp	freshly ground black pepper	2 mL
3 tbsp	freshly squeezed lemon juice	45 mL
8	6-inch (15 cm) corn tortillas, skillet-warmed (page 15)	8
2 cups	shredded butter lettuce	500 mL

1. *Tzatziki Sauce:* In a food processor, pulse yogurt, lemon juice, cucumber, garlic, oil, dill, capers, salt and pepper until fairly smooth but slightly chunky. Transfer to an airtight container and refrigerate for at least 30 minutes or for up to 2 days.

2. *Halibut:* Rinse halibut and pat dry with paper towel. Coat fish with oil. Season with salt and pepper. Drizzle with lemon juice. Grill fish, skin side down, for 5 minutes. Carefully turn and grill until fish easily flakes, 4 to 5 minutes. Transfer fish to a cutting board and let stand for 8 to 10 minutes. Cut into bite-size pieces.

3. To build tacos, divide fish equally among tortillas. Top with lettuce and tzatziki.

Tequila Shrimp Tacos (page 215)

Calabacitas Tacos (page 257)

Artichoke and Spinach Tacos (page 261)

Clockwise from left: Peach and Red Onion Salsa (page 302),
Chimichurri Sauce (page 328) and Tropical Salsa (page 299)

Spiced Fish Tacos in Lettuce Wraps

Makes 8 tacos

I love this light "low-carb" taco that doesn't use the traditional corn or flour tortilla. The spicy Asian sauce highlights the veggie and fish center, making them guilt-free and healthy.

Tip

Select a leafy lettuce like romaine or butter lettuce that is easy to roll and fold.

1½ lbs	skinless tilapia or cod fillets (see Tip, page 218)	750 g
½ tsp	kosher salt	2 mL
½ tsp	freshly ground black pepper	2 mL
2 tbsp	all-purpose flour	30 mL
3 tbsp	olive oil, divided	45 mL
2	cloves garlic, minced	2
⅓ cup	minced mushrooms	75 mL
3 tbsp	minced green onions, green parts only	45 mL
2 tbsp	minced drained canned water chestnuts	30 mL
1 tbsp	freshly squeezed lemon juice	15 mL
	Spicy Asian Sauce, divided (page 325)	
6	leaves leaf lettuce (see Tip, left)	

1. Rinse tilapia and pat dry with paper towel. Season fish with salt and pepper. Lightly dust with flour on both sides. In a large skillet, heat 2 tbsp (30 mL) of the oil over medium-high heat. Fry fish, turning once, until golden brown on the surface and opaque and flaky throughout, 4 to 5 minutes per side. Transfer fish to cutting board and mince.

2. In same skillet, heat remaining 1 tbsp (15 mL) of oil over medium-high heat. Sauté garlic, mushrooms, green onions, water chestnuts and lemon juice until onions are transparent and mushrooms are soft, 4 to 6 minutes. Add ½ cup (125 mL) of the Spicy Asian Sauce. Return fish to skillet. Gently mix well until heated through, 4 to 6 minutes.

3. To build tacos, divide fish mixture equally among lettuce leaves. Wrap and serve with remaining sauce.

Grilled Halibut Steak Tacos with Chile Basil Sauce

Makes 8 tacos

Grilling adds a rustic flavor to this halibut taco. Adding Italian herbs heightens the grilling influence and gives the fish filling robust flavor.

Tip

Taste, texture and freshness are the key elements in selecting the garnish for the perfect tacos. Tacos can be adorned with a variety of fresh leafy greens, tomatoes, onions, squash, zucchini, fresh herbs and succulent fruits, all adding an element of surprise to every bite.

• Preheat barbecue grill to medium-high heat

1½ lbs	halibut steaks	750 g
2 tbsp	olive oil	30 mL
2 tbsp	freshly squeezed lemon juice	30 mL
1 tbsp	minced basil	15 mL
1 tbsp	minced flat-leaf Italian parsley	15 mL
8	6- to 8-inch (15 to 20 cm) corn or flour tortillas, skillet-warmed (page 15)	8
	Chile Basil Sauce (page 328)	
2 cups	chopped salad mix	500 mL
1	tomato, seeded and diced	1

1. Rinse halibut and pat dry with paper towel. In a small bowl, combine oil, lemon juice, basil and parsley. Coat both sides of halibut with basil mixture.

2. Grill halibut, turning once, until fish flakes easily with a fork, 4 to 6 minutes per side, Transfer to a cutting board and cut into bite-size pieces.

3. To build tacos, divide fish equally among tortillas. Top with Chile Basil Sauce, salad mix and tomato. Fold tortillas in half.

Spicy Tuna Tacos
with Creamy Wasabi Sauce

Makes 8 tacos

There are vibrant flavors in this fish taco. Tasty tuna steaks grilled and topped with a fiery sauce are a delight to eat.

Tip
Creole seasoning, unlike Cajun, is a milder more traditional flavor from the South. It is usually a blend of cayenne pepper, garlic powder, black pepper, salt and paprika.

• Preheat barbecue grill to medium-high heat

2 tsp	Creole seasoning (see Tip, left)	10 mL
1 tsp	kosher salt	5 mL
½ tsp	cayenne pepper	2 mL
1½ lbs	tuna steaks, 1 inch (2.5 cm) thick	750 g
2 tbsp	olive oil	30 mL
8	6- to 8-inch (15 to 20 cm) corn or flour tortillas, skillet-warmed (page 15)	8
2 cups	chopped romaine lettuce	500 mL
	Creamy Wasabi Sauce (page 316)	

1. In a small bowl, combine seasoning, salt and cayenne.

2. Rinse tuna and pat dry with paper towel. Coat tuna steaks with oil and season both sides with seasoning mix.

3. Grill tuna, turning once, until opaque and firm, 5 to 6 minutes per side. Transfer to a cutting board and cut into bite-size pieces.

4. To build tacos, divide fish equally among tortillas. Top with lettuce and Creamy Wasabi Sauce. Fold tortillas in half.

Stir-Fried Shrimp and Catfish Tacos

Makes 8 tacos

This is a melt-in-your-mouth combination of fillet and shell fish. Tossed with a spicy sauce and a colorful salsa, this taco has a fiesta of flavors.

2 tbsp	olive oil, divided	30 mL
2 tbsp	butter, divided	30 mL
8 oz	medium shrimp, peeled and deveined	250 g
1 lb	skinless catfish fillets	500 g
	Salt and freshly ground black pepper	
8	6-inch (15 cm) corn tortillas, skillet-warmed (page 15)	8
	Cajun Sauce (page 327)	
2 cups	chopped romaine lettuce	500 mL
	Pico de Gallo (page 305)	

1. In a large skillet, heat 1 tbsp (15 mL) of the oil and 1 tbsp (15 mL) of the butter over medium-high heat. Sauté shrimp until pink and opaque throughout, 3 to 4 minutes. Transfer to a cutting board and cut into bite-size pieces. Set aside.

2. Rinse catfish and pat dry with paper towel. In same skillet, heat remaining 1 tbsp (15 mL) of oil and butter over medium-high heat. Add catfish and lightly season with salt and pepper. Fry, turning once, until fish is flaky and opaque in center, 4 to 5 minutes per side. Transfer to cutting board and cut into bite-size pieces.

3. To build tacos, divide shrimp and fish equally among tortillas. Top with Cajun Sauce, lettuce and Pico de Gallo. Fold tortillas in half.

Cedar-Planked Salmon Tacos with Sweet Pineapple Salsa

Makes 12 tacos

Grilling salmon on a cedar plank is actually easier than grilling directly on grill grates. You can cook and serve the fish right off the plank, which is a fun way to serve up these salmon tacos.

Tips

Make sure the cedar plank is untreated. You can often find them in the seafood department at the supermarket, at specialty kitchenware stores and at hardware stores where barbecue supplies are sold.

While grilling, check the wood plank occasionally to make sure it stays moist. Keep a spray bottle with water nearby. Spray the edges to keep them from burning.

- Preheat barbecue grill to medium heat.
- 1 cedar plank, soaked for 1 hour (see Tips, left)

1½ lbs	salmon fillet, 1½ inches (4 cm) thick	750 g
¼ cup	Dijon mustard	60 mL
¼ cup	packed brown sugar	60 mL
12	6- to 8-inch (15 to 20 cm) corn or flour tortillas (see Tips, 207), skillet-warmed (page 15)	12
2 cups	chopped romaine lettuce	500 mL
	Sweet Pineapple Salsa (page 309)	

1. Rinse salmon and pat dry with paper towel. Coat skin side of fillet with mustard and sprinkle with brown sugar. Place on plank, skin side down.

2. Grill fish, covered, until flakes easily, 20 to 25 minutes. Transfer to a cutting board and let cool slightly. Remove skin and cut fish into bite-size pieces.

3. To build tacos, divide salmon equally among tortillas. Top with lettuce and Sweet Pineapple Salsa. Fold tortillas in half.

Shrimp Fajita Tacos

Makes 8 tacos

Fajitas are a signature Tex-Mex favorite. Shrimp spiced up and sizzlin' with peppers makes an easy taco treasure.

Tip
Fajita seasoning is a combination of spices such as chile, cayenne, garlic and paprika.

Variation
Substitute 2 tsp (10 mL) Creole seasoning or garlic pepper seasoning for the fajita seasoning.

2 tbsp	olive oil	30 mL
1	onion, sliced into ¼-inch (0.5 cm) thick rings	1
1	red bell pepper, julienned	1
1	orange bell pepper, julienned	1
2 tsp	fajita seasoning (see Tip, left)	10 mL
24 to 32	medium shrimp, peeled and deveined (see Tip, page 231)	24 to 32
	Salt and freshly ground black pepper	
8	6- to 8-inch (15 to 20 cm) corn or flour tortillas, skillet-warmed (page 15)	8
1 cup	shredded Monterey Jack cheese	250 mL
2 cups	chopped romaine lettuce	500 mL
	Pico de Gallo (page 305)	
2	limes, each cut into 4 wedges	2

1. In a large skillet, heat oil over medium-high heat. Sauté onion, red and orange bell peppers and fajita seasoning until peppers are tender-crisp, 3 to 4 minutes. Add shrimp and sauté until vegetables are slightly charred and shrimp is pink and opaque throughout, 3 to 5 minutes. Season with salt and pepper to taste.

2. To build tacos, divide shrimp mixture equally among tortillas. Top with cheese, lettuce and Pico de Gallo. Fold tortillas in half. Serve with lime wedges.

Crispy Fried Shrimp Tacos

It is the crunchy texture that makes this fried shrimp delicious. Pile it high in a fresh tortilla, top with a heaping mound of cabbage and smother it in sauce for the perfect fish taco.

Tip

Shrimp are labeled by size according to how many are in an average pound (454 g). There are 31 to 35 medium shrimp in one pound (454 g). About 3 shrimp will fit in 6-inch (15 cm) tortillas and about 4 in 8-inch (20 cm) tortillas. Purchase the number you need based on the size of tortillas you have.

Variation

For a sweeter flavor, substitute the tomato and Creamy Wasabi Sauce with Tropical Salsa (page 299) or Orange Salsa (page 301).

• Candy/deep-fry thermometer

1 cup	milk	250 mL
½ cup	all-purpose flour	125 mL
1 cup	panko bread crumbs	250 mL
24 to 32	medium shrimp, peeled and deveined (see Tip, left)	24 to 32
8	6- to 8-inch (15 to 20 cm) corn or flour tortillas, skillet-warmed (page 15)	8
2 cups	shredded cabbage	500 mL
1	tomato, seeded and diced	1
	Creamy Wasabi Sauce (page 316)	

1. Place milk in a bowl, flour in a shallow dish and panko in a separate shallow dish. Working with 1 shrimp at a time, dip first in milk, dust in flour and dip in milk again, then roll in panko until well coated. Transfer to a platter. Discard any excess milk, flour and crumbs.

2. Fill a deep-fryer, deep heavy pot or deep with 3 inches (7.5 cm) of oil and heat to 350°F (180°C). Using tongs, gently place 4 to 6 shrimp at a time in the hot oil and deep-fry, turning once, until crust is golden brown and shrimp is pink and opaque, 2 to 3 minutes. Drain on paper towels.

3. To build tacos, divide shrimp among tortillas. Top with cabbage, tomato and Creamy Wasabi Sauce. Fold tortillas in half.

Fried Shrimp and Rice Tacos

One of my favorite Asian dishes is stir-fried shrimp, so creating this taco was fun! Generous flavors come through from the sesame oil and sweet and spicy sauce.

Variation

In Step 1, add 1 egg, slightly beaten, after oil. Continue with the recipe.

2 tbsp	sesame oil	30 mL
12 to 16	medium shrimp, peeled and deveined	12 to 16
¼ cup	cooked or frozen corn kernels, thawed if frozen	60 mL
¼ cup	frozen green peas, thawed	60 mL
1½ cups	cooked rice	375 mL
2 tbsp	freshly squeezed lemon juice	30 mL
	Salt and freshly ground black pepper	
8	6- to 8-inch (15 to 20 cm) flour tortilla, skillet-warmed (page 15)	8
2 cups	shredded red cabbage	500 mL
1 cup	shredded zucchini	250 mL
	Spicy Asian Sauce (page 325)	

1. In a large skillet, heat oil over medium-high heat. Sauté shrimp, corn and peas until shrimp turns pink and opaque throughout, 3 to 5 minutes. Transfer shrimp to a cutting board and dice into bite-size pieces. Return to skillet with peas and corn. Add rice and lemon juice and sauté until rice is heated through, 4 to 6 minutes. Season with salt and pepper to taste.

2. To build tacos, divide shrimp mixture equally among tortillas. Top with cabbage and zucchini. Drizzle with Spicy Asian Sauce. Fold tortillas in half.

Shrimp and Artichoke Tacos

Makes 8 tacos

This is a tangy combination of artichoke hearts and delicate shrimp loaded in a fresh tortilla. Freshness goes a long way with chopped romaine and tangy citrus salsa.

Tip

You can use canned or thawed frozen artichoke hearts. Drain artichokes well before chopping.

2 tbsp	olive oil	30 mL
1	clove garlic, minced	1
2 tbsp	freshly squeezed lemon juice	30 mL
24 to 32	medium shrimp, peeled and deveined (see Tip, page 231)	24 to 32
1 cup	chopped artichoke hearts (see Tip, left)	250 mL
	Salt	
8	6- to 8-inch (15 to 20 cm) corn or flour tortillas, skillet-warmed (page 15)	8
2 cups	chopped romaine lettuce	500 mL
1	lemon, each cut into 8 wedges	1
	Citrus Salsa (page 301)	

1. In a large skillet, heat oil over medium heat. Sauté garlic, lemon juice, shrimp and artichoke hearts until shrimp is pink and opaque throughout, 6 to 8 minutes.

2. To build tacos, with a slotted spoon, divide shrimp equally among tortillas. Top with lettuce. Fold tortillas in half. Serve with lemon wedges and Citrus Salsa.

Crab, Spinach and Artichoke Tacos

There is no doubt, this is a rich-flavored succulent taco that is perfect for entertaining. Fresh garlic pulls together the crab and fresh spinach. A creamy mild cheese adds more flavor to this indulgent taco.

Variation
Substitute Monterey Jack cheese for the panela cheese.

1 tbsp	olive oil	15 mL
1	clove garlic, minced	1
1 cup	chopped artichoke hearts (see Tip, page 233)	250 mL
½ cup	chopped fresh spinach	125 mL
1 lb	lump crabmeat (see Tip, page 208)	500 g
8	6- to 8-inch (15 to 20 cm) corn tortillas, skillet-warmed (page 15)	8
1 cup	shredded panela cheese	250 mL
2	avocados, sliced	2
	Pico de Gallo (page 305)	
2	limes, each cut into 4 wedges	2

1. In a large skillet, heat oil over medium-high heat. Sauté garlic, artichokes and spinach until spinach is wilted, about 2 minutes. Add crab and sauté until heated through, 6 to 8 minutes.

2. To build tacos, divide crab mixture equally among tortillas. Top with cheese, avocados and Pico de Gallo. Fold tortillas in half. Serve with a wedge of lime.

Chipotle Shrimp Tacos

Makes 8 tacos

Lightly grilled shrimp glazed with a smoked chile sauce has a smooth, distinctive taste. I love this filling topped with a sweet yet fiery corn salsa.

Tip

Flat skewers work best so shrimp does not flip around while turning. You can also thread shrimp on two skewers parallel to each other.

- Preheat greased barbecue grill to medium-high
- 4 wooden skewers, soaked in water for 30 minutes (see Tip, left)

8	chipotle chile peppers in adobo sauce, puréed	8
¼ cup	liquid honey	60 mL
2 tbsp	olive oil	30 mL
16 to 24	medium shrimp, peeled and deveined (see Tips, page 231)	16 to 24
8	6- to 8-inch (15 to 20 cm) flour tortillas, skillet-warmed (page 15)	8
2 cups	shredded cabbage	500 mL
	Fiery Corn Relish (page 311)	

1. In a medium bowl, combine chipotle purée, honey and oil.

2. Thread 4 to 6 shrimp on each skewer. Grill, turning once, until shrimp turns pink, 3 to 4 minutes per side. Brush shrimp with chile glaze and grill, turning once, until shrimp are opaque throughout, for 1 minute more per side. Transfer to a platter.

3. To build tacos, divide shrimp equally among tortillas. Top with cabbage and Fiery Corn Relish. Fold tortillas in half.

Shrimp and Chorizo Tacos

Stove top cooking makes this taco quick and easy. Authentic Mexican sausage is loaded with spices that glaze the shrimp.

Tip

Look for Mexican chorizo sausage for the most authentic flavor. If you can't find it, Spanish or Portuguese chorizo will also work.

8 oz	fresh Mexican chorizo sausage, removed from casings (see Tip, left)	250 g
24 to 32	medium shrimp, peeled and deveined (see Tips, page 231)	24 to 32
8	6-inch (15 cm) corn tortillas, skillet-warmed (page 15)	8
	Chile Cream Sauce (page 327)	
2 cups	chopped romaine lettuce	500 mL
¼ cup	sliced radishes	60 mL
¼ cup	minced onion	60 mL

1. In a large skillet, sauté chorizo over medium-high heat until lightly browned and heated through, 4 to 6 minutes. Add shrimp and sauté until shrimp turns pink and opaque throughout, 3 to 5 minutes. Drain off excess fat.

2. To build tacos, divide shrimp mixture equally among tortillas. Top with lettuce, radishes and onion. Drizzle with Chile Cream Sauce. Fold tortillas in half.

Mexican Shrimp Paella Tacos

Paella is a traditional rice dish very popular in Spain. The accent flavors of the fresh herbs, vegetables and seafood are simply to "garnish" the rice. This recipe incorporates Mexican flavors with the fresh chorizo, which adds just the right amount of spice to the rice.

Tip

Look for Mexican chorizo sausage for the most authentic flavor. If you can't find it, Spanish or Portuguese chorizo will also work.

8 oz	fresh Mexican chorizo sausage, removed from casings (see Tip, left)	250 g
1	onion, diced	1
4	cloves garlic, minced	4
1 cup	chopped flat-leaf Italian parsley	250 mL
1	can (15 oz/425 mL) diced tomatoes, drained, fire-roasted if possible	1
1½ cups	medium-grain white rice	375 mL
3 cups	chicken broth	750 mL
1 lb	medium shrimp, peeled and deveined	500 g
12	6- to 8-inch (15 to 20 cm) flour tortillas, skillet-warmed (page 15)	12

1. In a paella pan or large deep skillet over medium-high heat, sauté chorizo until lightly browned, 4 to 6 minutes.

2. In same skillet with chorizo, sauté onion, garlic and parsley until vegetables are tender-crisp, about 3 minutes. Add tomatoes and sauté until well blended, 3 to 4 minutes more. Add rice and sauté until grains are well coated.

3. Stir in broth, reduce heat and simmer, gently moving pan around so rice cooks evenly and most of liquid is absorbed, 10 to 12 minutes. Add shrimp, tucking them in and under rice. Simmer until rice puffs up, 12 to 15 minutes.

4. To build tacos, divide rice mixture equally among tortillas. Fold tortillas in half.

Tilapia Veracruz Tacos

Invite everyone over and enjoy this yummy taco. Layers of jalapeños, olives and spices top fresh tilapia and are reminiscent of Mediterranean flavors.

Tip

There are concerns about the sustainability of some fish and seafood so we recommend you check reliable sites such as www.seachoice.org for the latest information.

• Preheat greased barbecue grill to medium-high heat

1½ lbs	skinless tilapia fillets (see Tip, left)	750 g
3 tbsp	olive oil, divided	45 mL
1 tsp	kosher salt	5 mL
½ tsp	freshly ground black pepper	2 mL
2 tbsp	freshly squeezed lemon juice	30 mL
1	onion, thinly sliced	1
2	cloves garlic, minced	2
¼ cup	dry white wine	60 mL
¼ cup	chopped green olives	60 mL
1	tomato, seeded and diced	1
¼ cup	drained sliced pickled jalapeños	60 mL
1 tbsp	minced capers	15 mL
Pinch	granulated sugar	Pinch
8	6-inch (15 cm) corn tortillas, skillet-warmed (page 15)	8

1. Rinse tilapia and pat dry with paper towel. Brush fillets with 1 tbsp (15 mL) of the oil on both sides. Season with salt and pepper. Grill, turning once, until fish flakes easily, for 4 minutes per side. Transfer to a platter, baste with lemon juice and cover to keep warm.

2. In a skillet, heat remaining 2 tbsp (30 mL) of oil over medium-high heat. Sauté onion and garlic until onion is transparent, 6 to 8 minutes. Reduce heat to medium and add wine, olives, tomato, jalapeños, capers and sugar. Simmer, stirring often, until vegetables are tender-crisp, 12 to 15 minutes. Drain off excess liquid.

3. To build tacos, divide fish equally among tortillas. Top with tomato mixture. Fold tortillas in half.

Smoked Salmon Tacos

Makes 8 tacos

Rich smoky flavors of tender salmon are wrapped with a creamy filling and accented with fresh romaine lettuce and a creamy cilantro-based sauce.

8 oz	smoked salmon, chopped	250 g
¼ cup	minced onion	60 mL
1 tbsp	minced fresh cilantro	15 mL
8	6- to 8-inch (15 to 20 cm) flour tortillas	8
½ cup	whipped cream cheese	125 mL
2	English cucumbers, thinly sliced	2
2 cups	chopped romaine lettuce	500 mL
1	tomato, seeded and diced	1
	Cilantro Chile Sauce (page 325)	

1. In a large bowl, combine salmon, onion and cilantro.

2. Spread one side of each tortilla with a thin layer of cream cheese. Top each tortilla with 3 cucumber slices, salmon mixture, lettuce, tomato and Cilantro Chile Sauce. Fold tortillas in half.

Chilled Tuna Salad Tacos

Makes 8 tacos

This is a great lunch taco — quick, easy and refreshing. Enjoy this satisfying North American-style taco, dressed with a creamy sauce spiked with fresh herbs.

Variations

Substitute 1 tbsp (15 mL) minced fresh cilantro for parsley.

Add ¼ tsp (1 mL) ground cumin to the mayonnaise.

2	avocados, cubed	2
	Juice of 1 lime	
1 tbsp	minced flat-leaf Italian parsley	15 mL
1 tbsp	minced capers, rinsed	15 mL
2	cans (each 6 oz/170 g) water-packed light tuna, drained and flaked	2
3 tbsp	mayonnaise	45 mL
	Salt and freshly ground black pepper	
8	6- to 8-inch (15 to 20 cm) flour tortillas	8
2 cups	chopped salad mix	500 mL
½ cup	diced onion	125 mL
1	tomato, seeded and diced	1

1. In a large bowl, combine avocados, lime juice, parsley and capers. Add tuna and mayonnaise and season with salt and pepper to taste. Mix well. Cover and refrigerate for 30 minutes or for up to 2 hours to allow flavors to blend.

2. To build taco, skillet warm tortillas (page 15). Divide tuna mixture equally among tortillas. Top with salad mix, onion and tomato. Fold tortillas in half.

Parmesan Scallop Tacos

Makes 8 tacos

Simple sautéed scallops are quick to deliver big taste on this taco. Accented with cheese and lemony cream sauce, scallops fold well into the taco family.

Tip

The perfect size tortilla for a taco is 6 inches (15 cm). It is generally more available in corn rather than flour. Buy 8-inch (20 cm) flour tortillas and trim them with a pair of kitchen shears to 6 inches (15 cm) using a corn tortilla as a template.

1 lb	large dry sea scallops, trimmed if necessary	500 g
1 tbsp	olive oil	15 mL
1 tbsp	butter	15 mL
¼ cup	minced flat-leaf Italian parsley	60 mL
¾ tsp	salt	3 mL
½ tsp	freshly ground black pepper	2 mL
½ cup	freshly grated Parmesan cheese	125 mL
8	6- to 8-inch (15 to 20 cm) flour tortillas (see Tip, left), skillet-warmed (page 15)	8
2	tomatoes, seeded and diced	2
	Lemon Jalapeño Sauce (page 322)	

1. Remove the large abductor muscle from the side of each scallop. Rinse and pat dry with a paper towel.

2. In a large skillet, heat oil and butter over medium-high heat. Add scallops and season with parsley, salt and pepper. Fry until scallops are golden brown, about 3 minutes. Flip scallops and fry until just firm and opaque throughout, 2 to 3 minutes. Remove from skillet and dust with cheese. Slice into quarters.

3. To build tacos, divide scallops equally among tortillas. Top with tomatoes and Lemon Jalapeño Sauce.

Vegetarian

continued…

Peanut Butter and Berry Tacos

These tacos are heavenly. Peanut butter lovers will enjoy this crispy, peanutty treat! I love them deep-fried but they are just as delicious lightly grilled.

Variations

For a lighter version, follow Step 1. Heat a skillet over medium-high heat. Coat with cooking spray. Cook each taco until both sides are lightly browned, 3 to 5 minutes. Remove from heat. Let cool and remove toothpicks.

For a sweeter dessert version, dust with confectioner's (icing) sugar.

• Instant-read thermometer

8	6- to 8-inch (15 to 20 cm) flour tortillas, skillet-warmed (page 15)	8
½ cup	peanut butter	125 mL
⅓ cup	raspberry jam	75 mL
½ cup	blueberries	125 mL
½ cup	raspberries	125 mL
	Vegetable oil	

1. To build tacos, spread one side of each tortilla with a thin layer of peanut butter, about 1 tbsp (15 mL), leaving a ½ inch (1 cm) border around the edge. In center of each tortilla, place 2 tsp (10 mL) of the jam. Divide berries equally among tortillas. Fold tortillas in half and secure with toothpicks around edges.

2. Fill deep-fryer, deep heavy pot or deep skillet with 3 inches (7.5 cm) of oil and heat to 350°F (180°C). Using tongs, gently place 2 tacos at a time in the hot oil and deep-fry, turning once, until crispy and golden brown, about 2 minutes. Drain on paper towels.

Guacamole Tossa Tacos

Guacamole was known by early Spanish settlers as the "butter of the poor" for it smooth consistency and rich flavor. This taco is full of the same and is truly for avocado lovers.

Tip

Jicama is a root vegetable that adds texture. It has little flavor but takes on the flavor of the spices, herbs and juices around it.

2	jalapeños, minced	2
1 cup	chopped peeled jicama (see Tip, left)	250 mL
1/3 cup	minced red onion	75 mL
	Juice of 2 limes	
1 tbsp	minced fresh cilantro	15 mL
3	avocados	3
	Salt and freshly ground black pepper	
8	taco shells	8
	Guacamole (page 316)	
1 cup	shredded sharp Cheddar cheese	250 mL

1. In a large bowl, combine jalapeño, jicama, red onion, lime juice and cilantro. Cover and refrigerate for 30 minutes to allow flavors to blend or for up to 2 hours. Just before serving, cut avocados into cubes and gently fold into jicama mixture. Season with salt and pepper to taste.

2. To build tacos, warm tacos (page 15). Divide avocado mixture equally among taco shells. Top with Guacamole and cheese.

Sautéed Spinach, Veggie and Garlic Tacos

Makes 8 tacos

I love tacos with innovative combinations of fresh ingredients. These have an aromatic herb that heightens the flavor of the slow-simmered vegetables.

Tips

Cotija is a flavorful, slightly salty Mexican cheese. Feta or goat cheese are milder substitutes.

A fresh tomato salsa adds another dimension of flavor to this taco. Try Roasted Tomato Salsa (page 299) or Tomato Relish (page 311).

2 tbsp	olive oil	30 mL
2	cloves garlic, minced	2
1½ cups	chopped spinach	375 mL
1 cup	chopped zucchini	250 mL
1 cup	chopped mushrooms	250 mL
2 tsp	minced fresh rosemary	10 mL
	Salt and freshly ground black pepper	
8	6-inch (15 cm) corn tortillas, skillet-warmed (page 15)	8
1 cup	crumbled Cotija or feta cheese (see Tips, left)	250 mL

1. In a large skillet, heat oil over medium-high heat. Sauté garlic, spinach, zucchini, mushrooms and rosemary until vegetables are tender-crisp, 8 to 10 minutes. Season with salt and pepper to taste.

2. To build tacos, divide spinach mixture equally among tortillas. Top with cheese. Fold tortillas in half.

Chilled Veggie and Vinaigrette Tacos

This quick, easy salad taco is teamed with a saucy tangy dressing spiked with chile.

Tip

Rinse and thoroughly dry corn, zucchini and onion on a paper towel. This will keep excess moisture from diluting the dressing mixture.

14	grape tomatoes, cut in half	14
1 cup	cooked corn kernels (see Tip, left and page 257)	250 mL
1 cup	chopped zucchini	250 mL
3	green onions, green parts only, minced	3
½ cup	balsamic vinaigrette	125 mL
	Salt and freshly ground black pepper	
8	6- to 8-inch (15 to 20 cm) flour tortillas	8
1 cup	shredded iceberg lettuce	250 mL
	Jalapeño Cream Sauce (page 323)	

1. In a large bowl, combine tomatoes, corn and zucchini. Add green onions and vinaigrette. Toss gently. Season with salt and pepper to taste. Cover and refrigerate for 1 hour to allow flavors to blend or for up to 2 hours.

2. To build tacos, skillet warm tortillas (page 15). Divide corn mixture equally among tortillas. Top with lettuce and Jalapeño Cream Sauce. Fold tortillas in half.

Veggie Burger Tacos

This taco is a meatless wonder. It has all the flavor of a classic ground beef taco. Accents of chile and a creamy sauce bring it all together for delicious hearty flavor.

Tip

You can find vegetable based ground meat replacement in the frozen food or produce section of the supermarket.

12 oz	vegetarian ground beef replacement (see Tip, left)	375 g
1 tsp	ground cumin	5 mL
1/4 tsp	cayenne powder	1 mL
	Salt	
8	6- to 8-inch (15 to 20 cm) flour or corn tortillas, skillet-warmed (page 15)	8
2	avocados, cubed	2
1	tomato, seeded and diced	1
2 cups	chopped salad mix	500 mL
	Spicy Ranch Sauce (page, 326)	

1. In a large skillet, bring 1/4 cup (60 mL) water to a boil over medium-high heat. Add vegetarian ground beef, cumin and cayenne and cook until well blended and heated through, 6 to 8 minutes. Season with salt to taste.

2. To build tacos, divide vegetarian ground beef equally among tortillas. Top with avocados, tomato, salad mix and Spicy Ranch Sauce. Fold tortillas in half.

Portobello Tacos

The portobello is truly the "steak" of the mushroom family. The superb flavor is enhanced even more with grilling. It makes a delicious taco filling.

Tip

Queso Fresco is a Mexican fresh cheese with a crumbly texture that tastes like a combination of Monterey Jack and mozzarella cheese. Its main characteristic is that it does not melt, but will get soft when warmed.

Variation

Substitute feta cheese for the Queso Fresco.

• Preheat greased barbecue or indoor grill to medium-high

4	portobello mushroom caps	4
2 tbsp	olive oil	30 mL
3	cloves garlic, minced	3
1 tbsp	minced fresh oregano	15 mL
	Salt and freshly ground black pepper	
8	6-inch (15 cm) corn tortillas, skillet-warmed (page 15)	8
1 cup	crumbled Queso Fresco cheese (see Tip, left)	250 mL
2 cups	chopped spinach	500 mL
	Jalapeño Relish (page 310)	

1. Clean mushrooms with a damp paper towel.

2. In a small bowl, combine oil, garlic and oregano. Brush caps with oil mixture and season with salt and pepper to taste.

3. Grill mushrooms, stem side down, until well marked from grill, 3 to 5 minutes. Turn and grill until tender, about 3 minutes. Transfer to a cutting board and cut into $\frac{1}{4}$-inch (0.5 cm) slices.

4. To build tacos, divide mushrooms equally among tortillas. Top with cheese, spinach and Jalapeño Relish. Fold tortillas in half.

Roasted Corn and Green Chile Taco Steamers

Add an intense corn flavor by serving this corn filling in a double-steamed corn tortilla. Steaming tortillas with a bit of moisture gives them a softer, velvety texture, perfect for this taco.

Variations
Top sauce with Jalapeño Relish (page 310).

• **Preheat greased barbecue grill to medium-high**

1 tbsp	olive oil	15 mL
1 tbsp	butter, melted	15 mL
5 to 6	ears corn, husk and silk removed	5 to 6
1 cup	shredded Monterey Jack cheese	250 mL
	Salt and freshly ground black pepper	
16	6-inch (15 cm) corn tortillas, micro-warmed (page 15)	16
1 cup	roasted green chile pepper strips (see page 250)	250 mL
	Chile Basil Sauce (page 328)	

1. In a small bowl, combine oil and butter.

2. Grill corn, covered, turning with tongs and brushing occasionally with butter mixture, until nicely browned and slightly charred, 8 to 12 minutes. Transfer corn to a cutting board and remove kernels with a sharp knife.

3. In a large bowl, combine corn and cheese. Season with salt and pepper to taste.

4. To build tacos, stack 2 tortillas together per taco. Divide corn mixture equally among tortillas. Top with chile strips and drizzle with Chile Basil Sauce. Fold tortillas in half.

Grilled Eggplant and Red Pepper Tacos

Makes 8 tacos

The natural flavors of Italy shine through in this recipe. Eggplant adds a familiar earthiness along with the peppers and herbs.

Tip

To roast bell peppers, see Roasting Chiles, right. This method also works for bell peppers.

Variation

Sometimes I like to add a rich buttery flavor. Start by spreading a thin layer of butter on the outside of each tortilla. Then fill as in Step 2 and toast as in Step 3. The butter will give the outside of the taco a grilled buttery flavor.

1 tbsp	olive oil	15 mL
1 lb	eggplant, cut crosswise into ¼-inch (0.5 cm) slices	500 g
	Salt and freshly ground black pepper	
8 oz	mozzarella cheese, thinly sliced into 8 slices	250 g
8	6- to 8-inch (15 to 20 cm) flour tortillas, skillet-warmed (page 15)	8
½ cup	chopped roasted red bell peppers (see below and Tip, left)	125 mL
2 tbsp	chopped fresh basil	30 mL

1. In a large skillet, heat oil over medium-high heat. Sauté eggplant until tender, 4 to 6 minutes. Season with salt and pepper to taste.

2. To build tacos, divide cheese slices equally among tortillas. Top with equal amounts of eggplant and peppers. Garnish with basil. Fold tortillas in half.

3. In a clean large skillet over medium heat, toast tacos until crispy on both sides and cheese has melted in the middle.

Roasting Chiles

To roast chiles, such as New Mexico, Anaheim, poblano, jalapeño and habanero: Preheat greased outdoor grill to medium or preheat broiler. Place fresh chiles on outdoor grill or gas stovetop over medium heat or arrange on a baking sheet and place 2 to 3 inches (5 to 7.5 cm) away from heat under broiler. Grill or broil, turning often with tongs, until surfaces of skin are lightly charred and blistered. Immediately place peppers in a paper or plastic bag, or an airtight container and close tightly. Let peppers cool for 12 to 15 minutes. Peel off charred skin and remove stems and seeds. Tear into strips or chop as needed according to the recipe. Wash your hands thoroughly after handling chiles. Refrigerate peppers for up to 3 days or freeze in airtight container for up to 6 months.

Fried Tomato and Green Chile Tacos

Contemporary flavors of the garden are wrapped up in this taco. Lightly breaded tomatoes complement the earthy flavor of the chile.

Tip

The perfect size tortilla for a taco is 6 inches (15 cm). It is generally more available in corn rather than flour. Buy 8-inch (20 cm) flour tortillas and trim them with a pair of kitchen shears to 6 inches (15 cm) using a corn tortilla as a template.

6 to 8	tomatoes, ends removed and cut into $\frac{1}{4}$-inch (0.5 cm) slices	6 to 8
	Salt and freshly ground black pepper	
1 cup	dry Italian bread crumbs	250 mL
2 tbsp	all-purpose flour	30 mL
$\frac{1}{2}$ cup	milk	125 mL
4 tbsp	butter, divided	60 mL
8	6- to 8-inch (15 to 20 cm) flour or corn tortillas (see Tip, left), skillet-warmed (page 15)	8
$1\frac{1}{2}$ cups	pepper Jack cheese	375 mL
1 cup	chopped roasted green chile peppers, warmed (see page 250)	250 mL
2 cups	chopped salad mix	500 mL
	Chile Cream Sauce (page 327)	

1. Season both sides of tomato slices with salt and pepper. Let stand for 15 minutes. Spread bread crumbs out on a flat surface. Add flour and blend together with a fork.

2. Pour milk into a small bowl. Dip each tomato slice into milk then dredge in bread crumbs until well coated.

3. In a large skillet, heat 2 tbsp (30 mL) of the butter over medium-high heat. In batches, as necessary, sauté tomato slices until golden brown on each side, 4 to 6 minutes. Transfer to paper towels. Continue to sauté remaining tomatoes slices, adding 2 tbsp (30 mL) of butter and adjusting the heat, if necessary, between batches.

4. To build tacos, place 3 to 4 tomato slices on each tortilla. Top with cheese, chiles, salad mix and Chile Cream Sauce. Fold tortillas in half.

Mushroom, Green Chile and Swiss Tacos

I like to serve these tacos as appetizers — almost like a quesadilla. This taco is grilled lightly on both sides for a crispy finish.

Variation

Sometimes I like to add a rich buttery flavor. Start by spreading a thin layer of butter on the outside of each tortilla. Then fill as in Step 2 and toast as in Step 3. The butter will give the outside of the taco a grilled buttery flavor.

1 tbsp	olive oil	15 mL
2½ cups	chopped mushrooms	625 mL
½ cup	chopped roasted green chile peppers (see page 250)	125 mL
	Salt and freshly ground black pepper	
8	slices Swiss cheese	8
8	6- to 8-inch (15 to 20 cm) flour or corn tortillas, skillet-warmed (page 15)	8
2 cups	chopped salad mix	500 mL
	Pico de Gallo (page 305)	

1. In a large skillet, heat oil over medium-high heat. Sauté mushrooms and chiles until mushrooms are tender, 6 to 8 minutes. Season with salt and pepper to taste.

2. To build tacos, divide cheese slices equally among tortillas. Top with mushroom mixture. Fold tortillas in half.

3. In a clean large skillet over medium heat, toast tacos, turning carefully, until crispy on both sides and cheese is melted in the middle, 6 to 8 minutes. Gently garnish each taco with salad mix and Pico de Gallo.

Chile Relleno Soft Taco Bake

Corn tortillas add extraordinary texture and natural flavor to this dish. It is deliciously spicy, creamy and cheesy.

- Preheat oven to 375°F (190°C)
- 8-inch (20 cm) square glass baking dish, greased

3	eggs, lightly beaten	3
1½ cups	milk	375 mL
⅓ cup	all-purpose flour	75 mL
1 tsp	baking powder	5 mL
½ tsp	salt	2 mL
12	6-inch (15 cm) corn tortillas	12
	Vegetable cooking spray	
12	roasted whole green chile peppers, peeled (see page 250)	12
1 lb	Monterey Jack cheese, cut into 12 thick chunks	500 g
1½ cups	shredded Cheddar cheese	375 mL
2 cups	chopped salad mix	500 mL
2	tomatoes, seeded and chopped	2

1. In a large bowl, whisk together eggs and milk. Add flour, baking powder and salt and whisk until well blended.

2. Spray each tortilla lightly with cooking spray and skillet warm (page 15). Stack them on a platter.

3. Make a long slit in the side of each chile. Gently remove seeds and insert a piece of cheese. Place each filled chile in tortilla. Fold each tortilla in half and place side by side in prepared baking dish.

4. Pour egg mixture in and around each taco. Top with shredded cheese.

5. Bake in preheated oven until cheese is lightly browned and eggs are set, 30 to 35 minutes. Serve tacos on individual plates topped with salad mix and tomatoes.

Chile Relleno Tacos

Makes 8 tacos

Although chile rellenos are a lot of work, they are well worth it if you have the time. Here is a quick rendition of a wonderful Mexican treasure, an egg battered tortilla stuffed with chile and cheese.

Tips

This taco is so versatile. Serve them for breakfast, lunch or dinner. I have even served them as a side dish along with grilled meats and salad.

This chile cheese taco is delicious with Jalapeño Relish (page 310), Sweet Pineapple Salsa (page 309) or Fiesta Taco Sauce (page 324).

2 cups	chopped roasted green chile peppers (see page 250)	500 mL
1 cup	shredded Cheddar cheese	250 mL
1 cup	shredded Monterey Jack cheese	250 mL
8	6- to 8-inch (15 to 20 cm) flour tortillas, micro-warmed (page 15)	8
8	eggs, lightly beaten	8
1 cup	all-purpose flour	250 mL

1. To build tacos, divide chiles and Cheddar and Monterey Jack cheeses equally among tortillas, placing on one half of the tortilla. Fold over and secure edges with toothpicks. Deep-fry immediately or place filled tortillas in a large resealable plastic bag and refrigerate until ready to cook or for up to 8 hours.

2. Place eggs in a shallow dish. Place flour in another shallow dish. Dip each taco in the egg mixture quickly and then flour on both sides. Then dip into egg mixture again.

3. Spray a large skillet with cooking spray and heat over medium-high heat. Add each egg-dipped taco and toast until cheese is melted and tortilla is golden brown, 4 to 6 minutes per side.

Rolled Veggie Tacos with Spicy Asian Sauce

Makes 8 tacos

I call this my Mexican egg roll. I love it! A crispy golden corn tortilla stuffed with veggies and dipped in a spicy Asian sauce.

Variation

In a large skillet, heat 1 tbsp (15 mL) olive oil over medium-high heat, coating bottom of pan. Add 2 eggs and sauté until set. Let cool. Add to zucchini mixture (Step 1) and continue with the recipe.

- Candy/deep-fry thermometer

1 cup	shredded zucchini	250 mL
1 cup	shredded cabbage	250 mL
1	carrot, shredded	1
	Salt and freshly ground black pepper	
12	6-inch (15 cm) corn tortillas, micro-warmed (page 15)	12
	Vegetable oil	
	Spicy Asian Sauce (page 325)	

1. In a large bowl, combine zucchini, cabbage and carrot. Season with salt and pepper to taste.

2. To build tacos, place 2 heaping tbsp (30 mL) of zucchini mixture at one end of each tortilla, forming a thin straight line across end of tortilla. Gently roll tortilla and secure with a toothpick. Deep-fry immediately or place rolled tacos in a large resealable plastic bag to keep moist and refrigerate until ready to cook or for up to 24 hours.

3. Fill deep-fryer, deep heavy pot or deep skillet with 3 inches (7.5 cm) of oil and heat to 350°F (180°C). Using tongs, gently place 2 to 3 tacos at a time in the hot oil and deep-fry, turning once, until crispy and golden brown, 2 to 3 minutes. Drain on paper towels. Season lightly with salt. Serve with Spicy Asian Sauce.

Tomato and Mozzarella Taco Steamers with Chile Basil Sauce

This salad-inspired taco is delicious on a hot summer day. Intense flavors of tangy vinaigrette, chile and fresh veggies create a tantalizing taco.

2 tbsp	extra virgin olive oil	30 mL
1 tbsp	balsamic vinegar	15 mL
1	clove garlic, minced	1
	Kosher salt and freshly ground black pepper	
2	tomatoes, seeded and diced	2
1	zucchini, chopped	1
8 oz	mozzarella cheese, cubed	250 g
8	6-inch (15 cm) corn tortillas, micro-warmed (page 15)	8
2 cups	chopped romaine lettuce	500 mL
	Chile Basil Sauce (page 328)	

1. In a small bowl, whisk together oil, vinegar, garlic and salt and pepper to taste.

2. In a large bowl, combine tomatoes, zucchini and cheese. Add vinegar mixture and blend well.

3. To build tacos, divide tomato mixture equally among tortillas. Top with lettuce and Chile Basil Sauce. Fold tortillas in half.

New Mexico Garden Tacos

Makes 8 tacos

This taco is fast and simple and can be made in minutes. Adding intense flavor to the vegetable filling is made effortless by including a spicy salsa.

1 tbsp	olive oil	15 mL
1	clove garlic, minced	1
3 cups	chopped zucchini	750 mL
1 cup	chunky tomato salsa or Roasted Tomato Salsa (page 299)	250 mL
8	6-inch (15 cm) corn tortillas, skillet-warmed (page 15)	8
1½ cups	shredded Monterey Jack cheese	375 mL

1. In a large skillet, heat oil over medium-high heat. Add garlic, zucchini and salsa and sauté until zucchini is tender-crisp, 6 to 8 minutes. Drain off excess liquid.

2. To build tacos, divide zucchini mixture equally among tortillas. Top with cheese. Fold tortillas in half.

Calabacitas Tacos

Makes 8 tacos

This is a traditional dish served with a grilled meat or chicken. It comes from the original casserole of corn and squash. The sweet corn and zucchini taste is heightened with the addition of black beans.

Tips

Drained canned or thawed frozen corn kernels work in this recipe. Grilled or fire-roasted corn will add additional flavor.

Increase zucchini to 2 cups (500 mL) if summer squash is out of season or hard to find.

1 tbsp	olive oil	15 mL
½ cup	chopped onion	125 mL
2	cloves garlic, minced	2
1 cup	chopped summer squash (see Tips, left)	250 mL
1 cup	chopped zucchini	250 mL
1 cup	cooked corn kernels (see Tips, left)	250 mL
1 tbsp	minced flat-leaf parsley	15 mL
1 cup	shredded Monterey Jack cheese	250 mL
8	6- to 8-inch (15 to 20 cm) flour or corn tortillas, skillet-warmed (page 15)	8
	Pico de Gallo (page 305)	

1. In a large skillet, heat oil over medium-high heat. Sauté onion, garlic, summer squash, zucchini, corn and parsley until vegetables are tender-crisp, 10 to 12 minutes. Remove skillet from heat and stir in cheese until melted.

2. To build tacos, divide corn mixture equally among tortillas. Top with Pico de Gallo. Fold tortillas in half.

Fried Zucchini Tacos

I love deep-fried zucchini! The simple batter creates a tasty, crispy, crusted vegetable, folded in a tortilla and topped with a creamy sauce.

• Candy/deep-fry thermometer

1 cup	all-purpose flour	250 mL
1 tsp	salt	5 mL
½ tsp	freshly ground pepper	2 mL
1¼ cups	beer	300 mL
	Vegetable oil	
3	zucchini, cut crosswise into ¼-inch (0.5 cm) slices	3
	Freshly grated Parmesan cheese	
8	6-inch (15 cm) corn tortillas, skillet-warmed (page 15)	8
	Spicy Ranch Sauce (page 326)	
2 cups	chopped salad mix	500 mL
	Pico de Gallo (page 305)	

1. In a small bowl, whisk together flour, salt and pepper. Add beer and whisk until smooth.

2. Fill deep-fryer, deep heavy pot or deep skillet with 3 inches (7.5 cm) of oil and heat to 350°F (180°C). Using tongs, gently dip zucchini slices into batter then in the hot oil and deep-fry, turning once, until crispy and golden brown, 1 to 2 minutes. Drain on paper towels. Sprinkle lightly with Parmesan cheese.

3. To build tacos, place 3 to 4 zucchini slices on each tortilla. Drizzle with Spicy Ranch Sauce. Top with salad mix and Pico de Gallo.

Grilled Peppers and Cheese Tacos

Grilled vegetables add a depth of flavor to these tacos. Top with melted Provolone, fresh lettuce and creamy sauce and you have a crowd pleaser.

- Preheat greased barbecue or indoor grill to medium-high
- Vegetable grate or heavy foil

2	green bell peppers, cored and cut in half	2
2	red bell pepper, cored and cut in half	2
1 tbsp	olive oil	15 mL
2 tsp	minced rosemary	10 mL
	Kosher salt and freshly ground black pepper	
8	6- to 8-inch (15 to 20 cm) flour tortillas	8
8	thin slices Provolone cheese	8
2 cups	chopped salad mix	500 mL
	Chile Cream Sauce (page 327)	

1. Coat green and red peppers with oil. Place in vegetable grate or foil and grill peppers until tender-crisp, 4 to 6 minutes per side. Sprinkle equally with rosemary. Lightly season with salt and pepper. Transfer to a cutting board and cut into bite-size pieces.

2. To build tacos, reduce heat on the grill to medium-low or use area without direct heat. Place tortillas on grill and top each with one slice of cheese. When cheese starts to melt, transfer tortillas to a cutting board and top with peppers, salad mix and Chile Cream Sauce. Fold tortillas in half.

Asparagus, Artichoke and Feta Tacos

Makes 8 tacos

This is a taco full of freshness. Artichoke hearts and sharp, crumbly cheeses add superb flavor.

Variations

Substitute Queso Fresco cheese for feta cheese.

1 lb	asparagus, trimmed and cut into 1-inch (2.5 cm) pieces	500 g
½ cup	chopped drained canned artichoke hearts	125 mL
2 tbsp	extra virgin olive oil	30 mL
2 tbsp	freshly grated Parmesan cheese	30 mL
½ cup	crumbled feta cheese	125 mL
	Juice of 1 lemon	
	Salt and freshly ground black pepper	
8	6-inch (15 cm) corn tortillas, skillet-warmed (page 15)	8

1. Fill a medium saucepan half full of water. Bring water to a boil over high heat. Add asparagus and boil for 2 minutes. Drain well.

2. Place asparagus in a large bowl. Add artichoke hearts, oil, Parmesan cheese, feta cheese and lemon juice and toss gently to coat. Season with salt and pepper to taste.

3. To build tacos, divide asparagus mixture equally among tortillas. Fold tortillas in half.

Artichoke and Spinach Tacos

This salad-style taco is fresh and inviting. Enjoy amazing textures accented with tangy lemon and creamy sauce spiked with chile.

Tips

Rinse and pat dry all vegetables with paper towel before chopping to prevent a soggy texture.

If you are short on time, use store-bought taco shells. There are a variety of brands to choose from. Check with your local grocer to see if and when they make them fresh.

1 cup	spinach leaves, trimmed and torn into bite-size pieces	250 mL
1 cup	chopped romaine lettuce (see Tips, left)	250 mL
1 cup	chopped drained canned artichoke hearts	250 mL
¼ cup	thinly sliced red onion	60 mL
¼ cup	chopped drained canned water chestnuts	60 mL
	Juice of 1 lemon	
	Jalapeño Cream Sauce (page 323)	
8	taco shells, warmed (see Tips, left)	8
½ cup	crumbled Cotija cheese (see Tip, page 245)	125 mL

1. In a bowl, combine spinach, lettuce, artichoke hearts, red onion and water chestnuts. Cover and refrigerate for 30 minutes or for up to 2 hours to allow flavors to blend.

2. Just before serving, toss spinach mixture with lemon juice and Jalapeño Cream Sauce.

3. To build tacos, divide spinach mixture equally among taco shells. Top with cheese. Fold tortillas in half.

Jicama and Cucumber Tacos with Chile Vinaigrette

Makes 8 tacos

Unusual textures accompany interesting flavors of chile and tangy sauces. This taco has layers of flavorful spices and fresh vegetables.

¼ cup	olive oil	60 mL
3 tbsp	rice vinegar	45 mL
1 tbsp	chopped fresh dill	15 mL
½ tsp	Dijon mustard	2 mL
Pinch	chipotle pepper powder	Pinch
2	cucumbers, peeled and chopped	2
1 cup	chopped peeled jicama	250 mL
8	6-inch (15 cm) corn tortillas, skillet-warmed (page 15)	8

1. In a small bowl, whisk together oil, vinegar, dill, mustard and chipotle powder.

2. In a large bowl, combine cucumbers and jicama. Add vinaigrette and toss gently.

3. To build tacos, divide cucumber mixture equally among tortillas. Fold tortillas in half.

Caesar Salad Tacos

This salad-inspired taco has become a popular choice. Tangy dressing laces the fresh greens. Jicama and artichoke hearts add texture and flavor.

Tips

Rinse and pat dry all vegetables before chopping for a crisp dry mixture.

This recipe contains a raw egg. If you are concerned about the safety of using raw eggs, use pasteurized eggs in the shell or pasteurized liquid whole eggs, instead.

If you are pressed for time, substitute ¾ cup (175 mL) Caesar salad dressing for the lemon, egg, anchovy and Worcestershire sauce in Step 1.

Variations

For more texture and fiber, add ½ cup (125 mL) chopped pecans or sliced almonds in Step 1.

For a spicier flavor, add ½ cup (125 mL) chopped roasted green chile in the dressing mix in Step 1.

3 tbsp	freshly squeezed lemon juice	45 mL
1	egg, slightly beaten (see Tips, left)	1
1 tsp	anchovy paste	5 mL
Dash	Worcestershire sauce	Dash
¾ cup	freshly grated Parmesan cheese, divided	175 mL
2 cups	chopped romaine lettuce (see Tip, left)	500 mL
1 cup	drained chopped canned artichoke hearts	250 mL
½ cup	diced (¼ inch/0.5 cm) peeled jicama	125 mL
8	taco shells, warmed (page 15)	8

1. In a small bowl, whisk together lemon juice, egg, anchovy paste, Worcestershire and ¼ cup (60 mL) of the cheese.

2. In a large bowl, combine lettuce, artichoke hearts and jicama. Add dressing and toss until well coated.

3. To build tacos, divide lettuce mixture equally among taco shells. Top with remaining ½ cup (125 mL) of cheese.

Three-Bean Tacos

Fresh garden herbs add superb flavor to this bean taco. Enjoy a healthy taco filled with veggies full of fiber.

Tips

If you are pressed for time, use canned pinto, red and black beans, rinsed and drained.

Panela is a fresh Mexican cheese that tastes like a combination of Monterey Jack and mozzarella cheese. It's main characteristic is that it does not melt, but will get soft when warmed.

Variation

Add more flavor to this taco by topping it with Pico de Gallo (page 305) or Green Chile Relish (page 312).

1 tbsp	olive oil	15 mL
¾ cup	cooked pinto beans (see Tips, left)	175 mL
½ cup	canned red beans, drained and rinsed	125 mL
½ cup	canned black beans, drained and rinsed	125 mL
¼ cup	diced seeded tomato	60 mL
⅓ cup	minced seeded jalapeño	75 mL
¼ cup	chopped fresh cilantro	60 mL
2 tbsp	chopped fresh basil	30 mL
	Salt and freshly ground black pepper	
8	6-inch (15 cm) corn tortillas, skillet-warmed (page 15)	8
2 cups	chopped salad mix	500 mL
1 cup	crumbled panela or shredded Monterey Jack cheese (see Tips, left)	250 mL

1. In a large skillet, heat oil over medium-high heat. Sauté pinto, red and black beans, tomato, jalapeño, cilantro and basil until beans are heated through, 8 to 10 minutes. Season with salt and pepper to taste. Drain off excess liquid.

2. To build tacos, divide bean mixture equally among tortillas. Top with lettuce and cheese. Fold tortillas in half.

Sweet Pepper Cheese Tacos

Unexpected sweet and savory flavors make this taco memorable. Enjoy fresh apple with Swiss cheese spiked with roasted jalapeño.

Variation
Sometimes I like to add a rich buttery flavor. Start by spreading a thin layer of butter on the outside of each tortilla. Then fill as in Step 1. The butter will give the outside of the taco a grilled buttery flavor.

8	thin slices Swiss cheese	8
8	thin slices Cheddar cheese	8
8	6- to 8-inch (15 to 20 cm) flour tortillas, skillet-warmed (page 15)	8
3	jalapeños, roasted, seeded and diced (see page 250)	3
1	Golden Delicious apple, cut lengthwise into 8 slices, then cut each in half	1
1	onion, thinly sliced	1
	Vegetable cooking spray	

1. To build tacos, divide Swiss and Cheddar cheeses equally among tortillas. Top with equal amounts of jalapeño, apple and onion. Fold tortillas in half.

2. Coat a large skillet with cooking spray and heat over medium heat. Toast tacos, turning carefully, until crispy on both sides and cheese is melted in the middle, 6 to 8 minutes.

Basic Pinto Beans

This is a simple recipe of basic mashed pinto beans.

Makes 6 cups (1.5 L)

3 cups	dried pinto beans	750 mL
1 tbsp	garlic powder	15 mL
1 tbsp	onion powder	15 mL

1. Place beans in a large pot. Add enough water to cover by 4 inches (10 cm) and bring to a boil over medium-high heat. Reduce heat and boil gently until soft (see Tips, below), $2\frac{1}{2}$ to 3 hours. Let cool completely to room temperature, about 2 to 3 hours.

Tips
Test beans by smashing one bean between thumb and index finger.

Store beans in an airtight container and refrigerate for up to 2 days or freeze for up to 4 months.

Variation
Substitute black beans or kidney beans for the pinto beans. Follow Step 1.

Avocado and Corn Tacos

Makes 8 tacos

Chile-spiced avocado flavors these tacos. A light corn filling spiked with sweet bell pepper is the perfect backdrop.

Variations

Substitute feta cheese for the Queso Fresco.

Add more flavor by topping this taco with Jalapeño Relish (page 310), Fiesta Taco Sauce (page 324) or Roasted Tomato Salsa (page 299).

	Juice of 1 lime	
2 tbsp	olive oil	30 mL
¼ cup	crumbled Queso Fresco cheese (see Tip, page 248)	60 mL
1 tsp	ground cumin	5 mL
2 cups	cooked corn kernels (see Tip, page 267)	500 mL
2	avocados, cubed	2
¼ cup	minced red bell pepper	60 mL
	Salt and freshly ground black pepper	
8	6-inch (15 cm) corn tortillas, skillet-warmed (page 15)	8

1. In a small bowl, combine lime juice, oil, cheese and cumin.

2. In a large bowl, combine corn, avocados and bell pepper. Add lime juice mixture and toss to coat. Season with salt and pepper to taste. Cover and refrigerate for 1 hour or for up to 3 hours to allow flavors to meld.

3. To build tacos, divide corn mixture equally among tortillas. Fold tortillas in half.

Toasted Corn and Onion Tacos

Makes 8 tacos

This toasted taco reminds me of an amazing grilled cheese sandwich. Stuffed with sautéed onions and buttery corn, it is a toasty treat.

Tip
Drained canned or thawed frozen corn kernels work in this recipe. Grilled or fire-roasted corn will add additional flavor.

Variation
Sometimes I like to add a rich buttery flavor. Start by spreading a thin layer of butter on the outside of each tortilla. Then fill as in Step 2 and toast as in Step 3. The butter will give the outside of the taco a grilled buttery flavor.

1 tbsp	olive oil	15 mL
1 tbsp	butter	15 mL
1 tsp	chipotle pepper powder	5 mL
2	onions, thinly sliced	2
1 cup	cooked corn kernels (see Tip, left)	250 mL
1 cup	shredded Monterey Jack cheese	250 mL
8	6- to 8-inch (15 to 20 cm) corn or flour tortillas, skillet-warmed (page 15)	8
½ cup	crumbled Cotija or feta cheese	125 mL
	Vegetable cooking spray	

1. In a large skillet, heat oil, butter and chipotle powder over medium heat. Sauté onions until transparent, 10 to 12 minutes. Add corn and sauté until heated through.

2. To build tacos, divide Monterey Jack cheese equally among tortillas. Top with corn mixture and Cotija cheese. Fold tortillas in half.

3. Coat a large skillet with cooking spray and heat over medium heat. Toast tacos, turning carefully, until crispy on both sides and cheese is melted in the middle, 6 to 8 minutes.

Black-Eyed Pea Tacos

Makes 8 tacos

Enjoy the combination of peas, spinach and onion, accented with sharp cheese and tangy lemon. Tradition says to serve black-eyed peas on New Year's Day for good luck in the upcoming year. This is the perfect taco for that special day.

1½ cups	canned or cooked black-eyed peas, drained and rinsed	375 mL
3	green onions, green parts only, chopped	3
1 cup	chopped spinach	250 mL
½ cup	sliced black olives	125 mL
½ cup	crumbled feta cheese	125 mL
	Juice of 1 lemon	
	Salt and freshly ground black pepper	
8	6- to 8-inch (15 to 20 cm) flour tortillas, skillet-warmed (page 15)	8

1. In a large bowl, combine black-eyed peas, green onions, spinach, olives and cheese. Add lemon juice and season with salt and pepper to taste and toss to coat.

2. To build tacos, divide pea mixture equally among tortillas. Fold tortillas in half.

Spicy Tofu Tacos

Makes 8 tacos

Tofu is a superb source of protein and the perfect alternative to meat tacos. A simple garnish of Cheddar and tomato add freshness, and the Asian sauces deliver heightened flavor and heat in this taco filling.

Tip

There are variety of teriyaki sauces on the market. Infused flavors range from spicy miso to garlic, green onion and ginger. Test a few and find your favorite.

1 tbsp	olive oil	15 mL
½ cup	minced onion	125 mL
1 lb	firm tofu, cubed	500 g
¼ cup	teriyaki sauce (see Tip, left)	60 mL
Dash	soy sauce	Dash
8	6- to 8-inch (15 to 20 cm) corn or flour tortillas	8
1 cup	shredded sharp Cheddar cheese	250 mL
2 cups	chopped salad mix	500 mL
1	tomato, seeded and diced	1

1. In a large skillet, heat oil over medium-high heat. Sauté onion until transparent, 4 to 6 minutes. Add tofu, teriyaki sauce and soy sauce and sauté until tofu is well coated and heated through, 4 to 6 minutes.

2. To build tacos, divide tofu mixture equally among tortillas. Top with cheese, salad mix and tomato. Fold tortillas in half.

Navajo Tacos

This Native American taco is a staple of the native culture. The flat leavened dough is deep-fried. The soft crust bread is piled high with pinto beans and fresh produce.

Variation
Add 1 lb (500 g) seasoned cooked lean ground beef and 2 cups (500 mL) seasoned shredded cooked beef or chicken.

• Candy/deep-fry thermometer

Fry Bread

3 cups	all-purpose flour	750 mL
2 tsp	baking soda	10 mL
1 tsp	salt	5 mL
½ cup	melted butter	125 mL
2 cups	cooked or canned whole pinto beans, drained and rinsed (see page 265)	500 mL
2 cups	shredded lettuce	500 mL
1½ cups	shredded Cheddar cheese	375 mL
1	tomato, chopped	1
2	ripe avocados, cubed	2
8	radishes, thinly sliced	8

1. In a large bowl, combine flour, baking soda and salt until smooth. Slowly add ¾ cup (175 mL) water and butter, stirring, until dough comes together. In the bowl, knead with your hands just until dough is smooth. Divide into eight portions and shape each into a 6-inch (15 cm) flat round. Keep dough covered.

2. Fill a deep-fryer, deep heavy pot or large deep skillet with 3 inches (7.5 cm) of oil and heat to 350°F (180°C). Using tongs, fry each dough round, one at a time, turning once, until golden brown, about 2 minutes. Drain on paper towels.

3. To build tacos, divide beans among fry bread rounds. Top with lettuce, cheese, tomato, avocados and radishes.

Spaghetti Tacos

This crazy combination is addictive! Crunchy taco shells stuffed with tomato-laced pasta are fun and delicious. Kids of all ages go crazy for these tacos.

Tip

I like serving this taco with store-bought taco shells. They are crispier and add a better texture. Look for high-quality prepared taco shells. Check your local grocery store and test the different brands. I tend to like the true Mexican brands because they taste more authentic to me.

Variations

For a meat taco, add 24 slices round pepperoni. Follow recipe and top each taco with 3 slices of pepperoni.

Add 8 oz (250 g) cooked, drained and crumbled ground beef to sauce in Step 2.

4 to 6 oz	spaghetti noodles	125 to 175 g
1	can (15 oz/425 mL) tomato sauce (1¾ cups/425 mL)	1
1 tsp	minced basil	5 mL
1 tsp	garlic powder	5 mL
½ tsp	ground oregano	2 mL
½ tsp	freshly ground black pepper	2 mL
Pinch	granulated sugar	Pinch
8	taco shells, warmed (see Tip, left)	8
¼ cup	freshly grated Parmesan cheese	60 mL

1. Fill a large pot three-quarters full of water and bring to a boil over high heat. Add noodles and cook until tender or al dente, 10 to 12 minutes. Drain. Transfer to a medium bowl and cover.

2. In a small saucepan over medium heat, combine tomato sauce, basil, garlic powder, oregano and pepper. Bring to a gentle boil. Reduce heat to medium-low and simmer for 6 to 8 minutes. Pour sauce over pasta and toss until well coated.

3. To build tacos, divide pasta equally among taco shells. Top with Parmesan.

Heart Healthy Veggie and Bean Tacos

This is a delicious filling that is full of fiber and nutrients. The corn tortilla, which is low in fat and high in fiber as well, makes the perfect wrap for this healthy taco.

1 tbsp	olive oil	15 mL
½ cup	minced green bell pepper	125 mL
½ cup	diced seeded tomato	125 mL
4	green onions, green parts only, minced	4
1	can (14 to 19 oz/398 to 540 mL) pinto beans, rinsed and drained	1
	Salt and freshly ground black pepper	
8	6-inch (15 cm) corn tortillas, skillet-warmed (page 15)	8
2 cups	chopped romaine lettuce	500 mL
	Fiesta Taco Sauce (page 324)	

1. In a large skillet, heat oil over medium-high heat. Sauté bell pepper, tomato and green onions until tender-crisp, 6 to 8 minutes. Add beans and sauté until beans are heated through, 8 to 10 minutes. Season with salt and pepper to taste.

2. To build tacos, divide bean mixture equally among tortillas. Top with lettuce and Fiesta Taco Sauce. Fold tortillas in half.

Sonoran Bean and Cheese Tacos

Makes 16 rolled tacos

This light, flaky crisp taco is a favorite among kids. Creating a rolled taco with a fried flour tortilla is a mainstay in Sonoran-style cooking. Also known as a flauta, these vegetarian tacos are delicious.

Tip

Serve with Fiesta Taco Sauce (page 324), Tomatillo Avocado Salsa (page 304) or Cilantro Chile Sauce (page 325).

- Candy/deep-fry thermometer

2 cups	Quick Refried Beans or Stove Top Refried Beans (page 273)	500 mL
16	6-inch (15 cm) flour tortillas, micro- or skillet-warmed (page 15)	16
1 cup	shredded Monterey Jack cheese	250 mL
	Vegetable oil	
	Salt	

1. To build tacos, place 2 tbsp (30 mL) of the beans at one end of each tortilla, shaping the filling into a short, straight line. Top with cheese. Gently roll tortilla and beans, and secure with a toothpick. Repeat with remaining tortillas. Deep-fry immediately or place rolled tacos in a resealable plastic bag to keep moist. Refrigerate until ready to cook for up to 2 days or place in freezer for up to 4 months. Thaw completely before cooking.

2. Fill deep-fryer, deep heavy pot or deep skillet with 3 inches (7.5 cm) of oil and heat to 350°F (180°C). Using tongs, gently place 4 to 6 tacos at a time in the hot oil and deep-fry until crispy and golden brown, about 2 minutes. Drain on paper towels. Lightly season with salt.

Stove Top Refried Beans

These beans can be whipped up in minutes. A true authentic Mexican flavor is best achieved by refrying these beans in lard. They are delicious.

Makes 2 cups (500 mL)

2 cups	cooked pinto beans, drained, reserving liquid (page 265)	500 mL
2 tbsp	lard	30 mL
	Salt	

1. In a large skillet, heat beans and ¼ cup (60 mL) reserved liquid over medium-high heat. Bring to a boil and boil for 2 minutes. Reduce heat to medium-low. Using a potato masher, gently mash beans. Beans should be like a thick paste, not runny. If too thick, add more reserved liquid, 1 tsp (5 mL) at a time, until bean mixture is thick, but not stiff. Repeat until all beans are mashed.

2. In another large skillet, melt lard over medium-high heat. Add mashed beans and stir until well blended and bubbling, 4 to 6 minutes. Season with salt to taste.

Variation
Substitute 2 tbsp (30 mL) vegetable or canola oil for lard.

Quick Refried Beans

I like taking shortcuts with good results when I'm cooking. Here is a quick way to get an authentic tasting batch of refried beans in a hurry.

Makes about 2 cups (500 mL)

2	cans (each 14 to 19 oz/398 to 540 mL) pinto beans, slightly drained, reserving liquid (see Tip, below)	2
1½ tbsp	lard	22 mL
	Salt	

1. In a large skillet, bring beans to a boil over medium-high heat and boil for 2 minutes. Reduce heat to medium-low. Using a potato masher, gently mash beans. Beans should be like a thick paste, not runny. If too thick, add reserved liquid, 1 tsp (5 mL) at a time, until just thick, but not stiff.

2. Increase heat to medium. Scoop beans to one side of skillet and add lard. Let lard start melting and slowly stir beans and lard until well blended and bubbling. Season with salt to taste.

Tip
I also like the dehydrated refried beans. They are quick to prepare and have a great flavor. You can find them in your Mexican food section at the supermarket. I usually add ½ cup (125 mL) less water than directed when rehydrating them for a firmer consistency.

Variation
Substitute vegetable or canola oil for lard for a vegetarian option.

Red Beans and Rice Soft Tacos with Cajun Sauce

Cajun cooking is so popular and this regional favorite makes the best tacos. Enjoy tasty beans and tender rice loaded in fresh tortillas.

1 tbsp	olive oil	15 mL
1	clove garlic, minced	1
1½ cups	canned or cooked red beans, rinsed and drained	375 mL
1 cup	cooked white rice	250 mL
¼ cup	minced green bell pepper	60 mL
Pinch	cayenne pepper	Pinch
	Salt and freshly ground black pepper	
8	6- to 8-inch (15 to 20 cm) flour tortillas, skillet-warmed (page 15)	8
2 cups	chopped romaine lettuce	500 mL
1	onion, chopped	1
	Cajun Sauce (page 327)	

1. In a large skillet, heat oil over medium-high heat. Sauté garlic, beans, rice, bell pepper and cayenne pepper until vegetables are tender and beans are heated through, 10 to 12 minutes. Season with salt and pepper to taste.

2. To build tacos, divide bean mixture equally among tortillas. Top with lettuce, onion and Cajun Sauce. Fold tortillas in half.

Crispy Black Bean and Basil Tacos

Makes 8 tacos

The contemporary flavor of this taco is fresh and fun. The garden fresh herbs blend well with the tangy vinaigrette dressing.

2½ cups	rinsed drained canned black beans	625 mL
½ cup	chopped fresh basil	125 mL
¼ cup	olive oil	60 mL
3 tbsp	balsamic vinegar	45 mL
2	cloves garlic, minced	2
¼ tsp	salt	1 mL
¼ tsp	freshly ground black pepper	1 mL
8	taco shells (page 15)	8
2 cups	chopped salad mix	500 mL
	Chile Basil Sauce (page 328)	

1. In a large bowl, combine beans, basil, oil, vinegar, garlic, salt and pepper.

2. To build tacos, divide bean mixture equally among taco shells. Top with lettuce and Chile Basil Sauce.

Black Bean Soft Tacos with Fiery Corn Relish

Makes 8 tacos

This soft taco is superb with the spicy corn relish. This makes a wonderful appetizer or side dish.

Variation
Substitute feta cheese for the Queso Fresco.

1 tbsp	olive oil	15 mL
2	cloves garlic, minced	2
1 cup	sliced white button mushrooms	250 mL
½ cup	minced onion	125 mL
1	can (14 to 19 oz/398 to 540 mL) black beans, drained and rinsed	1
8	6-inch (15 cm) corn tortillas, skillet-warmed (page 15)	8
	Fiery Corn Relish (page 311)	
½ cup	crumbled Queso Fresco cheese	125 mL

1. In a large skillet, heat oil over medium-high heat. Sauté garlic, mushrooms and onion until onion is transparent, 8 to 10 minutes. Add beans and sauté until heated through, 4 to 6 minutes.

2. To build tacos, divide bean mixture equally among tortillas. Top with Fiery Corn Relish and cheese. Fold tortillas in half.

Refried Bean, Goat Cheese and Cabbage Taquitos

Strong distinctive cheese with smooth authentic refried beans creates a taste that is memorable. I like to garnish with cabbage for a good texture.

Variation

Substitute Queso Fresco or feta cheese for the goat cheese.

- Candy/deep-fry thermometer

3 cups	Quick Refried Beans or Stove Top Refried Beans (page 273)	750 mL
36	6-inch (15 cm) corn tortillas, micro-warmed (page 15)	36
	Vegetable oil	
	Salt	
2 cups	shredded cabbage	500 mL
1½ cups	crumbled goat cheese	375 mL
	Fiesta Taco Sauce (page 324)	

1. To build tacos, place 1 heaping tbsp (15 mL) of the beans at one end of each tortilla. Gently roll tortilla and secure with a toothpick. Deep-fry immediately or place rolled tacos in a resealable plastic bag to keep them moist. Repeat with remaining tortillas. Refrigerate for up to 2 days or place in freezer for up to 4 months. Thaw completely before cooking.

2. Fill deep-fryer, deep heavy pot or deep skillet with 3 inches (7.5 cm) of oil and heat to 350°F (180°C). Using tongs, gently place 3 to 4 tacos at a time in the hot oil and deep-fry, turning once, until golden brown and crispy on the ends and a bit soft in the middle, 2 to 3 minutes. Drain on paper towels. Lightly season with salt.

3. To serve, place 3 taquitos side by side on a plate. Top with cabbage and cheese. Serve Fiesta Taco Sauce on the side.

Refried Bean and Rice Crispy Tacos

Folded tacos take on a new identity here, loaded with a cheesy, fiber-filled center. They are quick to make and fun to eat.

- Candy/deep-fry thermometer

1 cup	Quick Refried Beans or Stove Top Refried Beans (page 273)	250 mL
8	6-inch (15 cm) corn tortillas, micro-warmed (page 15)	8
1 cup	cooked white rice	250 mL
1 cup	shredded Monterey Jack cheese	250 mL
	Vegetable oil	
	Fiesta Taco Sauce (page 324)	

1. To build tacos, place 2 tbsp (30 mL) of the beans on one half of each tortilla, spread out slightly, staying away from the edges. Top with equal amounts of rice and cheese. Fold tortillas in half and secure edges with toothpicks. Deep-fry immediately or place filled tortillas in resealable plastic bag to keep moist. Refrigerate for up to 2 days.

2. Fill deep-fryer, deep heavy pot or deep skillet with 3 inches (7.5 cm) of oil and heat to 350°F (180°C). Using tongs, gently place 2 to 3 tacos at a time in the hot oil and deep-fry, turning once, until crispy and golden brown, 2 to 3 minutes. Drain on paper towels. Serve with Fiesta Taco Sauce.

Crispy Corn Tacos
with Cilantro Chile Sauce

Makes 8 tacos

Fresh corn lends an added flavor that blends well with fresh herbs, lime and chile sauce. Tucked into a crispy corn shell this flavor combination gives you double the flavor and texture.

Tips

When fresh corn is not available, substitute 3 cups (750 mL) canned or frozen corn.

I prefer making my own crispy taco shells. They will be hot, crispy and delicious. Directions on taco shell "how-tos" are on page 14. However, when I am short on time I do buy high-quality prepared taco shells. Check your local grocery store and test the different brands. I tend to like the true Mexican brands because they taste more authentic to me.

6	ears corn, shucked (see Tips, left)	6
2	tomatoes, seeded and diced	2
¼ cup	chopped fresh basil	60 mL
3 tbsp	olive oil	45 mL
	Juice of 1 lime	
1 tsp	hot pepper flakes	5 mL
	Salt and freshly ground black pepper	
8	taco shells (see Tips, left)	8
2 cups	chopped romaine lettuce	500 mL
	Cilantro Chile Sauce (page 325)	

1. In a large pot over medium-high heat, fill half full of water and bring to a boil. Add corn and boil until tender, 5 to 8 minutes. Transfer corn to a cutting board and remove kernels with a knife.

2. In a large bowl, combine corn, tomatoes, basil, oil, lime juice and hot pepper flakes. Season with salt and pepper to taste.

3. To build tacos, divide corn mixture equally among taco shells. Top with lettuce and drizzle with Cilantro Chile Sauce.

Crispy Refried Bean and Spanish Rice Tacos

Makes 12 tacos

Combining Mexican favorites in this taco make perfect sense. These quick little tacos are full of flavor and texture.

Tip
When I am pressed for time I use a packaged Spanish rice mix found in the grocery store.

- Candy/deep-fry thermometer

1 cup	Quick Refried Beans or Stove Top Refried Beans (page 273)	250 mL
1 cup	Spanish rice (page 281) (see Tips, left)	250 mL
12	corn tortillas, micro-warmed (page 15)	12
	Vegetable oil	
	Roasted Tomato Salsa (page 299)	

1. To build tacos, place 1 heaping tbsp (15 mL) of the bean mixture at one end of each tortilla. Place 1 heaping tbsp (15 mL) of rice on top of beans. Mash beans and rice together, forming a thin straight line across the end of the tortilla. Gently roll the tortilla and secure with a toothpick. Deep-fry immediately or place rolled tacos in a resealable plastic bag to keep moist. Refrigerate for up to 2 days.

2. Fill deep-fryer, deep heavy pot or deep skillet with 3 inches (7.5 cm) of oil and heat to 350°F (180°C). Using tongs, gently place 2 to 3 tacos at a time in the hot oil and deep-fry, turning once, until crispy and golden brown, 2 to 3 minutes. Drain on paper towels. Serve with Roasted Tomato Salsa.

Spinach Rice Taquitos with Roasted Tomato Salsa

Makes 24 tacos

This tasty little taco makes a wonderful appetizer. I like to serve it with a variety of taco sauces.

Variations

In addition to Fiesta Taco Sauce, I also recommend Lemon Jalapeño Sauce (page 322), Spicy Asian Sauce (page 325), Chipotle Ranch Sauce (page 326) or Chile Cream Sauce (page 327).

- Candy/deep-fry thermometer

1 tbsp	olive oil	15 mL
1	clove garlic, minced	1
1½ cups	chopped spinach	375 mL
1½ cups	cooked Spanish rice (see page 281 and Tip, page 279)	375 mL
1 cup	shredded Monterey Jack cheese	250 mL
24	6-inch (15 cm) corn tortillas, micro-warmed (page 15)	24
	Vegetable oil	
	Salt	
	Roasted Tomato Salsa (page 299)	

1. In a large skillet, heat oil over medium heat. Sauté garlic and spinach until spinach is wilted, 4 to 6 minutes. Add rice and sauté until heated through, 6 to 8 minutes. Drain off any excess liquid. Transfer to a bowl and let cool completely, about 1 hour. Add cheese and mix well.

2. To build tacos, place 1 heaping tbsp (15 mL) of the rice mixture at one end of each tortilla. Gently roll tortilla and secure with a toothpick. Deep-fry immediately or place rolled tacos in a resealable plastic bag to keep moist. Refrigerate for up to 2 days.

3. Fill deep-fryer, deep heavy pot or deep skillet with 3 inches (7.5 cm) of oil and heat to 350°F (180°C). Using tongs, gently place 3 to 4 tacos at a time in the hot oil and deep-fry, turning once, until golden brown and crispy on the ends and a bit soft in the middle, 2 to 3 minutes. Drain on paper towels. Lightly season with salt. Serve with Roasted Tomato Salsa.

Spanish Rice

Spanish rice is lightly spiced with tomato, garlic and onion. These simple flavors create a light flavorful dish that can be used in fillings or served as a side dish for any taco gathering.

Makes about 3 cups (750 mL)

2 tbsp	light olive oil	30 mL
½ cup	onion, chopped	125 mL
3	cloves garlic, minced	3
1¼ cups	long-grain white rice	300 mL
1 cup	tomato sauce	250 mL
	Salt	

1. In a large skillet, heat oil over medium heat. Sauté onion and garlic until onion is transparent, 4 to 6 minutes. Add rice and sauté until rice starts to brown lightly, 4 to 6 minutes.

2. Add tomato sauce and 3 cups (750 mL) water and blend well. Bring to a boil. Reduce heat to medium-low. Cover and simmer until rice is tender and liquid has evaporated, 15 to 20 minutes. Fluff rice with a fork. Season with salt to taste.

Tips

If rice does not have a soft texture, reduce heat and cook, covered, for another 5 to 10 minutes, careful not to burn the rice on the bottom of pan.

If rice does have a soft texture but liquid remains in pan, continue cooking rice, uncovered, until liquid has evaporated.

Black Bean, Avocado and Tomato Tacos

Makes 8 tacos

A tossed taco filling is perfect laced with spicy vinaigrette. This taco is quick for entertaining.

Tip

For this quantity of black beans, use 1 can (14 to 19 oz/398 to 540 mL) drained and rinsed, or cook 1 cup (250 mL) dried black beans.

Variation

Substitute your favorite tomato-based salsa for Tomato Table Salsa.

2 cups	canned or cooked black beans, rinsed and drained (see Tip, left)	500 mL
2	tomatoes, seeded and diced	2
¼ cup	Italian vinaigrette	60 mL
¼ cup	Tomato Table Salsa (page 302)	60 mL
3	avocados	3
	Salt and freshly ground black pepper	
8	taco shells, warmed (see Tips, page 278)	8
1 cup	shredded Manchego or Monterey Jack cheese	250 mL
¼ cup	chopped fresh cilantro	60 mL

1. In a large bowl, combine beans, tomatoes, vinaigrette and Tomato Table Salsa. Cover and refrigerate for at least 1 hour to allow flavors to blend or for up to 4 hours. Just before serving, cube avocado and gently stir in. Season with salt and pepper to taste.

2. To build tacos, divide bean mixture equally among taco shells. Top with cheese and cilantro.

Potato Taquitos with Cotija Cheese

Makes 16 tacos

This is my version of a favorite potato taco served in an old pool hall in Arizona. It is a savory, salty little appetizer that pairs well with an ice cold Mexican beer.

Tips

Wash and cut 2 medium potatoes into ¼-inch (0.5 cm) cubes. Fill a large pot half full of water. Bring water to a boil over high heat. Add potatoes and boil until soft, about 15 minutes. Drain and cool completely.

You can also bake 2 medium-size potatoes for 1½ hours in a preheated 350°F (180°C) oven until tender throughout. Let cool and then dice.

You do not need to seal the ends. The taco looks like a small flute.

- Candy/deep-fry thermometer

2½ cups	diced cooked potatoes, slightly mashed (see Tips, left)	625 mL
16	6-inch (15 cm) corn tortillas, micro-warmed (page 15)	16
	Vegetable oil	
	Salt	
2 cups	shredded cabbage	500 mL
1 cup	crumbled Cotija cheese (see Tip, page 245)	250 mL
	Fiesta Taco Sauce (page 324)	

1. To build tacos, place 2 heaping tbsp (30 mL) of the potatoes at one end of each tortilla. Gently roll tortilla and secure with a toothpick. Deep-fry immediately or place taquitos in a resealable plastic bag to keep moist. Refrigerate until ready to cook for up to 2 days.

2. Fill deep-fryer, deep heavy pot or deep skillet with 3 inches (7.5 cm) of oil and heat to 350°F (180°C). Using tongs, gently place 3 to 4 taquitos at a time in the hot oil and deep-fry, turning once, until golden brown and crispy, 2 to 3 minutes. Drain on paper towels. Lightly season with salt.

3. To serve, place 3 to 4 taquitos on a plate. Top with equal amounts of cabbage and cheese. Drizzle with Fiesta Taco Sauce.

Spicy Spud Tacos

This is like a baked potato wrapped in a crispy corn tortilla shell. Enjoy a chewy, crispy texture that gives way to a light, spicy potato filling.

- Candy/deep-fry thermometer

2½ cups	diced cooked potatoes, slightly mashed (see Tips, page 283)	625 mL
1 tsp	hot pepper flakes	5 mL
	Salt	
8	6- to 8-inch (15 to 20 cm) corn tortillas, micro-warmed (page 15)	8
	Vegetable oil	
	Chipotle Ranch Sauce (page 326)	

1. In a large bowl, combine potatoes and hot pepper flakes. Season with salt to taste.

2. To build tacos, divide potato mixture equally among tortillas, placing mixture on one half of tortilla. Fold over and secure edges with a toothpicks. Deep-fry immediately or place folded tacos in a resealable plastic bag to keep moist. Refrigerate until ready to cook for up to 2 days.

3. Fill deep-fryer, deep heavy pot or deep skillet with 3 inches (7.5 cm) of oil and heat to 350°F (180°C). Using tongs, gently place 2 to 3 tacos at a time in the hot oil and deep-fry, turning once, until golden brown and crispy, 2 to 3 minutes. Drain on paper towels. Season lightly with salt. Serve with Chipotle Ranch Sauce.

Shredded Potato Rolled Tacos with Chile con Queso

Makes 12 tacos

I enjoy light, snack-style meals, which makes this taco the perfect choice. It can be made in minutes and served with a warm, rich queso for dipping.

• Candy/deep-fry thermometer

2 cups	frozen shredded hash brown potatoes, thawed	500 mL
½ cup	shredded sharp Cheddar cheese	125 mL
3 tbsp	minced onion	45 mL
	Salt and freshly ground black pepper	
12	6-inch (15 cm) corn tortillas, skillet-warmed (page 15)	12
	Vegetable oil	
	Salt	
	Chile con Queso (page 315)	

1. In a large bowl, combine potatoes, cheese and onion. Season with salt and pepper to taste.

2. To build tacos, place 2 heaping tbsp (30 mL) of the potato mixture at one end of each tortilla, forming a thin straight line across end of tortilla. Gently roll tortilla and secure with a toothpick. Deep-fry immediately or place rolled tacos in a resealable plastic bag to keep moist. Refrigerate for up to 2 days.

3. Fill deep-fryer, deep heavy pot or deep skillet with 3 inches (7.5 cm) of oil and heat to 350°F (180°C). Using tongs, gently place 2 to 3 tacos at a time in the hot oil and deep-fry, turning once, until crispy and golden brown, 2 to 3 minutes. Drain on paper towels. Lightly season with salt. Serve with Chile con Queso.

Red Chile Potato Tacos

Makes 8 tacos

Potatoes simmered in red chile is a familiar offering in the Southwest. This taco is chock full of red chile goodness.

Tip

The perfect size tortilla for a taco is 6 inches (15 cm). It is generally more available in corn rather than flour. Buy 8-inch (20 cm) flour tortillas and trim them with a pair of kitchen shears to 6 inches (15 cm) using a corn tortilla as a template.

2 tbsp	olive oil, divided	30 mL
2	cloves garlic, minced	2
1 cup	red enchilada sauce or New Mexico Red Chile Sauce (page 319)	250 mL
2½ cups	diced cooked potatoes, slightly mashed (see Tip, page 283)	625 mL
	Kosher salt	
8	6- to 8-inch (15 to 20 cm) flour tortillas (see Tip, left), skillet-warmed (page 15)	8
1 cup	shredded Cheddar cheese	250 mL

1. In a skillet, heat 1 tbsp (15 mL) of the oil over medium heat. Sauté garlic until soft, about 1 minute. Add sauce and sauté until sauce is heated through, 3 to 4 minutes. Set aside.

2. In same skillet, heat remaining 1 tbsp (15 mL) oil over medium-high heat. Add potatoes and sauté until golden brown and crispy, 12 to 14 minutes. Reduce heat to medium-low. Add sauce and sauté until well blended. Season with salt to taste.

3. To build tacos, divide potato mixture equally among tortillas. Top with cheese. Fold tortillas in half.

Chipotle Sweet Potato Tacos

This is a bright-tasting taco to serve during the holidays. Its sweet-savory filling is extraordinarily spiced with two types of chile. Enjoy layers of unexpected flavor.

3 tbsp	freshly grated Parmesan cheese	45 mL
½ tsp	chipotle pepper powder	2 mL
2 tbsp	olive oil	30 mL
2½ cups	diced sweet potatoes	625 mL
½ cup	diced onion	125 mL
	Salt and freshly ground black pepper	
8	6- to 8-inch (15 to 20 cm) flour tortillas, skillet-warmed (page 15)	8
	Poblano Sauce (page 320)	

1. In a small bowl, combine Parmesan and chipotle powder.

2. In a large skillet, heat oil over high heat. Gently add sweet potatoes and onion and sauté until sweet potatoes are golden brown and crispy, 12 to 14 minutes. Transfer to a paper towel-lined platter, then to a bowl and season with cheese mixture and salt and pepper to taste.

3. To build tacos, divide sweet potato mixture equally among tortillas. Fold tortillas in half. Serve with Poblano Sauce.

Arroz Verde Tacos

Makes 8 tacos

This taco is fresh from the garden. Enjoy a light and tasty rice filling spiked with fresh green chile and cilantro stuffed into a fresh tortilla.

- Food processor

½ cup	roasted green chile peppers (see page 250)	125 mL
½ cup	minced fresh cilantro	125 mL
2	cloves garlic, minced	2
3 tbsp	olive oil	45 mL
2 cups	cooked white or brown rice	500 mL
8	taco shells, warmed	8
2 cups	chopped salad mix	500 mL
1	tomato, seeded and diced	1

1. In a food processor, combine chile, cilantro, garlic and oil and process until smooth with a little texture, 1 to 2 minutes.

2. In a large microwave-safe bowl, combine rice and chile mixture. Cover with plastic wrap and microwave on High for 1 minute. Remove and stir. Repeat until rice is heated through, 3 to 4 minutes.

3. To build tacos, divide rice mixture equally among taco shells. Garnish with salad mix and tomato.

Fiery Corn Relish (page 311)
and Guacamole (page 316)

Peachy Praline Soft Tacos (page 351)

Mango-Raspberry Cupitas (page 352)

Pomegranate Margarita (page 371)
and Mojito de Mexico (page 374)

Huevos Rancheros Soft Tacos

Makes 8 tacos

Some said it could not be done — a "hand held" Huevos Rancheros? Lightly fried eggs, covered in fresh green chile and rich, melted cheese and wrapped in a warm corn tortilla. Here it is and it is delicious!

Variation

For a fresh vegetable flavor, substitute Roasted Tomato Salsa (page 299) and Jalapeño Relish (page 310) for the green chile.

- Preheat broiler

8	6-inch (15 cm) corn tortillas	8
	Vegetable cooking spray	
¼ cup	vegetable oil, divided	60 mL
8	eggs	8
1 cup	chopped roasted green chile peppers (see page 250)	250 mL
1 cup	shredded Cheddar cheese	250 mL

1. Spray both sides of each tortilla with cooking spray. In a large skillet over high heat, warm tortillas on both sides until they are pliable and slightly toasted around the edges. Arrange side by side on a baking sheet.

2. In same skillet, add 1 tbsp (15 mL) of the oil and fry each egg, turning once for "over medium" finish, 1 to 2 minutes per side. Place each egg on a platter. Add remaining oil as needed and repeat with remaining eggs.

3. To build tacos, place 1 egg on top of each tortilla. Top equally with green chile peppers. Divide cheese equally among tortillas and place on top of each egg. Broil until cheese is melted, about 1 minute. Fold tortillas in half.

Crispy Breakfast Tacos

Spuds and green chile are a favorite Mexican flavor combination. A crispy corn tortilla loaded with potato, chile and cheese makes this taco a favorite.

Variation

Substitute 2 cooked potatoes, peeled and shredded, instead of the hash browns.

- Candy/deep-fry thermometer

2 cups	frozen shredded hash brown potatoes, thawed	500 mL
¾ cup	chopped roasted green chile peppers (page 250)	175 mL
½ tsp	salt	2 mL
Pinch	freshly ground black pepper	Pinch
1 cup	shredded Cheddar cheese	250 mL
8	6-inch (15 cm) corn tortillas, micro-warmed (page 15)	8
	Vegetable oil	
	Tomato Table Salsa (page 302)	

1. In a large bowl, combine hash browns and chile peppers. Season with salt and pepper. Add cheese and toss until well blended.

2. To build tacos, divide potato mixture equally among tortillas, placing it on one half of the tortilla. Fold over and secure the edges with a toothpicks. Deep-fry immediately or place filled tortillas in a large resealable plastic bag to keep moist.

3. Fill deep-fryer, deep heavy pot or deep skillet with 3 inches (7.5 cm) of oil and heat to 350°F (180°C). Using tongs, gently place 2 to 3 tacos at a time in the hot oil and deep-fry, turning once, until crispy and golden brown, 1 to 2 minutes. Drain on paper towels. Serve with Tomato Table Salsa.

Veggie and Egg Soft Tacos

Makes 8 tacos

This is a colorful vegetarian breakfast taco. It is full of sautéed peppers and fluffy eggs, then topped with the freshness of avocado and a chile cream sauce.

2 tbsp	olive oil	30 mL
½ cup	chopped roasted red bell pepper (see page 250)	125 mL
½ cup	chopped and roasted green chile pepper (see page 250)	125 mL
½ cup	chopped zucchini	125 mL
8	eggs, lightly beaten	8
	Salt and freshly ground black pepper	
8	6- to 8-inch (15 to 20 cm) flour tortillas, skillet-warmed (page 15)	8
2	avocados, cubed	2
	Cilantro Chile Sauce (page 325)	

1. In a skillet, heat oil over medium heat. Sauté red and green bell peppers, green chile peppers and zucchini until vegetables are tender, 3 to 4 minutes. Add eggs and cook, stirring, until scrambled and set. Season with salt and pepper to taste.

2. To build tacos, divide egg mixture equally among tortillas. Top with avocado and Cilantro Chile Sauce. Fold tortillas in half.

Cheesy Egg and Herb Tacos

Makes 8 tacos

This simple taco starts with an egg filling with a light cheesy flavor accented with a more intense cheese flavor. Garden fresh herbs and veggies top it off nicely.

Variation
Substitute Parmesan cheese for the Cotija.

1 tbsp	olive oil	15 mL
8	eggs, lightly beaten	8
4 oz	whipped cream cheese	125 g
8	6- to 8-inch (15 to 20 cm) flour or corn tortillas, skillet-warmed (page 15)	8
½ cup	freshly crumbled Cotija cheese	125 mL
1 tbsp	minced fresh basil	15 mL
1	tomato, seeded and diced	1

1. In a large skillet, heat oil over medium-high heat. Add eggs and cream cheese and cook, stirring, until eggs are scrambled and set, 6 to 8 minutes.

2. To build tacos, divide eggs equally among tortillas. Top with cheese, basil and tomatoes. Fold tortillas in half.

Egg and Spinach Taco Steamers

This breakfast taco is inspired by my love for Italian flavors. The fresh herbs and vegetables come together with a hint of garlic. Steaming the corn tortillas creates a soft velvety texture to wrap around the fluffy egg filling.

1 tbsp	olive oil	15 mL
1	clove garlic, minced	1
1 cup	chopped spinach	250 mL
8	eggs, lightly beaten	8
16	6-inch (15 cm) corn tortillas, micro-warmed (page 15)	16
1 cup	shredded mozzarella cheese	250 mL
1	tomato, seeded and diced	1
2 tbsp	minced fresh basil	30 mL

1. In a skillet, heat oil over medium heat. Sauté garlic and spinach until spinach is wilted, 6 to 8 minutes. Add eggs and cook, stirring, until scrambled and set.

2. To build tacos, stack 2 tortillas per taco. Divide egg mixture equally among tortillas. Top with cheese, tomato and basil. Fold tortillas in half.

Egg and Potato with Tomato

Tomato gives this breakfast taco an unexpected taste. Enjoy this egg stuffed delight topped with a green chile sauce.

3 tbsp	olive oil	45 mL
1 cup	shredded potato	250 mL
6	eggs, lightly beaten	6
1	tomato, seeded and diced	1
	Salt and freshly ground black pepper	
8	6-inch (15 cm) corn tortillas, skillet-warmed (page 15)	8
	Salsa Verde (page 300)	

1. In a large skillet, heat oil over medium-high heat. Sauté potato until golden brown, 8 to 10 minutes. Move potato to one side of skillet and add eggs and cook, stirring, until eggs are almost set. Slowly mix potato into eggs. Add tomato. Cook egg mixture, stirring, until eggs are set. Season with salt and pepper to taste.

2. To build tacos, divide egg mixture equally among tortillas. Top with Salsa Verde. Fold tortillas in half.

Scrambled Veggie Tacos

Makes 8 tacos

This hearty vegetarian taco is overflowing with flavor. Lightly sautéed vegetables wrapped in soft scrambled eggs and fresh flour tortilla is the essence of a Southwest breakfast treat.

2 tbsp	olive oil	30 mL
½ cup	chopped green bell pepper	125 mL
½ cup	diced seeded tomato	125 mL
4	green onions, green parts only, minced	4
4	mushrooms, thinly sliced	4
6	eggs, lightly beaten	6
	Salt and freshly ground black pepper	
8	6-inch (15 cm) flour tortillas, skillet-warmed (page 15)	8
½ cup	shredded Monterey Jack cheese	125 mL
½ cup	shredded sharp Cheddar cheese	125 mL
	New Mexico Green Chile Sauce (page 320)	

1. In a large skillet, heat oil over medium heat. Sauté bell pepper, tomato, green onions and mushrooms until tender, 8 to 10 minutes. Push vegetables to one side of skillet and add eggs. Cook, stirring, until they begin to set. Slowly stir vegetables into eggs and sauté until eggs are scrambled and set, about 4 minutes. Season with salt and pepper to taste.

2. To build tacos, divide egg mixture equally among tortillas. Top with Monterey Jack and Cheddar cheeses and New Mexico Green Chile Sauce. Fold tortillas in half.

Cowgirl Miga Tacos

This is an easy eatin', on the go sandwich taco. If you love egg sandwiches you will enjoy this delightful chilled egg taco.

Tip

Refrigerate for 30 minutes or for up to 1 hour; any longer could cause tortillas to get soggy.

8	eggs	8
¼ cup	mayonnaise	60 mL
¼ cup	minced drained pickled jalapeños	60 mL
3	green onions, green parts only, minced	3
2	stalks celery, chopped	2
	Salt and freshly ground black pepper	
8	6- to 8-inch (15 to 20 cm) flour tortillas, skillet-warmed (page 15)	8
2 cups	chopped romaine lettuce	500 mL
1	tomato, seeded and chopped	1

1. Gently place eggs in a pot. Add enough cold water to cover by 1 inch (2.5 cm). Bring to a gentle boil over medium-high heat. Turn off heat, cover and let eggs stand for 15 minutes. Meanwhile, fill a large bowl with ice water. Transfer eggs to ice water and let stand for 3 to 4 minutes until cool.

2. Peel eggs and place in a medium bowl. Lightly mash eggs, but do not overdo it. Gently fold in mayonnaise, jalapeños, green onions and celery. Season with salt and pepper to taste.

3. To build tacos, divide egg mixture equally among tortillas. Top with lettuce and tomato. Refrigerate for up to 1 hour (see Tip, left).

Tacos Benedict

I created this for all the eggs Benedict fans out there that want a little something new. It is all here, poached egg, savory bacon (see Variations, below) and rich buttery cream sauce wrapped in a flour tortilla. Ole!

Variations

For a non-vegetarian version, you can also make this taco with 8 slices Canadian bacon. In Step 4, place 1 slice of bacon on top of each tortilla and continue with the recipe.

Top each taco with a slice of pickled jalapeño.

- Preheat oven to 400°F (200°C)
- Blender
- Baking sheet, greased

Quick Hollandaise Sauce

4	egg yolks	4
1 tbsp	freshly squeezed lemon juice	15 mL
10 tbsp	butter, melted	150 mL
Pinch	cayenne pepper	Pinch
8	6- to 8-inch (15 to 20 cm) flour tortillas	8
	Vegetable cooking spray	
8	eggs	8
½ cup	shredded Cheddar cheese	125 mL

1. *Quick Hollandaise Sauce:* In a blender, combine egg yolks and lemon juice and blend on medium-high speed until eggs are lighter in color, about 30 seconds. Turn blender speed to low and slowly drizzle in butter through hole in lid until incorporated. Add cayenne and taste. Add more lemon juice, if needed. Transfer to a serving container.

2. Spray both sides of each tortilla with cooking spray. In a large skillet over high heat, warm tortillas on both sides until pliable and slightly toasted around edges. Arrange side by side on a baking sheet.

3. *To poach eggs:* In a saucepan over medium-high, bring water to a boil. Gently crack each egg into a bowl and add first egg to boiling water, wait 1 minute, then add another, cooking up to 4 eggs at a time, being sure they aren't crowded in the pan. Remove from heat and cover for 4 minutes. Using a slotted spoon, transfer eggs to a platter. Repeat with remaining eggs.

4. To build tacos, place on a baking sheet. Top with 1 egg and divide Hollandaise sauce equally. Top with cheese. Broil until cheese is melted and bubbly, about 1 minute. Fold tortillas in half.

Potato and Egg Tacos with Jalapeño Relish

Makes 8 tacos

Fresh corn tortillas filled with lightly fried potatoes and whipped eggs is a taco that will get your attention in the morning.

- Preheat oven to 200°F (100°C)
- Ovenproof bowl

2 tbsp	olive oil	30 mL
2 cups	diced potatoes	500 mL
6	eggs, lightly beaten	6
	Salt and freshly ground black pepper	
8	6-inch (15 cm) corn tortillas, skillet-warmed (page 15)	8
	Jalapeño Relish (page 310)	

1. In a large skillet, heat oil over medium-high heat. Add potatoes and cook, covered, until soft, 6 to 8 minutes. Remove lid and sauté until crisp and golden brown, 6 to 8 minutes. Transfer to ovenproof bowl and keep warm in preheated oven.

2. Reduce heat to medium. In same skillet, add eggs and cook, stirring, until scrambled and set. Add to potatoes and stir gently to combine. Season with salt and pepper to taste.

3. To build tacos, divide potato mixture equally among tortillas. Fold tortillas in half. Serve with Jalapeño Relish.

Salsas, Relishes and Sauces

Salsas and Relishes

continued…

Sauces

Roasted Tomato Salsa

*Roasting the tomatoes in
this salsa heightens the
sweet and earthy flavors.
This basic tomato salsa is
delicious on grilled meats
and chicken. The charred
skin adds an earthy flavor
that blends well with
the roasted jalapeños. It
makes a great "chip and
dip" salsa as well.*

- Preheat broiler
- Blender

4 to 6	tomatoes, unpeeled	4 to 6
3 to 4	roasted jalapeños, skin on (see page 250)	3 to 4
1	onion, chopped	1
2	green onions, green parts only, chopped	2
1 tbsp	minced flat-leaf parsley	15 mL
	Salt	

1. Place tomatoes on a baking sheet and broil, turning often, until skins are charred, for 3 to 4 minutes.

2. In a blender, pulse charred tomatoes, jalapeños, onion and green onions until thick and slightly chunky. Pour into an airtight container. Add salt to taste. Refrigerate, stirring occasionally, for 1 hour or for up to 2 days.

Variation
Substitute 1 tbsp (15 mL) minced fresh cilantro for the parsley.

Tropical Salsa

*Refreshing tropical
flavors blend well with
the rich buttery texture
and flavor of fresh
avocado. This salsa
is perfect for fish or
chicken tacos.*

1 cup	diced mango	250 mL
1 cup	diced pineapple	250 mL
2 tsp	minced fresh cilantro	10 mL
1	roasted habanero chile pepper, minced (see page 250)	1
1	avocado	1
	Juice of 1 lime	

1. In a large bowl, combine mango, pineapple and cilantro. Add chile, in small amounts, tasting after each for heat level. Pour into an airtight container and refrigerate, stirring occasionally, for 30 minutes or for up to 2 hours. Just before serving, cube avocado and add to salsa with lime juice and gently toss. Serve immediately.

Salsa Verde

Makes 2 cups
(500 mL)

Flavorful roasted green chile is spiked with extra heat from the jalapeños. I love this salsa. Served chilled, at room temperature or even heated, this salsa is very versatile.

Tip

If you buy roasted chiles in a jar, you'll need ½ cup (125 mL) chopped.

• Blender or food processor

12	roasted New Mexico or Anaheim green chile peppers (see Tip, left and page 250)	12
4	roasted jalapeños (page 250)	4
2	cloves garlic, minced	2
1 tbsp	olive oil	15 mL
1	onion, chopped	1
	Juice of 1 lime	
	Salt	

1. In a blender, pulse green chiles, jalapeños, garlic, olive oil, onion and lime juice until slightly chunky, 1 to 2 minutes. Pour into an airtight container. Add salt to taste. Refrigerate, stirring occasionally, for 1 hour or for up to 2 days.

Asian Pear Salsa

Makes 2 cups
(500 mL)

An Asian pear has a combination of pear flavor with a crisp apple texture. This salsa adds sweet, tart flavor to tacos with just a hint of spiciness.

	Juice of lime	
2 tbsp	rice wine vinegar	30 mL
1 tsp	finely grated gingerroot	5 mL
1 tsp	finely minced fresh jalapeño	5 mL
2	Asian pears, chopped	2
2 tbsp	minced fresh cilantro	30 mL
2	stalks celery, chopped	2
2	green onions, green part only, chopped	2

1. In a small bowl, combine lime juice, vinegar, ginger and jalapeño. Add pears, cilantro, celery and green onions. Toss until well blended. Place in an airtight container and refrigerate for 1 to 3 hours.

Citrus Salsa

**Makes 2 cups
(500 mL)**

*Citrus lovers will enjoy
the freshness of this
salsa spiked with chile.
Jicama and mango add
interesting textures and
great flavor to chicken
and fish tacos.*

2	oranges, cut into chunks	2
1	lime, cut into chunks	1
½	grapefruit, cut into chunks	½
¼ cup	chopped jicama (see Tip, page 244)	60 mL
2 tsp	hot pepper flakes, divided	10 mL
1	mango, diced	1

1. In a large bowl, combine oranges, lime, grapefruit, jicama and 1 tsp (5 mL) of the hot pepper flakes. Gently add mango and toss. Transfer to an airtight container and refrigerate, stirring occasionally, for 30 minutes or for up to 2 hours. Taste for heat levels and add remaining pepper flakes before serving, if desired.

Orange Salsa

**Makes 2 cups
(500 mL)**

*Tangy oranges work well
with a little heat. Onion
and jalapeño add flavor
and texture to this salsa.*

5	oranges, cut into chunks	5
4	limes, cut into chunks	4
1	jalapeño pepper, seeded and chopped	1
2 tsp	finely chopped onion	10 mL

1. In a large bowl, combine oranges, limes, jalapeño and onion. Transfer to an airtight container and refrigerate, stirring occasionally, for 30 minutes or for up to 2 hours.

Tomato Table Salsa

Makes 3½ cups (875 mL)

This is my girlfriend Donna's favorite table salsa. She serves it with almost every meal. It goes well with beef, chicken and veggie tacos. I like it on fresh, crispy tortilla chips.

Tip

Hot pepper flakes give this salsa its heat. The pepper flakes often vary in heat levels so add an additional 1 tsp (5 mL) for more heat, if desired.

1	can (28 oz/796 mL) diced tomatoes	1
½ cup	chopped roasted New Mexico or Anaheim green chile peppers (see page 250)	125 mL
3 to 4	green onions, white parts and a bit of green, chopped	3 to 4
1	onion, finely chopped	1
1	clove garlic, minced	1
2 tsp	hot pepper flakes (see Tip, left)	10 mL
	Salt	

1. In a large bowl, combine tomatoes, chiles, green onions to taste, onion, garlic, hot pepper flakes and salt. Transfer to an airtight container and refrigerate, stirring occasionally, for 30 minutes or for up to 2 hours.

Peach and Red Onion Salsa

Makes 3 cups (750 mL)

This salsa is full of a fiesta of textures. Smooth peaches and crispy onion make a tantalizing salsa. This is a favorite on pork or chicken tacos.

6	peaches, peeled and diced	6
1	red onion, diced	1
	Juice of 2 limes	
1	red bell pepper, diced	1
2	jalapeños, diced	2
½ cup	chopped jicama	125 mL

1. In a large bowl, gently combine peaches, red onion, lime juice, bell pepper, jalapeños and jicama. Transfer to an airtight container and refrigerate, stirring occasionally, for 30 minutes or for up to 2 hours.

Creamy Corn Salsa

**Makes 2 cups
(500 mL)**

*This salsa delivers layers
of flavor from the fresh
natural spices, the creamy
tasty sauce and the sweet
pepper. It's a perfect
pairing with chicken,
veggie or pork tacos.*

Tip

You can use canned corn,
drained; frozen corn,
thawed; or corn from the
cob, cooked on the stove
top. For an added smoky
flavor, use corn grilled on
the barbecue grill.

Variations

Substitute ¼ cup (60 mL)
drained canned jalapeños
for the fresh jalapeños.

Substitute ½ cup (125 mL)
ranch salad dressing for the
mayonnaise, sour cream
and cumin.

¼ cup	mayonnaise	60 mL
¼ cup	sour cream	60 mL
½ tsp	ground cumin	2 mL
1½ cups	corn kernels (see Tip, left)	375 mL
1	red bell pepper, diced	1
2 tbsp	minced jalapeño	30 mL
	Freshly ground black pepper	

1. In a large bowl, combine mayonnaise, sour cream and
   cumin. Add corn, bell pepper and jalapeño. Toss gently
   until well coated. Season with black pepper to taste.
   Transfer to an airtight container and refrigerate, stirring
   occasionally, for 30 minutes or for up to 2 hours.

Tomatillo Avocado Salsa

Amazingly, tomatillos have an intense citrusy flavor that blends well with the smooth, rich flavor of the avocado. I love the pungent flavor of fresh cilantro so the more the merrier for me!

Tips

Tomatillos are a small green tomato-like fruit covered in a green filmy husk. They have a citrusy flavor and are perfect for sauces and salsas. Remove the husks and wash tomatillos thoroughly to remove stickiness.

Cilantro is a leafy green flat-leaf herb that is has a distinctive pungent flavor and should be soaked and rinsed in water several times to clean before using to avoid gritty texture.

I prefer kosher or sea salt because it has a lighter, cleaner flavor.

Variation

For a milder version, substitute 1 poblano chile pepper, seeded and chopped, for the jalapeños.

• Blender or food processor

12	tomatillos, peeled, cored and chopped (see Tips, left)	12
6	green onions, ends removed, green parts only, chopped	6
3	jalapeños, seeded and chopped	3
1 to 2	cloves garlic, coarsely chopped	1 to 2
1 cup	cilantro leaves (see Tips, left)	250 mL
½ tsp	kosher salt (see Tips, left)	2 mL
2	avocados	2

1. In a blender, pulse tomatillos, green onions, jalapeños, garlic to taste, cilantro and salt until slightly chunky. Transfer to an airtight container and refrigerate, stirring occasionally, for 1 hour or for up to 2 hours. Before serving, cube avocados and gently fold in.

Cilantro and Chile Salsa

Fresh herbs and earthy roasted chiles crown this salsa with flavor. Grilled steak, chicken and fish tacos are delicious with a scoop on top.

Tips

Cilantro should be soaked and rinsed in water several times to clean before using to avoid gritty texture.

I prefer kosher or sea salt because it has a lighter, cleaner flavor.

• Blender or food processor

1½ cups	chopped roasted New Mexico or Anaheim green chile peppers (see page 250)	375 mL
3	roasted jalapeños (see page 250)	3
3	green onions, ends removed, white and light green parts only, chopped	3
2	cloves garlic, minced	2
1 cup	lightly packed fresh cilantro leaves (see Tips, left)	250 mL
1 tbsp	olive oil	15 mL
2 tsp	kosher salt	10 mL

1. In a blender, pulse green chiles, jalapeños, green onions, garlic, cilantro, oil and salt until slightly chunky. Transfer to an airtight container and refrigerate, stirring occasionally, for 1 hour or for up to 2 hours.

Pico de Gallo

This is a salsa I use more than any other. These flavors capture the true essence of Mexico, crisp and refreshing! I can't think of a taco this does not taste good on — well maybe a sweet one.

4	tomatoes, seeded and diced	4
4	green onions, greens parts only, minced	4
3	jalapeños, seeded and minced	3
2	serrano chile peppers, seeded and minced	2
1	onion, finely chopped	1
2 tbsp	minced fresh cilantro	30 mL
	Juice of 2 limes	
	Kosher salt	

1. In a large bowl, combine tomatoes, green onions, jalapeños, serrano chiles, onion and cilantro. Add lime juice and mix well. Transfer to an airtight container and refrigerate, stirring occasionally, for 1 hour or for up to 24 hours. Add salt to taste just before serving.

Onion Apple Salsa

Tangy and sweet is what this salsa offers. It is a tasty complement to pork and chicken tacos. But I have been known to pile it high on crispy, salty tortilla chips.

Tips

Apples can be peeled or skin can be left on. I usually peel one apple and leave one with the skin for good color and texture.

Prepare this salsa close to the serving time. Apples tend to turn brown quickly, although the lemon juice should preserve their color a bit longer.

Variation

I prefer a tart-tasting apple, however, you can substitute 2 Golden Delicious apples for a sweeter-tasting salsa.

3	jalapeños, seeded and minced	3
2	red bell peppers, minced	2
2	apples, such as Granny Smith, cored and chopped (See Tips, left)	2
1	onion, finely chopped	1
1 tbsp	freshly squeezed lemon juice	15 mL
1 tbsp	minced fresh cilantro	15 mL
½ cup	unsweetened apple juice	125 mL
	Kosher salt	

1. In a large bowl, combine jalapeños, bell peppers, apples, onion, lemon juice and cilantro. Add apple juice and mix well. Place in an airtight container. Refrigerate for 1 hour or for up to 2 hours (see Tips, left). Add salt to taste just before serving.

Red Onion Salsa

**Makes 1½ cups
(375 mL)**

This is my version of the traditional Mexican onion condiment: thin slices of onions marinated in fresh lemon juice. One bite will take you across the border.

Tip

I like flat-leaf Italian parsley over curly parsley because of the added flavor but also because it adds great color and texture.

1	red onion, minced	1
1	onion, minced	1
	Juice of 1 lemon	
	Juice of 1 lime	
2 tsp	olive oil	10 mL
1 tbsp	minced flat-leaf parsley (see Tip, left)	15 mL

1. In a large bowl, combine red onion, onion, lemon juice, lime juice, oil and parsley. Transfer to an airtight container and refrigerate, stirring occasionally, for 1 hour or for up to 24 hours.

Citrusy Lime Salsa

**Makes 2 cups
(500 mL)**

Fresh lime is one citrus fruit that is at the center of Mexican cooking. It is showcased in this light salsa with a hint of ginger. Pair it with grilled fish or fresh veggies and you have an enticing taco.

• Blender or food processor

4	limes, divided	4
6	tomatillos, peeled and chopped	6
2 tbsp	olive oil	30 mL
2	cloves garlic, minced	2
1 tsp	minced fresh gingerroot	5 mL
1 tbsp	minced fresh cilantro	15 mL
Pinch	Kosher salt	Pinch

1. Juice 2 limes and reserve juice. Remove skin and pith from 2 limes and cut into bite-size pieces.

2. In a blender, pulse tomatillos, oil, garlic and ginger until slightly chunky. Pour into a large bowl. Add lime juice, pieces of lime and cilantro. Mix gently. Transfer to an airtight container and refrigerate, stirring occasionally, for 1 hour or for up to 24 hours. Add salt to taste just before serving.

Veggie Salsa

**Makes 2 cups
(500 mL)**

*This salsa of veggies in
a light marinade is fresh
and appealing. It tops any
taco with flavor.*

Tip

You can use canned corn,
drained; frozen corn,
thawed; or corn from the
cob, cooked on the stove
top. For an added smoky
flavor, use corn grilled on
the barbecue grill.

1 tbsp	white vinegar	15 mL
1 tbsp	olive oil	15 mL
1 tsp	hot pepper flakes	5 mL
1 cup	chopped zucchini	250 mL
1 cup	corn kernels (see Tip, left)	250 mL
2	radishes, minced	2

1. In a large bowl, combine vinegar, oil and hot pepper
   flakes. Add zucchini, corn and radishes. Mix well.
   Transfer to an airtight container and refrigerate, stirring
   occasionally, for 1 hour or for up to 24 hours.

Strawberry Salsa

**Makes 2 cups
(500 mL)**

*This salsa is a sweet,
peppery ambrosial treat.
Fresh strawberries spiked
with chile and laced with
honey make a memorable
culinary experience. I
serve it on veggie tacos
as well as dessert tacos.
It is fabulous on hot fresh
corn tortilla chips!*

½ cup	liquid honey	125 mL
¼ cup	balsamic vinegar	60 mL
¼ tsp	coarsely ground black pepper	1 mL
4 cups	chopped strawberries	1 L
2	roasted jalapeños, minced (see page 250)	2

1. In a large bowl, combine honey, vinegar and pepper.
   Gently add strawberries and jalapeños. Transfer to an
   airtight container and refrigerate, stirring occasionally,
   for 1 hour or for up to 24 hours.

Sweet Pineapple Salsa

Sweet and savory flavor combinations are perfect for the world of tacos. This sweet salsa is tempting on everything from cheesy veggie tacos to spicy pork tacos, leaving a different impression every time.

2 cups	diced pineapple	500 mL
½ cup	minced fresh cilantro	125 mL
¼ cup	minced red onion	60 mL
¼ cup	diced red bell pepper	60 mL
1	jalapeño, seeded and minced	1

1. In a large bowl, combine pineapple, cilantro, red onion, bell pepper and jalapeño. Transfer to an airtight container and refrigerate, stirring occasionally, for 1 hour or for up to 24 hours.

Jicama Salsa

Jicama, an edible root, adds a crispy texture along with the mild flavor of leek. Enjoy both tossed in a citrusy bath and scooped up on a beefy taco.

Variation

For a spicier flavor, add ½ tsp (1 mL) ground cumin, and salt and freshly ground pepper to taste.

1	leek, white part and a bit of green, thinly sliced	1
1 cup	diced jicama	250 mL
1 tbsp	minced flat-leaf parsley	15 mL
	Juice of 2 lemons	

1. In a large bowl, combine leek, jicama, parsley and lemon juice. Transfer to an airtight container and refrigerate, stirring occasionally, for 1 hour or for up to 24 hours.

Margarita Melon Salsa

Makes 2 cups (500 mL)

The luscious flavors of margaritas are poured over the melon in this salsa. The sweet and tangy composition is delicious on fresh fish tacos.

Tip

A medium sweet and sour margarita liquid mix works best for this recipe.

1 cup	diced honeydew	250 mL
1/2 cup	diced cantaloupe	125 mL
1	mango, diced	1
1	green onion, green part only, minced	1
1	jalapeño, diced	1
1/3 cup	liquid margarita mix (see Tip, left)	75 mL
	Juice of 1 lime	
2 tbsp	freshly squeezed orange juice	30 mL

1. In a large bowl, combine honeydew, cantaloupe, mango, green onion, jalapeño, margarita mix, lime juice and orange juice. Transfer to an airtight container and refrigerate, stirring occasionally, for 1 hour or for up to 24 hours.

Jalapeño Relish

Makes 2 1/2 cups (625 mL)

Tangy and hot relish packs a punch you won't forget. Make it a few days ahead for the best flavor.

6	jalapeños, seeded and chopped	6
4	green onions, ends removed, green parts only, chopped	4
2	tomatoes, seeded and diced	2
3 tbsp	olive oil	45 mL
2 tbsp	red wine vinegar	30 mL
	Salt and freshly ground black pepper	

1. In a large bowl, combine jalapeños, green onions, tomatoes, oil and vinegar. Toss until jalapeño mixture is well coated. Season with salt and pepper to taste. Serve immediately or transfer to an airtight container and refrigerate, stirring occasionally, for up to 2 days.

Fiery Corn Relish

*Refreshing sweet corn
makes a crisp crunchy
salsa for tacos. It is fresh
tasting and colorful.*

Tip

You can use canned corn,
drained; frozen corn,
thawed; or corn from the
cob, cooked on the stove
top. For an added smoky
flavor, use corn grilled on
the barbecue grill.

¼ cup	olive oil	60 mL
3 tbsp	freshly squeezed lime juice	45 mL
2 tsp	minced fresh cilantro	10 mL
3	tomatoes, seeded and diced	3
1½ cups	corn kernels (see Tip, left)	375 mL
2 to 3	jalapeños, seeded and diced	2 to 3
	Salt and freshly ground black pepper	

1. In a large bowl, combine oil, lime juice and cilantro.
   Add tomatoes, corn and jalapeños to taste. Mix well
   until corn mixture is well coated. Season with salt and
   pepper to taste. Transfer to an airtight container and
   refrigerate, stirring occasionally, for 1 hour or for up to
   2 days.

Tomato Relish

*This is "Salsa 101," the
starting point for salsa
and Mexican relish. It
is quick and easy and
delicious every time!*

4	tomatoes, seeded and diced	4
½ cup	chopped roasted New Mexico or Anaheim green chile peppers (see page 250)	125 mL
2	green onions, ends removed, green parts only, chopped	2
1	onion, finely chopped	1
2 tsp	minced flat-leaf parsley	10 mL
1 tsp	minced fresh cilantro	5 mL
	Kosher salt and freshly ground black pepper	

1. In a large bowl, combine tomatoes, chiles, green onions,
   onion, parsley and cilantro. Season with salt and pepper
   to taste. Transfer to an airtight container and refrigerate,
   stirring occasionally, for 1 hour or for up to 2 days.

Green Chile Relish

**Makes 2 cups
(500 mL)**

*I have been snacking on
this relish for years. I
serve it on grilled steak
tacos, fried fish tacos
and even veggie tacos.*

2 cups	chopped roasted New Mexico or Anaheim green chile peppers (see page 250)	500 mL
¼ cup	olive oil	60 mL
5	cloves garlic, minced	5
1 tsp	crushed Mexican oregano	5 mL
	Kosher salt	

1. In a large bowl, combine chiles, oil, garlic, oregano and salt to taste. Transfer to an airtight container and refrigerate, stirring occasionally, for 1 hour or for up to 2 days.

Blue Cheese and Onion Relish

**Makes 2 cups
(500 mL)**

*I like to start this relish
a day ahead of time.
Marinating the onions
assures a better tasting
relish with good texture.*

Variation
Substitute ¾ cup (175 mL)
Italian dressing for oil,
vinegar, sugar, salt and
pepper.

¾ cup	red wine vinegar	175 mL
½ cup	olive oil	125 mL
½ tsp	granulated sugar	2 mL
½ tsp	salt	2 mL
Pinch	freshly ground black pepper	Pinch
2	onions, sliced into thin rings	2
1 cup	crumbled blue cheese	250 mL

1. In a large bowl, whisk together vinegar, oil, sugar, salt and pepper. Add onion and toss until well coated. Transfer to an airtight container. Refrigerate overnight.

2. Remove onion mixture from refrigerator. Let onion mixture stand at room temperature for 15 minutes before serving. Add blue cheese and toss until well blended.

Garlic and Jalapeño Relish

Makes 1 cup (250 mL)

This sautéed relish is rich in flavor. Serve it warm or at room temperature.

1 tbsp	olive oil	15 mL
5	cloves garlic, minced	5
5	jalapeños, seeded and minced	5
¾ cup	chopped green onion, green parts only	175 mL
	Kosher salt and freshly ground black pepper	

1. In a large skillet, heat oil and garlic over medium heat. Sauté jalapeños and green onion until vegetables are tender-crisp, 6 to 8 minutes. Season with salt and pepper to taste. Serve warm or let cool to room temperature. Transfer to an airtight container and refrigerate, stirring occasionally, for 1 hour or for up to 2 days.

Apple, Onion and Garlic Relish

Makes 2 cups (500 mL)

This sweet salsa is perfect for pork or veggie tacos.

2	apples, peeled and diced	2
2	green onions, ends removed, green parts only, diced	2
2	cloves garlic, minced	2
½ cup	fresh pineapple chunks	125 mL
½ tsp	grated lime zest	2 mL
2 tbsp	freshly squeezed lime juice	30 mL

1. In a large bowl, combine apples, green onions, garlic, pineapple, lime zest and lime juice. Serve at room temperature or transfer to an airtight container and refrigerate, stirring occasionally, for up to 4 days.

Cabbage Relish

Shredded cabbage can take on so many flavors, from Asian to Mexican. Here are several variations you can try once you have the shredded cabbage.

Variations

Asian 1: Toss cabbage with 3 tbsp (45 mL) rice vinegar, 2 tbsp (30 mL) olive oil and ¼ cup (60 mL) toasted sesame seeds

Asian 2: Toss cabbage with ¼ cup (60 mL) Spicy Asian Sauce (page 325).

Italian: Toss cabbage with ¼ cup (60 mL) balsamic vinaigrette and 1 tbsp (15 mL) minced onion.

Mexican: Toss cabbage with 3 tbsp (45 mL) freshly squeezed lime juice, 2 tbsp (30 mL) olive oil and 1 tsp (5 mL) hot pepper flakes.

2 cups	finely shredded green cabbage	500 mL
1 cup	finely shredded red cabbage	250 mL

1. In a small bowl, combine your preferred dressing ingredients from Variations (left) and whisk until well blended.

2. In a large bowl, combine cabbage. Add dressing mixture and toss until cabbage is well coated. Transfer to an airtight container and refrigerate, stirring occasionally, for up to 2 days.

Red Onion Relish

Makes 2 cups (500 mL)

This sweet savory relish is a family favorite. Try it on your favorite taco.

1 cup	red wine vinegar	250 mL
¼ cup	vegetable oil	60 mL
¼ cup	granulated sugar	60 mL
2	red onions, diced	2

1. In a large bowl, whisk together vinegar, oil and sugar. Add red onions and toss until well coated. Transfer to an airtight container and refrigerate, stirring occasionally, for 1 hour or for up to 2 days.

Chile con Queso

Makes 3½ cups (875 mL)

Chile con Queso must have a balance of good texture and taste. It has to be smooth and creamy yet thick enough to cling to a taco or chip. This combination of cheeses ensures a good consistency and blends fresh chile and tomato flavors throughout.

2 cups	shredded Cheddar cheese	500 mL
1 cup	shredded Monterey Jack cheese	250 mL
1½ tsp	cornstarch	7 mL
¾ cup	chicken broth	175 mL
¾ cup	chopped roasted New Mexico or Anaheim green chile peppers (see page 250)	175 mL
1	tomato, seeded and diced	1
12 oz	pasteurized prepared cheese product, such as Velveeta, cut into cubes	375 g

1. In a large bowl, combine Cheddar and Monterey Jack cheeses with cornstarch. Mix well until cheese is well coated.

2. In a large pot, heat broth over medium-high heat. Sauté chiles and tomato until tomato is soft, 4 to 6 minutes. Reduce heat to medium-low and stir in shredded cheese mixture. Add processed cheese, a few cubes at a time, stirring until smooth. Serve immediately or let cool completely at room temperature. Transfer to an airtight container and refrigerate for up to 4 days. To reheat, place in a microwave-safe bowl and microwave on Medium for 30 seconds. Repeat until queso is completely melted.

Guacamole

A good guacamole has to have balance in flavor. The avocados, fresh vegetables and chile blend well with the flavors of the citrusy juices.

6	avocados, mashed	6
1	tomato, seeded and chopped	1
¼ cup	minced onion	60 mL
1	large jalapeño, diced	1
2	green onions, green parts only, chopped	2
2 tbsp	freshly squeezed lime juice	30 mL
	Kosher or sea salt	
	Minced fresh cilantro	

1. In a large bowl, gently combine avocados, tomato, onion, jalapeño and green onions. Add lime juice and mix well. Add salt and cilantro to taste. Serve immediately or transfer to an airtight container and refrigerate, stirring occasionally, for 30 minutes or for up to 2 hours.

Creamy Wasabi Sauce

This sauce has an indescribable spicy flavor. This version of Japanese horseradish is perfect for fish tacos.

Tip

This might seem like a lot of wasabi sauce but it is much milder than wasabi paste, which is more concentrated. Wasabi sauce is a combination of water, soybean oil and a root blend of wasabi and horseradish. Look for it in the deli section of your supermarket.

| ¾ cup | wasabi sauce (see Tip, left) | 175 mL |
| ⅓ cup | sour cream | 75 mL |

1. In a medium bowl, combine wasabi sauce and sour cream. Transfer to an airtight container and refrigerate for 1 hour or for up to 2 days.

Apple Chipotle Sauce

This sauce has a rich smoky sweet flavor and is best served warm. I like to serve it on grilled pork tacos.

- Blender or food processor

2 tbsp	butter	30 mL
2	Golden Delicious apples, peeled and diced	2
2 tsp	puréed chipotle chile peppers in adobo sauce	10 mL
1 tbsp	liquid honey	15 mL
1 tsp	brandy	5 mL

1. In a saucepan, melt butter over medium heat. Add apples, chile, honey, brandy and ¼ cup (60 mL) water and bring to a simmer. Reduce heat and simmer until apples are soft, 6 to 8 minutes. Let mixture cool slightly.

2. In a blender, blend apple mixture until smooth. Serve immediately or let cool completely and transfer to an airtight container or squeeze bottle. Refrigerate for 1 hour or for up to 4 days.

Fresh Red Chile Sauce

Anaheim or New Mexico green chiles turn red on the vine in late August. If you are lucky enough to get your hands on them, you have got to try this sauce. It is an entirely different flavor than that of the dried red chile. Use it as an enchilada sauce or a warm dipping sauce for tacos.

- Blender or food processor

6	fresh New Mexico or Anaheim red chile peppers	6
¼ cup	olive oil	60 mL
4	cloves garlic, minced	4
	Kosher salt	

1. In a large pot, cover chiles with water and bring to a boil over medium-high heat. Reduce heat and boil gently until chiles are soft, 15 to 20 minutes. Transfer to a cutting board. Remove stem and seeds.

2. In a blender, pulse chiles until smooth. Chile should be a thick, pourable consistency. Add water if chile is too thick and blend.

3. In a large skillet, heat oil and garlic over medium heat. Sauté red chile mixture until sauce is heated through, 8 to 10 minutes. Season with salt to taste. Let cool. Serve immediately or transfer to an airtight container and refrigerate, stirring occasionally, for up to 2 days or freeze for up to 4 months.

New Mexico Red Chile Sauce

**Makes 2 cups
(500 mL)**

*This authentic sauce
is traditional in the
Southwest. Made from
dried red chiles, it is a
time-consuming process
but worth the effort.*

• Blender or food processor

6	dried New Mexico red chile peppers, stems removed	6
6 tbsp	vegetable oil, divided	90 mL
4	cloves garlic, minced	4
2 tbsp	all-purpose flour	30 mL
	Kosher salt and freshly ground black pepper	

1. Place chiles in a bowl and cover with 1 quart (1 L) of water. Refrigerate overnight. This will soften the chiles.

2. Drain soaking liquid from chiles, reserving liquid. In a blender, purée chiles with 1½ cups (375 mL) reserved liquid until smooth. Purée should be thick but pourable. Add additional soaking liquid, if needed. Press chile purée through a fine-mesh sieve or a strainer, discarding skin and seeds.

3. In a large skillet, heat 2 tbsp (30 mL) of the oil over medium heat. Add chile purée and garlic. Bring to a gentle boil. Reduce heat to low and simmer, stirring occasionally, until flavors are well blended, 8 to 10 minutes. Set aside.

4. In a small saucepan, heat remaining ¼ cup (60 mL) of oil over medium heat. Gradually stir in flour, creating a roux (a thick paste). Remove from heat.

5. Increase heat to medium. Gradually stir roux into chile sauce. Reduce heat and simmer, stirring, until thick and smooth, 6 to 8 minutes. Serve immediately or let cool to room temperature. Transfer to an airtight container and refrigerate for up to 2 days.

New Mexico Green Chile Sauce

**Makes 2 cups
(500 mL)**

*This smooth spicy
sauce highlights fresh
green chile peppers. It
is good for dipping and
smothering the best
tacos.*

1	tomato, seeded and diced	1
1½ cups	chopped roasted New Mexico or Anaheim green chile peppers (see page 250)	375 mL
2	cloves garlic, minced	2
1 cup	chicken broth	250 mL
2 tbsp	olive oil	30 mL
¼ cup	all-purpose flour	60 mL

1. In a large skillet, combine tomato, chile, garlic and broth and bring to a boil over medium-high heat. Reduce heat and bring to a gentle boil, until vegetables are tender, 6 to 8 minutes.

2. In a small saucepan, heat oil over medium heat. Gradually stir in flour, creating a roux (a thick paste). Remove from heat.

3. Gradually stir roux into chile sauce over medium heat, whisking until smooth and thick, 6 to 8 minutes. Serve immediately or let cool to room temperature. Transfer to an airtight container and refrigerate for up to 2 days.

Poblano Sauce

**Makes 1 cup
(250 mL)**

*Poblano chiles have a
milder, earthier flavor
than most green chiles
and make an exquisite
creamy chile sauce.*

• Blender or food processor

2	roasted poblano chile peppers (see page 250)	2
3	cloves garlic, minced	3
¼ cup	olive oil	60 mL
¼ cup	mayonnaise	60 mL
¼ cup	minced fresh cilantro	60 mL
	Salt and freshly ground black pepper	

1. In a blender, pulse chiles, garlic, oil, 1 tbsp (15 mL) water, mayonnaise and cilantro until smooth. Transfer to an airtight container or squeeze bottle and refrigerate, stirring occasionally, for 1 hour or for up to 2 days.

Creamy Garlic Spread

**Makes 1 cup
(250 mL)**

*Roasted garlic folded into
a smooth, buttery rich
spread is heavenly. I like
to serve it on fresh flour
tortillas. Be adventurous
and try it on beef or fish
tacos.*

• Preheat 400°F (200°C) oven

1	head garlic	1
1 tbsp	olive oil	15 mL
8 oz	whipped cream cheese	250 g
1 tbsp	chopped chives	15 mL
1 tbsp	minced roasted jalapeño (see page 250)	15 mL
	Kosher salt	

1. Remove papery skin from garlic head. Cut top off garlic bulb, exposing garlic cloves.

2. Place bulb in center of large piece of foil. Drizzle with oil and wrap to enclose, sealing edges tightly. Roast in preheated oven for 35 to 40 minutes or until fragrant and soft.

3. Unwrap garlic. Gently remove garlic cloves. Mash 5 cloves with a fork, creating a paste. Reserve remaining garlic for another recipe.

4. In a medium bowl, combine paste, cream cheese, chives and jalapeño. Season with salt to taste. Taste and add more garlic cloves, if desired. Transfer to an airtight container and refrigerate for 1 hour or for up to 4 days.

Basic Taco Cream Sauce

¾ cup	mayonnaise	175 mL
½ cup	plain yogurt	125 mL
	Juice of 1 lime	

This is a basic tasty cream sauce typically served on fish tacos in various parts of Baja, Mexico. I like to drizzle it on top of my chicken and fish tacos. Add the spices that you prefer to customize it for your taste (see Variations, below).

1. In a medium bowl, combine mayonnaise and yogurt. Add lime juice and whisk until smooth. Transfer to an airtight container or squeeze bottle. Refrigerate, stirring occasionally, for 1 hour or for up to 4 days.

Variations
Add any or all of the following: 2 garlic cloves, minced; 1 tsp (5 mL) chile powder; or ½ tsp (2 mL) each cumin, hot pepper flakes or fresh cilantro. Season with salt to taste.

Lemon Jalapeño Sauce

This sauce is light and citrusy with just a little spicy flavor. It is perfectly pleasing on fish or veggie tacos.

- Blender or food processor

¾ cup	mayonnaise	175 mL
½ cup	plain yogurt	125 mL
2	roasted jalapeños (see page 250)	2
1 tsp	grated lemon zest	5 mL
	Juice of 1 lemon	

1. In a blender, pulse mayonnaise, yogurt, jalapeños, lemon zest and lemon juice until smooth. Transfer to an airtight container or squeeze bottle. Refrigerate, stirring occasionally, for 1 hour or for up to 4 days.

Jalapeño Cream Sauce

Makes 1¼ cups (300 mL)

Hot and spicy condiments crown tacos with extra flavor. This combination is no exception, with roasted peppers and cream.

• Blender or food processor

¾ cup	mayonnaise	175 mL
½ cup	plain yogurt	125 mL
3	roasted jalapeños (see page 250)	3
1 tbsp	minced fresh cilantro	15 mL
	Salt and freshly ground black pepper	

1. In a blender, pulse mayonnaise, yogurt, jalapeños and cilantro until smooth. Season with salt and pepper to taste. Transfer to an airtight container or squeeze bottle. Refrigerate, stirring occasionally, for 1 hour or for up to 4 days.

Habanero Cream Sauce

Makes 1 cup (250 mL)

Now we are talking hot! The habanero chile is one of the hottest in the world. I like the flavor but use it sparingly. The yogurt tones the heat down a bit.

• Blender or food processor

¾ cup	mayonnaise	175 mL
½ cup	plain yogurt	125 mL
1	roasted habanero chile pepper (see page 250)	1
1 tbsp	minced flat-leaf parsley	15 mL
	Salt and freshly ground black pepper	

1. In a blender, pulse mayonnaise, yogurt, 1 tsp (5 mL) habanero and parsley until smooth. Taste for level of heat desired. Season with salt and pepper to taste. Transfer to an airtight container or squeeze bottle. Refrigerate for 1 hour or for up to 4 days.

Spicy Mushroom Sauce

This rich, buttery sauce is full of mushrooms and will make any beefy taco enticing. Spiked with chile, it is a savory condiment.

1 tbsp	butter	15 mL
1 tbsp	olive oil	15 mL
1½ cups	chopped mushrooms	375 mL
¼ cup	red wine	60 mL
1 tsp	hot pepper flakes	5 mL

1. In a saucepan, heat oil and butter over medium heat. Add mushrooms, wine and hot pepper flakes. Reduce heat medium-low. Cover and simmer, stirring occasionally, until mushrooms are soft, 6 to 8 minutes. Serve warm immediately or let cool completely and transfer to an airtight container. Refrigerate for up to 2 days.

Fiesta Taco Sauce

Makes 3½ cups (875 mL)

I love to drench my rolled tacos in this spicy tomato sauce. It is a unique balance of flavors, accented with Mexican oregano. Hot pepper flakes add heat while the onion adds texture and taste.

Tips

Mexican oregano is dried but sometimes it comes with big pieces that need to be crushed or minced.

This taco sauce has a thinner consistency than most. For a thicker sauce, add less water.

* **Blender or food processor**

1¾ cups	tomato sauce	425 mL
1	onion, chopped	1
1 tbsp	crushed Mexican oregano (see Tips, left)	15 mL
1 tbsp	minced garlic	15 mL
1	can (28 oz/796 mL) crushed or diced tomatoes	1
2 tbsp	hot pepper flakes	30 mL
1 tbsp	kosher salt	15 mL

1. In a large bowl, combine tomato sauce, onion, oregano, garlic and tomatoes. Add hot pepper flakes and salt.

2. In a blender, in batches, pulse tomato mixture until smooth. Pour into a large bowl and add up to 1½ cups (375 mL) of water depending on the consistency you desire (see Tips, left). Mix well. Repeat until all tomato mixture has been blended with water. Transfer sauce to a large airtight container. Cover and refrigerate, stirring occasionally, for 1 hour or for up to 4 days.

Spicy Asian Sauce

**Makes 1½ cups
(375 mL)**

I add this sauce to meat, chicken and fish fillings for my tacos. I also toss it with fresh produce, such as cabbage and lettuce. It is a spicy sauce full of Asian flavors with a little chile for some kick.

¾ cup	granulated sugar	175 mL
2 tbsp	cornstarch	30 mL
½ cup	soy sauce	125 mL
⅓ cup	red wine vinegar	75 mL
1 tbsp	ketchup	15 mL
2 tsp	hot pepper flakes	10 mL

1. In a small bowl, combine sugar and cornstarch.

2. In a saucepan, combine ⅔ cup (150 mL) water, soy sauce, vinegar, ketchup and hot pepper flakes. Add sugar mixture and mix well. Bring to a boil over medium-high heat. Reduce heat and boil gently, stirring, until sauce thickens, 4 to 6 minutes. Let sauce cool. Serve immediately or transfer to an airtight container or squeeze bottle and refrigerate, stirring occasionally, for up to 4 days.

Cilantro Chile Sauce

**Makes 2 cups
(500 mL)**

Fresh herbs and spicy chile blend well to create a sassy sauce. Avocado adds a creamy texture you will enjoy.

Tip
Cilantro should be soaked and rinsed in water several times to clean before using to avoid gritty texture. Pat dry on paper towels.

• Blender or food processor

2 cups	whole leaves lightly packed fresh cilantro (see Tip, left)	500 mL
1 cup	chopped roasted New Mexico or Anaheim green chile peppers (see page 250)	250 mL
½ cup	olive oil (approx.)	125 mL
2	cloves garlic, minced	2
1	avocado, cubed	1
	Juice of 2 limes (approx.)	
	Kosher salt and freshly ground black pepper	

1. In a blender, pulse cilantro, chiles, oil, garlic, avocado and lime juice until smooth. If mixture is too thick, add 1 tbsp (15 mL) olive oil and 1 tbsp (15 mL) fresh lime juice. Season with salt and pepper to taste. Serve immediately or transfer to an airtight container or squeeze bottle and refrigerate, stirring occasionally, for up to 4 days.

Chipotle Ranch Sauce

Ranch dressing has a salty savory flavor that works well with the smoky chile flavor of chipotle.

Variation

For added heat, add 1 tsp (5 mL) hot pepper flakes.

1½ cups	ranch salad dressing	375 mL
2 tsp	puréed chipotle chile pepper in adobo sauce	10 mL

1. In a large bowl, whisk together ranch dressing and chile. Serve immediately or transfer to an airtight container or squeeze bottle and refrigerate, stirring occasionally, for up to 4 days.

Spicy Ranch Sauce

Savory herb flavors get a kick from the spicy taste of fresh green chiles.

- Blender or food processor

1½ cups	ranch salad dressing	375 mL
½ cup	chopped roasted New Mexico or Anaheim green chile peppers (see page 250)	125 mL

1. In a blender, blend dressing and chiles until smooth. Serve immediately or transfer to an airtight container or squeeze bottle and refrigerate, stirring occasionally, for up to 4 days.

Cajun Sauce

Cajun seasoning is made up of three different chile flavors, adding a savory spicy taste to this creamy sauce.

• Blender or food processor

½ cup	plain yogurt	125 mL
½ cup	mayonnaise	125 mL
1 tsp	Cajun or Creole seasoning	5 mL

1. In a blender, pulse yogurt, mayonnaise and seasoning until smooth and well blended. Serve immediately or transfer to an airtight container or squeeze bottle and refrigerate, stirring occasionally, for up to 4 days.

Chile Cream Sauce

Rich thick creamier sauces leave a lasting impression with me. Spiked with green chile, this cream sauce is heavenly on any taco.

• Blender or food processor

½ cup	mayonnaise	125 mL
⅓ cup	plain yogurt	75 mL
¼ cup	small-curd cottage cheese	60 mL
¼ cup	chopped roasted New Mexico or Anaheim green chile pepper (see page 250)	60 mL

1. In a blender, pulse mayonnaise, yogurt, cottage cheese and chile until smooth and well blended. Serve immediately or transfer to an airtight container or squeeze bottle and refrigerate, stirring occasionally, for up to 4 days.

Chile Basil Sauce

The rich taste of fresh basil imparts intense flavor to this cream sauce. The blend of garlic and fresh herbs makes this a delectable condiment.

- Blender or food processor

¾ cup	mayonnaise	175 mL
½ cup	plain yogurt	125 mL
1 cup	chopped fresh basil	250 mL
2	roasted jalapeños (see page 250)	2
1	clove garlic, minced	1
	Salt and freshly ground black pepper	

1. In a blender, pulse mayonnaise, yogurt, basil, jalapeño and garlic until smooth and well blended. Season with salt and pepper to taste. Serve immediately or transfer to an airtight container or squeeze bottle and refrigerate, stirring occasionally, for up to 4 days.

Chimichurri Sauce

I could eat this sauce by the spoonful! Its fresh herb combination is soothing and refreshing. It is a delicate balance of cilantro, fresh herbs, garlic, lime and olive oil. Delicious!

Tips

Cilantro should be soaked and rinsed in water several times to clean before using to avoid gritty texture. Pat dry on paper towels.

I prefer kosher or sea salt because it has a lighter, cleaner flavor.

- Blender or food processor

2 cups	chopped fresh cilantro (see Tips, left)	500 mL
1½ cups	chopped flat-leaf parsley	375 mL
3	green onions, ends removed, green parts only, chopped	3
3	cloves garlic, minced	3
½ cup	olive oil	125 mL
	Juice of 2 limes	
	Kosher salt and freshly ground black pepper	

1. In a blender, pulse cilantro, parsley, green onions, garlic, oil and lime juice until smooth and well blended. Season with salt and pepper to taste. Serve immediately at room temperature or transfer to an airtight container and refrigerate, stirring occasionally, for 1 hour or for up to 24 hours. Bring to room temperature before serving.

Hot Pineapple Sauce

Makes 1 cup (250 mL)

Habanero peppers are more about heat than flavor. Just a pinch will get attention in this sweet, fruity sauce. It is perfect for a grilled shrimp or chicken taco, adding a sweet savory finish.

• Blender or food processor

1 cup	drained pineapple chunks	250 mL
½ cup	mango chunks	125 mL
1	roasted habanero chile pepper, diced (see page 250)	1
	Kosher salt	

1. In a blender, pulse pineapple, mango and 1 tsp (5 mL) of the habanero until smooth. Taste for level of heat desired. Add more chile pepper, if needed. Season with salt and pulse until well blended. Serve immediately or transfer to an airtight container and refrigerate, stirring occasionally, for 1 hour or for up to 24 hours.

Spicy BBQ Sauce

Makes 1 cup (250 mL)

OK, this is truly a "quickie"! I always keep the three items in this recipe in the pantry. Just grab your favorite barbecue sauce and spice it up. Perfect for a grilled beef, chicken or pork taco.

Tip
There are some wonderful barbecue sauces on the market. Select one that is medium in flavor without any extra flavorings like mesquite or hickory. Select a mild barbecue sauce that you enjoy.

1 tbsp	olive oil	15 mL
1 cup	barbecue sauce (see Tip, left)	250 mL
2 tsp	puréed chipotle chile peppers in adobo sauce	10 mL

1. In a small saucepan, heat oil over medium-low heat. Add barbecue sauce and chiles and cook, stirring, until sauce is heated through, 6 to 8 minutes.

Ancho Bourbon Sauce

Makes 1 cup (250 mL)

This savory and spicy sauce is exquisite on a beefy taco. The buttery, beefy flavors are laced with chile and crowned with bourbon.

Tip

Ancho chile powder has a sweet fruity flavor that is mildly hot.

3 tbsp	butter, divided	45 mL
2 tbsp	olive oil	30 mL
¼ cup	minced onion	60 mL
1 tbsp	ancho chile powder (see Tip, left)	15 mL
1 tsp	ground cumin	5 mL
1	clove garlic, minced	1
¼ cup	bourbon	60 mL
2 tbsp	beef broth	30 mL
	Salt and freshly ground black pepper	

1. In a small saucepan, heat 2 tbsp (30 mL) of the butter and oil. Add onion, chile powder, cumin, garlic, bourbon and beef broth. Bring to a gentle boil, stirring, 6 to 8 minutes. Remove from heat. Add remaining 1 tbsp (15 mL) of butter, stirring to blend. Season with salt and pepper to taste. Let sauce cool slightly. Serve immediately or let cool completely and transfer to an airtight container and refrigerate for up to 4 days.

Quick Mole Sauce

Makes 2 cups (500 mL)

There are a lot of variations of mole sauce throughout Mexico. My version is savory-sweet and easy to make. Enjoy it on chicken and beef tacos.

Tips

Add a pinch of cinnamon and ½ tsp (5 mL) granulated sugar for a sweeter version.

Top with toasted sesame seeds.

2 cups	red enchilada sauce	500 mL
1 tsp	hot pepper flakes	5 mL
1 tsp	dried oregano	5 mL
1 tsp	ground cumin	5 mL
1 tsp	garlic powder	5 mL
1 tsp	onion powder	5 mL
1½ oz	semisweet chocolate, chopped into small pieces	45 g

1. In a saucepan, heat sauce over medium heat. Add hot pepper flakes, oregano, cumin, garlic powder and onion powder, stirring, until well blended, 3 to 5 minutes. Reduce heat to low and add chocolate. Stir until chocolate is melted. Remove from heat.

Jalapeño Mustard

I like yellow mustard just the way it is most of the time. But the pickled jalapeños give it a tangy vinegar flavor and a little heat, which I love!

| 1 cup | prepared yellow mustard | 250 mL |
| ½ cup | minced drained pickled jalapeños | 125 mL |

1. In a small bowl, combine mustard and jalapeños. Serve immediately or transfer to an airtight container and refrigerate for up to 3 days.

Honey Mustard Glaze

This is a rich glaze with a little zing to it. It is delicious on pork and chicken tacos.

4 tbsp	butter	60 mL
½ cup	grated onion	125 mL
½ cup	prepared yellow mustard	125 mL
⅓ cup	packed brown sugar	75 mL
½ tsp	cayenne pepper	2 mL

1. In a skillet, heat butter over medium heat until bubbling. Sauté onion until soft, 4 to 6 minutes. Add mustard, brown sugar and cayenne and simmer, stirring, about 8 minutes. Let cool to room temperature. Serve immediately or transfer to an airtight container and refrigerate for up to 4 days.

Spicy Mayonnaise

**Makes 1 cup
(250 mL)**

1 cup	mayonnaise	250 mL
2 tsp	freshly squeezed lemon juice	10 mL
2 tsp	minced chipotle chile pepper in adobo sauce	10 mL

I love to whip up a spicy mayo. It is the perfect spread for tortillas and adds flavor to taco fillings. In the Variations (below) I offer two different spreads I enjoy. As well as the chipotle peppers in the original recipe that add a smoky flavor, you can also use habanero pepper which adds heat or jalapeño and lime which add a zesty citrus taste.

1. In a small bowl, combine mayonnaise, lemon juice and chiles. Transfer sauce to a large airtight container. Cover and refrigerate for 1 hour or for up to 4 days.

Variations

Substitute 1 tsp (5 mL) minced fresh habanero chile pepper for the chipotle.

Add 1 tbsp (15 mL) freshly squeezed lime juice and a pinch of dried Mexican oregano.

Dessert Tacos

Banana-Caramel Soft Tacos

Crispy light shells filled with a warm banana caramel filling leaves a lasting memory after dinner. You will enjoy this simple to make dessert.

¼ cup	butter	60 mL
½ cup	packed brown sugar	125 mL
1 tbsp	half-and-half (10%) cream	15 mL
3	bananas, sliced ¼ inch (0.5 cm) thick	3
4	flour taco shells (page 14)	4
4	scoops vanilla ice cream	4

1. In a large skillet, heat butter over medium heat. Add brown sugar and bring to a boil, stirring to dissolve sugar. Reduce heat and simmer, stirring, for 3 minutes. Reduce heat to low and gradually stir in cream. Simmer, stirring, until mixture is slightly thickened, 2 to 3 minutes. Remove from heat. Gently fold in bananas.

2. Place shells on individual plates. Divide banana mixture equally among shells. Garnish each plate with a scoop of ice cream.

Banana Cream Tacos

Makes 4 tacos

This dessert is a snap to make. You will love the yummy rich cream in this delicious crispy shell.

Tip
For a lighter, flakier shell, try the fried shell (see Variation, page 335).

- Blender or electric mixer
- Pastry bag and tip

1 cup	whipped nondairy topping	250 mL
1 cup	half-and-half (10%) cream	250 mL
1	package (4-serving size) instant banana cream pudding mix	1
1 tbsp	milk, optional	15 mL
4	rolled flour tortilla dessert shells (page 335) (see Tip, left)	4
2	bananas, sliced ¼ inch (0.5 cm) thick	2
¼ cup	confectioner's (icing) sugar	60 mL

1. In blender or with an electric mixer, combine whipped topping and cream until blended. Gradually add pudding mix and blend until smooth. If mixture is too thick, add 1 tbsp (15 mL) milk for desired consistency.

2. Transfer filling to pastry bag. Pipe filling evenly into each shell. Place shells on individual plates and garnish with banana slices. Dust with confectioner's sugar.

Rolled Dessert Shells

Tortillas are so versatile. Baked or deep-fried, I love creating dessert tacos with these fun shells.

Makes 4 tortillas

- Preheat oven to 400°F (200°C)
- Four 8- by 6-inch (20 by 15 cm) pieces of heavy-duty foil

| 4 | 6-inch (15 cm) flour or corn tortillas (see Tips, below) | 4 |
| | Vegetable cooking spray | |

1. To create a foil mold, roll each piece of foil into a cylinder 8 inches (20 cm) long and about $\frac{3}{4}$ inch (2 cm) in diameter (about the size of a nickel).

2. Lightly coat tortillas with cooking spray on both sides. Place tortillas, 2 at a time, in a small plastic bag and microwave on High for 15 seconds. Tortillas should be moist and pliable, but not too hot to handle. Remove from plastic bag. Place foil cylinder at one end of the tortilla. Gently roll tortilla around foil cylinder and secure with a toothpick (see Tips, below). Repeat with remaining tortillas and place on a baking sheet in preheated oven immediately.

3. Bake until tortilla is crispy and light golden brown, 12 to 15 minutes. Repeat with remaining tortillas. Transfer to a platter. Let cool slightly. Gently remove toothpicks and foil.

Tips

It can be very difficult to find 6-inch (15 cm) flour tortillas, unless you make them yourself. When I am pressed for time, I buy high-quality 8-inch (20 cm) flour tortillas and trim them to a 6-inch (15 cm) size. An 8-inch (20 cm) tortilla is too large for the dessert tacos.

When cutting and rolling the foil for the mold, make sure it is longer than your tortillas are wide. You want some foil to stick out both ends of the rolled-up tortilla.

Variations

For a crispy flakier flour shell, fill a deep-fryer, deep heavy pot or deep skillet with 3 inches (7.5 cm) of oil and heat to 350°F (180°C). Follow Steps 1 and 2. Then, using tongs, gently place 3 to 4 rolls at a time in the hot oil and deep-fry, turning once, until golden brown and crispy, 2 to 3 minutes. Drain on paper towels. Carefully remove the toothpick and foil.

Rolled Taquito Shells: For smaller taquitos, roll the foil to a cylinder $\frac{1}{2}$ inch (1 cm) in diameter.

Flan Cupitas with Fresh Berries

Cupita is Mexican slang for small corn or flour tortillas shaped into a cup form. Traditions of Mexico come through in the flavor of this easy-to-make flan dessert.

1	package (3 oz or 104 g) flan or crème caramel mix	1
4	flour cupitas (page 337)	4
2 cups	milk	500 mL
1 cup	mixed berries, such as blueberries, boysenberries and raspberries	250 mL

1. Sprinkle caramel sauce from flan mix equally in bottom of each cupita.

2. In a saucepan, heat milk over medium heat. Add flan mix, stirring constantly, and bring to a boil. Remove from heat and pour slowly over caramel mix in each cupita.

3. Refrigerate for at least 1 hour until set or for up to 4 hours. Before serving, top with berries.

Lemon Cream Cupitas

This lemony delight is quick to whip up. I like to garnish it with fresh fruit for a delectable treat.

• Blender or electric mixer

1 cup	whipped nondairy topping	250 mL
1 cup	sour cream	250 mL
	Grated zest of 1 lemon	
1 tbsp	milk, optional	15 mL
1	package (4-serving size) instant lemon pudding mix	1
4	flour cupitas (page 337)	4
1 cup	raspberries	250 mL

1. In blender or with an electric mixer, combine whipped topping, sour cream and lemon zest until blended. Gradually add pudding mix and blend until smooth. If mixture is too thick, add 1 tbsp (15 mL) milk for desired consistency.

2. To build cupitas, divide cream filling equally among cupitas. Refrigerate for at least 1 hour until set or for up to 4 hours. Before serving, garnish with raspberries.

Cupitas

Small tortillas make the perfect shell for fruit and creamy fillings.
These little cups are quick to make and delicious.

Makes 4 cupitas

- Preheat oven to 400°F (200°C)
- 4 deep ovenproof cereal bowls

| 4 | 6-inch (15 cm) flour or corn tortillas (see Tip, below) | 4 |
| | Vegetable cooking spray | |

1. Lightly coat tortillas with cooking spray on both sides. Place tortillas, 2 at a time, in a small plastic bag and microwave on High for 15 seconds. Tortillas should be moist and pliable, but not too hot to handle. Remove from plastic bag. Fit each tortilla in deep bowl, carefully using your fingers to fold and mold the edges into a curvy shape. Place bowls in preheated oven immediately.

2. Bake in preheated oven until tortillas are crispy and golden brown, 10 to 12 minutes. Let cool in bowls. Transfer to platter.

Tip

It can be very difficult to find 6-inch (15 cm) flour tortillas, unless you make them yourself. When I am pressed for time, I buy a high-quality 8-inch (20 cm) flour tortilla and trim it to a 6-inch (15 cm) size. An 8-inch (20 cm) tortilla is too large for the dessert tacos.

Apple-Caramel Flautas

Apple pie lovers will enjoy these little flautas. Fruit-filled tortillas, deep-fried and topped with ice cream, are soulfully satisfying.

Variations

Drizzle equally with ½ cup (125 mL) caramel sauce and sprinkle with ½ cup (125 mL) minced pecans as garnish.

For a lighter version, preheat oven to 350°F (180°C). Follow Steps 1 and 2. Then lightly spray each flauta with cooking spray. Place on a greased baking sheet and bake until golden brown, 10 to 12 minutes. Apple filling may ooze out a bit.

- Candy/deep-fry thermometer

3 tbsp	granulated sugar	45 mL
2 tsp	ground cinnamon	10 mL
1 cup	canned chopped apple pie filling	250 mL
4	6- to 8-inch (15 to 20 cm) flour tortillas, micro-warmed (page 15)	4
	Vegetable oil	
4	scoops French vanilla ice cream	4

1. In a shallow bowl, combine sugar and cinnamon. Spread out to a thin layer.

2. Place ¼ cup (60 mL) of the apple filling in a thin line across one end of each tortilla. Gently roll tortilla and secure with a toothpick.

3. Fill a deep-fryer, deep heavy pot or deep skillet with 3 inches (7.5 cm) of oil and heat to 350°F (180°C). Using tongs, gently place flautas, 2 at a time, in the hot oil and deep-fry, turning once, until golden brown and crispy, 2 to 3 minutes. Drain on paper towels, then quickly toss in sugar mixture. Place on individual serving plates with a scoop of ice cream.

Peach Cobbler Tacos

These little sweet treats remind me of the fruity empanadas of Mexico. I use puff pastry here instead of the traditional taco shell to create a flaky crust filled with tangy fruit.

Tip

You'll need half a package (16 to 18 oz/454 to 540 g) puff pastry for this recipe. If your puff pastry isn't pre-rolled, roll it out to about a 12-inch (30 cm) circle or square then cut into circles.

• Preheat oven to 375°F (190°C)

1	sheet puff pastry, thawed (see Tip, left)	1
3 tbsp	butter, softened	45 mL
1 cup	canned sliced peaches, drained	250 mL
3 tbsp	packed brown sugar	45 mL
	Pralines and cream ice cream	

1. On a lightly floured surface, cut puff pastry into four 6-inch (15 cm) circles. Spread butter equally on one half of each pastry circle. Divide peaches and brown sugar equally on top of butter. Fold opposite side of pastry over filling to make a half moon shape and press edges to seal.

2. Place on a baking sheet. Bake in preheated oven until golden brown, 12 to 15 minutes.

3. Transfer each pastry to an individual plate and top with ice cream.

Fresco de Fruit Taco Cupitas

Mexico is famous for adding a hint of chile to unsuspecting dishes. Enjoy this fresh fruit bowl laced with lime and hot pepper flakes.

2 cups	sliced strawberries	500 mL
1 cup	diced pineapple	250 mL
1/2 cup	chopped jicama	125 mL
2	kiwis, peeled and cut into chunks	2
	Grated zest and juice of 1 lime	
1/2 tsp	hot pepper flakes	2 mL
4	corn cupitas (page 337)	4
1/4 cup	sweetened shredded coconut	60 mL

1. In a large bowl, combine strawberries, pineapple, jicama, kiwis, lime zest, lime juice and hot pepper flakes. Let stand for 10 minutes to let hot pepper flakes soften and bloom.

2. Divide fruit equally among cupitas. Top with coconut.

Cinnamon Taco Triangles and Strawberry Salsa

This simple pleasure has superb flavor. The sweet cinnamon chips are highlighted with the tangy peppery flavor of the fruit salsa.

• Candy/deep-fry thermometer

2 cups	granulated sugar	500 mL
¼ cup	ground cinnamon	60 mL
4	6- to 8-inch (15 to 20 cm) flour tortillas, each cut into 6 wedges	4
	Vegetable oil	
	Strawberry Salsa (page 308)	

1. In a medium bowl, combine sugar and cinnamon.

2. Fill a deep-fryer, deep heavy pot or deep skillet with 3 inches (7.5 cm) of oil and heat to 350°F (180°C). Using tongs, gently place 4 to 6 tortilla wedges at a time in the hot oil and deep-fry, turning once, until golden brown and crispy, 1 to 2 minutes. Drain on paper towels, then quickly toss in sugar mixture.

3. Arrange chips on a serving platter and serve with a bowl of Strawberry Salsa.

Cinnamon Taco Triangles and Pineapple Salsa

Makes 24 triangles

This is a sweet appetizer your guests will enjoy. Tangy salsa spiked with chile is terrific teamed with sweet chips and creamy cheese.

- Candy/deep-fry thermometer

2 cups	granulated sugar	500 mL
¼ cup	ground cinnamon	60 mL
4	6- to 8-inch (15 to 20 cm) flour tortillas, each cut into 6 wedges	4
	Vegetable oil	
8 oz	whipped cream cheese	250 g
	Sweet Pineapple Salsa (page 309)	

1. In a medium bowl, combine sugar and cinnamon.

2. Fill a deep-fryer, deep heavy pot or deep skillet with 3 inches (7.5 cm) of oil and heat to 350°F (180°C). Using tongs, gently place 4 to 6 tortilla wedges at a time in the hot oil and deep-fry, turning once, until golden brown and crispy, 1 to 2 minutes. Drain on paper towels, then quickly toss in sugar mixture.

3. Spread cream cheese in a shallow serving bowl and top with Sweet Pineapple Salsa.

4. Arrange chips on a serving platter and serve with cream cheese and salsa in a bowl in center.

Blueberry Corn Tacos with Vanilla Ice Cream

Makes 4 tacos

This fruit-filled taco is like an empanada. It is a sweet crispy dessert cooked to perfection.

Tips

For the ready-to-eat cheesecake filling, you can substitute ¼ cup (60 mL) whipped cream cheese mixed with 1 tsp (5 mL) granulated sugar and ½ tsp (2 mL) vanilla extract.

Garnish with ½ cup (125 mL) blueberries divided equally among tacos.

- Candy/deep-fry thermometer

1 cup	granulated sugar	250 mL
2 tbsp	ground cinnamon	30 mL
4	6-inch (15 cm) corn tortillas, micro-warmed (page 15)	4
¼ cup	ready-to-eat cheesecake filling, divided (see Tip, left)	60 mL
½ cup	blueberries	125 mL
4	scoops vanilla ice cream	4

1. In a shallow bowl, combine sugar and cinnamon. Spread out to a thin layer.

2. Spread 1 tbsp (15 mL) of the cheesecake filling on one half of each tortilla. Top with 1 tbsp (15 mL) of blueberries. Fold each tortilla in half and secure with 3 toothpicks around the edges.

3. Fill a deep-fryer, deep heavy pot or deep skillet with 3 inches (7.5 cm) of oil and heat to 350°F (180°C). Using tongs, gently place 2 tacos at a time in the hot oil and deep-fry, turning once, until golden brown and crispy, 1 to 2 minutes. Drain on paper towels, then quickly toss in sugar mixture. Serve tacos on individual plates. Top each with 1 scoop of ice cream.

Kiwi and Strawberry Margarita Taco Cupitas

A sweet and refreshing reminder of Mexico's famous cocktail, this dessert will be a hit. It is full of flavor and color.

3 tbsp	granulated sugar	45 mL
1 tsp	kosher salt	5 mL
1 tbsp	butter, melted	15 mL
4	flour cupitas (page 337)	4
4	scoops lime sorbet	4
3	kiwis, peeled and diced	3
2 cups	sliced strawberries	500 mL

1. On a small plate, combine sugar and salt. Pour butter into another small plate. Dip rim of each cupita in butter then in sugar mixture. Gently tap to get rid of excess sugar.

2. Place one scoop of sorbet in each cupita. Chill in freezer for 1 hour or for up to 4 hours. Just before serving, divide kiwis and strawberries equally among cupitas.

Mini Margarita Cream Cupitas

This little delight is like a taste of margarita pie. Tangy sweet custard fills these little crispy tortilla cups.

• **Preheat oven to 350°F (180°C)**

2	egg yolks	2
1	egg	1
1	can (14 oz or 300 mL) sweetened condensed milk	1
½ cup	freshly squeezed lime juice	125 mL
3	drops green food coloring	3
8	mini flour cupitas (page 344)	8
1	lime, thinly sliced	1

1. In a bowl, whisk together egg yolks and egg. Whisk in condensed milk, lime juice and food coloring until smooth.

2. Place cupitas on a baking sheet. Pour mixture equally into cupita shells. Bake in preheated oven until filling is firm, for 15 minutes. Let cupitas cool. Refrigerate for at least 1 hour until chilled or for up to 2 hours. Garnish with lime twist.

Mini Cupitas

These shells take no time at all to make. Fruit fillings and creamy custards are fabulous in these mini cups.

Makes 8 mini cupitas

- Preheat oven to 400°F (200°C)
- Muffin pan

| 8 | 4-inch (10 cm) flour or corn tortillas (see Tip, below) | 8 |
| | Vegetable cooking spray | |

1. Lightly coat tortillas with cooking spray on both sides. Place tortillas, 2 at a time, in a small plastic bag and microwave on High for 15 seconds. Tortillas should be moist and pliable, but not too hot to handle. Remove from plastic bag. Gently fit each tortilla into a muffin cup, carefully using your fingers to fold and mold the edges into a curvy shape. Place pan in the oven immediately.

2. Bake in preheated oven until golden brown, 10 to 12 minutes. Let cool in pan. Transfer to platter.

Tip

It can be very difficult to find 4-inch (10 cm) flour tortillas, unless you make them yourself. When I am pressed for time, I buy high-quality 8-inch (20 cm) flour tortillas and trim them very carefully into two 4-inch (10 cm) tortillas. An 8-inch (20 cm) tortilla is too large for the dessert tacos.

Decadent Chocolate Taco Chips

Makes 24 chips

My daughter and I like making these for a quick candy treat. Just layer caramel, nuts and chocolate and in minutes, you've created a delicious delight.

Tips

If you are pressed for time, substitute 1 cup (250 mL) semisweet chocolate chips for the 6 oz (175 g) chocolate. Place chips in a microwave-safe bowl and microwave on Medium (50%) for 1 to 1½ minutes, stirring every 30 seconds, or until chocolate is melted.

I have found dipping chocolate, mainly for fresh fruit, usually found in the produce department of your grocery store, works well. It is tasty and easy to work with.

Variations

Substitute ¼ cup (60 mL) roasted salted chopped pistachios for pecans.

- Preheat oven to 400°F (200°C)

4	6- to 8-inch (15 to 20 cm) flour tortillas, cut into 6 wedges	4
	Vegetable cooking spray	
20	soft caramel candy pieces	20
¼ cup	finely chopped pecans	60 mL
6 oz	semisweet chocolate (see Tips, left)	175 g

1. Spray both sides of tortilla wedges lightly with cooking spray and place on a baking sheet. Bake in preheated oven until crisp and golden brown, 8 to 10 minutes.

2. In a small microwave-safe bowl, microwave caramel candies and 1 tsp (5 mL) water on Medium (50%) for 30 seconds. Stir and repeat until candy is melted.

3. Drizzle each chip equally with caramel. Immediately, sprinkle with pecans. Let cool until set, about 20 minutes.

4. In a heavy saucepan, heat chocolate over low heat, stirring frequently, until smooth. Remove pan from heat. Drizzle each chip equally with chocolate. Let cool.

Berry-Almond Flautas

Sweet berries and cream are delicious with a hint of almond flavor. I like deep-fried shells for this taco, which gives a flakier shell.

- Blender or electric mixer
- Pastry bag and tip

1 cup	whole milk	250 mL
1 cup	whipped nondairy topping	250 mL
1	package (4-serving size) instant vanilla pudding mix	1
1 tsp	almond extract	5 mL
1/3 cup	raspberry jam	75 mL
1 cup	mixed fruit, such as raspberries, boysenberries, strawberries or blueberries	250 mL
8	rolled flour dessert shells, deep-fried (see Variations, page 335)	8
1/4 cup	confectioner's (icing) sugar	60 mL

1. In blender or with an electric mixer, combine milk and whipped topping until blended. Gradually add pudding mix and almond extract and blend until smooth.

2. In a small saucepan, heat jam over medium-low heat. Add berries, stirring until heated through, 6 to 8 minutes. Let cool slightly.

3. Transfer filling to pastry bag. Pipe filling evenly into each shell. Place 2 shells on individual plates, lightly dust with confectioner's sugar and garnish with raspberry sauce.

White Chocolate Raspberry Tacos

Makes 4 tacos

Gourmet ice creams can make a dessert spectacular. Layers of flavor are added with this raspberry ice cream laced with white chocolate.

Variation

Substitute raspberry ripple ice cream for white chocolate raspberry truffle ice cream. Follow Step 1 and top raspberry sauce with ¼ cup (60 mL) chopped white chocolate divided equally among tacos.

Raspberry Sauce

½ cup	raspberry jam	125 mL
¼ cup	fresh raspberries	60 mL
1 tsp	freshly squeezed lemon juice	5 mL
4	flour taco shells (page 14)	4
8	scoops white chocolate raspberry truffle ice cream	8

1. *Raspberry Sauce:* In a small saucepan, heat jam over medium-low heat. Add raspberries and lemon juice, stirring until heated through, 6 to 8 minutes. Let cool slightly.

2. Carefully fill shells with ice cream. Transfer to individual plates. Drizzle with Raspberry Sauce.

Peanut Butter Chocolate Taco Bowl

Makes 4 cupitas

This favorite flavor combination is rich salty and sweet. Top it with salty nuts and enjoy!

Tip
I have also found dipping chocolate, mainly for fresh fruit, usually found in the produce department of your grocery store, works well. It is tasty and easy to work with.

Variations
Drizzle with Mexican Chocolate Sauce (page 354).

6 oz	semisweet chocolate chips (see Tip, left)	175 g
4	flour cupitas (page 337)	4
4	scoops chocolate peanut butter ice cream	4
¼ cup	roasted salted peanuts, preferably Spanish, chopped	60 mL

1. Place chips in a microwave-safe shallow bowl and microwave on Medium (50%) for 1 to 1½ minutes, stirring every 30 seconds, or until chocolate is melted. Dip rim of each cupita bowl in chocolate. Shake off excess chocolate. Let stand until chocolate is set.

2. Place 1 scoop of ice cream in each cupita. Top with nuts.

Cheesecake Sweet Taquitos

These taquitos are creamy, dreamy and easy! Cheesecake lovers will marvel at the simplicity of this dessert.

Tip

For the ready-to-eat cheesecake filling, substitute 1 cup (250 mL) whipped cream cheese mixed with 1 tbsp (15 mL) granulated sugar and ½ tsp (2 mL) vanilla extract.

- Pastry bag and tip

1 cup	ready-to-eat cheesecake filling (see Tip, left)	250 mL
8	rolled taquito shells (see Variations, page 335)	8
	Confectioner's (icing) sugar	

1. Place cheesecake filling in pastry bag. Pipe filling equally into taquito shells. Place taquitos side by side on a serving platter and sprinkle with confectioner's sugar.

Pumpkin Pecan Cheesecake Tacos

This flavor combination makes me yearn for the fall season. This is a wonderful treat full of spices and creamy goodness.

- Pastry bag and tip

1 cup	ready-to-eat cheesecake filling (see Tip, above)	250 mL
3 tbsp	pumpkin pie filling	45 mL
4	rolled flour dessert shells (page 335)	4
½ cup	caramel topping	125 mL
¼ cup	chopped pecans	60 mL

1. In a large bowl, combine cheesecake filling and pumpkin pie filling.

2. Place filling in pastry bag and pipe into shells. Place filled tacos on individual plates and drizzle with caramel topping. Top with pecans.

Simple Caramel Sauce

This recipe is quick and easy. It has a buttery delicious flavor.

Tips

This is a fast cooking process so be sure to have all ingredients ready and near the stove before starting.

A deep pan and long-handled spoon are necessary for safety because mixture will foam up when the butter and cream are added.

- Large, deep, heavy-bottomed saucepan
- Long-handled spoon (see Tips, left)

1 cup	granulated sugar	250 mL
6 tbsp	butter	90 mL
½ cup	heavy or whipping (35%) cream	125 mL

1. In saucepan, combine sugar and 1 tsp (5 mL) water. Once sugar starts to melt, stir vigorously with a wooden, long-handled spoon. Bring to a rolling boil over high heat, stirring vigorously. Boil, without stirring, until all the sugar crystals have melted and turned a dark, caramel color, 6 to 8 minutes. Add butter and whisk until melted, 2 to 3 minutes. Remove from heat.

2. Gradually add cream, whisking to blend well until smooth. Serve immediately or let cool completely. Place in an airtight container and refrigerate for up to 4 days.

Vanilla Cream Tacos with Sweet Pineapple Salsa

This fluffy sweet cream filling is delicious. Accents of pineapple add a tropical flavor.

1 cup	granulated sugar	250 mL
1 tbsp	all-purpose flour	15 mL
1 cup	heavy or whipping (35%) cream	250 mL
1 tsp	vanilla extract	5 mL
4	folded flour tortilla shells (page 14)	4
1 cup	pineapple chunks	250 mL
	Sweet Pineapple Salsa (page 309)	

1. In a large bowl, combine sugar and flour. In a chilled bowl, combine cream and vanilla. Using an electric mixer, beat cream mixture, gradually adding sugar mixture. Beat on High until stiff peaks form.

2. Divide cream equally among taco shells. Gently tuck pineapple chunks into cream in each taco. Serve with a bowl of Sweet Pineapple Salsa.

Peachy Praline Soft Tacos

This reminds me of dessert after a good Sunday dinner. It is a simple stove top version of a fruity cobbler.

Tip

If peaches are out of season, use 2 cups (500 mL) canned sliced peaches, drained.

1 tbsp	butter	15 mL
4	peaches, peeled and diced (see Tip, left)	4
8	flour tortillas, micro-warmed (page 15)	8
1/3 cup	packed brown sugar	75 mL
1 tsp	ground cinnamon	5 mL
1/2 tsp	vanilla extract	2 mL
	Vegetable cooking spray	
1/2 cup	caramel topping	125 mL
1/2 cup	chopped pecans	125 mL

1. In a saucepan, heat butter and peaches over medium heat. Add brown sugar, cinnamon and vanilla. Bring to a gentle boil. Boil for 2 minutes.

2. Using a slotted spoon, fill each tortilla equally with peach mixture, discarding liquid. Fold tortilla in half and secure with 3 toothpicks, securing edges. Lightly coat both sides with cooking spray.

3. In a large skillet over medium heat, grill filled tortillas on each side until golden brown, 3 to 4 minutes per side. Carefully remove toothpicks and serve on individual plates. Drizzle with caramel topping and top with pecans.

Chilled Choco Tacos

Rich, creamy chocolate mousse fills these crispy shells. I like to indulge, so I make sure I have extra creamy filling for dipping. Enjoy!

Tip

Garnish with ½ cup (125 mL) sliced strawberries and ¼ cup (60 mL) slivered almonds.

- Blender or electric mixer
- Pastry bag and tip

1 cup	whipped nondairy topping	250 mL
1 cup	half-and-half (10%) cream	250 mL
1	package (4-serving size) instant chocolate pudding mix	1
1 tbsp	milk, optional	15 mL
4	rolled flour dessert shells (page 335)	4

1. In blender or with an electric mixer, combine topping and cream until blended. Gradually add pudding mix and blend until smooth. If mixture is too thick, add 1 tbsp (15 mL) milk for desired consistency.

2. Place filling in pastry bag. Pipe filling equally into each shell from both ends. Transfer to a serving platter or individual plates. Place any remaining filling in a bowl and serve on the platter for dipping.

Mango-Raspberry Cupitas

Lush tangy mango sorbet topped sweet raspberry sauce highlights these cupitas.

½ cup	raspberry jam	125 mL
1 cup	raspberries	250 mL
1 tbsp	freshly squeezed lemon juice	15 mL
4	scoops mango sorbet	4
4	corn or flour cupitas (page 337)	4
4	fresh mint leaves	4

1. In a small saucepan, heat jam over medium heat until melted. Add raspberries and lemon juice and heat, stirring gently, until hot and bubbling, 3 to 6 minutes.

2. Place 1 scoop of sorbet in each cupita. Top with warm sauce. Garnish with mint leaves.

Lemon Dream Wontons

This little bite of dessert is just enough after a big taco dinner. The tart lemony filling reminds me of sweet lemon meringue pie.

• Candy/deep-fry thermometer

¼ cup	lemon curd	60 mL
12	wonton wrappers	12
	Vegetable oil	
¼ cup	confectioner's (icing) sugar	60 mL

1. Place 1 tsp (5 mL) lemon curd in the center of a wonton wrapper (keep remaining wraps covered with a damp towel while working to prevent drying out). Brush all edges of wrap with water to dampen. Fold into a triangle and seal edges, pressing out any air inside. Repeat with remaining wraps.

2. Fill a deep-fryer, deep heavy pot or deep skillet with 3 inches (7.5 cm) of oil and heat to 350°F (180°C). Using tongs, gently place 3 to 4 wontons at a time in the hot oil and deep-fry, turning once, until golden brown and crispy, 2 to 3 minutes. Drain on paper towels. Transfer to a serving platter and dust with confectioner's sugar.

Sundae Tacos with Mexican Chocolate Sauce

Mexican chocolate traditionally has a hint of cinnamon. Drizzle this rich sauce over a combination of creamy ice creams and crispy flour tortillas.

Tip

I use this Mexican chocolate sauce on a lot of desserts. This sauce can be stored in an airtight container in the refrigerator for up to 5 days.

Variation

Sprinkle ½ cup (125 mL) chopped pecans equally over top.

Mexican Chocolate Sauce

2 tbsp	butter	30 mL
1	can (14 oz or 300 mL) sweetened condensed milk	1
1 cup	semisweet chocolate chips	250 mL
¼ tsp	ground cinnamon	1 mL
4	folded flour taco shells (page 14)	4
4	scoops vanilla ice cream	4
4	scoops coffee ice cream	4

1. *Mexican Chocolate Sauce:* In a small saucepan, melt butter over medium-low heat. Add condensed milk, chocolate chips and cinnamon, stirring constantly, until smooth (see Tip, left).

2. Carefully place 1 scoop of each ice cream in each shell and transfer to individual serving plates. Drizzle with warm sauce.

Ice Cream Bowl with Sweet Taco Triangles

Makes 4 cupitas

This is a fun and easy dessert that makes a great presentation. Choose your favorite ice cream combinations and enjoy!

• Candy/deep-fry thermometer

2 cups	granulated sugar	500 mL
¼ cup	ground cinnamon	60 mL
4	8-inch (20 cm) four tortillas, each cut into 6 wedges	4
	Vegetable oil	
4	scoops dulce de leche ice cream	4
4	scoops French vanilla ice cream	4
4	scoops chocolate ice cream	4
4	flour cupitas (page 337)	4

1. In a medium bowl, combine sugar and cinnamon.

2. Fill a deep-fryer, deep heavy pot or deep skillet with 3 inches (7.5 cm) of oil and heat to 350°F (180°C). Using tongs, gently place 4 to 6 tortilla wedges at a time in the hot oil and deep-fry, turning once, until golden brown and crispy, 1 to 2 minutes. Drain on paper towels, then quickly toss in sugar mixture.

3. Place one scoop of each flavor of ice cream in cupitas. Garnish ice cream scoops with tortilla wedges.

Orange Crème Brûlée Mini Cupitas

This flavor combination is impressive. Enjoy creamy vanilla accented with a mild citrusy sauce.

Variation
Substitute French vanilla ice cream for crème brûlée ice cream.

½ cup	orange marmalade	125 mL
1 tbsp	freshly squeezed lemon juice	15 mL
4	small scoops crème brûlée ice cream	4
4	mini flour cupitas (page 344)	4

1. In a small saucepan, heat marmalade over medium-low heat until melted. Stir in lemon juice.

2. Place 1 scoop of ice cream in each cupita. Drizzle with sauce.

Chocolate Mousse Cupitas

Creamy chocolate crowned with sweet and tart strawberries is unforgettable. Delight in this light creamy dessert.

• Blender or electric mixer

1 cup	whipped nondairy topping	250 mL
1 cup	half-and-half (10%) cream	250 mL
1	package (4-serving size) instant sugar-free chocolate pudding mix	1
1 tbsp	milk, optional	15 mL
4	flour cupitas (page 337)	4
¼ cup	shaved chocolate	60 mL
4	whole strawberries	4

1. In blender or with an electric mixer, combine topping and cream until blended. Slowly add pudding and blend until smooth. If mixture is too thick, add 1 tbsp (15 mL) milk for desired consistency.

2. Divide mousse equally among cupitas. Top with shaved chocolate and garnish with a strawberry.

Cinnamon Taquitos with Dulce de Leche Ice Cream

Makes 4 servings

Cinnamon and caramel make a tantalizing combination. Treat your guests to this sophisticated indulgence.

• Candy/deep-fry thermometer

½ cup	granulated sugar	125 mL
1 tbsp	ground cinnamon	15 mL
8	wonton wrappers	8
	Vegetable oil	
4	scoops dulce de leche or caramel ice cream	4

1. In a medium bowl, combine sugar and cinnamon.

2. Brush one edge of each wonton wrapper with water to dampen. Starting at opposite edge, roll up, pressing seam to seal, and secure with a toothpick.

3. Fill a deep-fryer, deep heavy pot or deep skillet with 3 inches (7.5 cm) of oil and heat to 350°F (180°C). Using tongs, gently place 3 to 4 taquitos at a time in the hot oil and deep-fry, turning once, until golden brown and crispy, 1 to 2 minutes. Drain on paper towels. Roll in sugar mixture.

4. Place ice cream in dessert bowls. Insert 2 taquitos into each scoop.

Creamy Cinnamon Dessert Tacos

Makes 4 tacos

Spices and peppers add a contemporary freshness to this dessert. Sweet berries laced with a peppery accent are heightened by the creamy frozen filling.

Variation

Substitute cinnamon ice cream with 8 scoops of French vanilla, softened and blended with 2 tsp (10 mL) cinnamon. Mix well and refreeze until firm. Rescoop into 8 scoops.

4	flour taco shells (page 14)	4
8	scoops cinnamon ice cream	8
	Strawberry Salsa (page 308)	
4	orange slices	4

1. Carefully fill shells with ice cream. Transfer to individual plates. Top with Strawberry Salsa and garnish with an orange slice.

Cherry Cheesecake Cupitas

Makes 8 mini cupitas

This simple, velvety filling is topped with a tart fruity glaze. This special dessert is an American favorite.

¾ cup	ready-to-eat cheesecake filling, divided (see Tip, page 349)	175 mL
8	mini flour cupitas (page 344)	8
½ cup	cherry pie filling	125 mL

1. Divide cream cheese filling equally among cupitas. Top with pie filling. Refrigerate for at least 1 hour, until chilled, or for up to 4 hours. Transfer to a serving platter.

Fruit and Sweet Cream Nachitos

Makes 24 nachitos

A plate full of sweet cream, crunchy chips and fresh fruit makes an impressive presentation at any gathering. Fun and tasty!

• Preheat oven to 400°F (200°C)

4	6- to 8-inch (15 to 20 cm) flour tortillas, each cut into 6 wedges	4
	Vegetable cooking spray	
12 oz	whipped cream cheese	375 g
3 tbsp	confectioner's (icing) sugar	45 mL
1 tsp	ground cinnamon	5 mL
1 cup	raspberries	250 mL
1 cup	boysenberries or blackberries	250 mL
1 cup	blueberries	250 mL

1. Spray both sides of tortilla wedges lightly with cooking spray and place on a baking sheet. Bake in preheated oven until crisp and golden brown, 8 to 10 minutes. Let cool.

2. In a large bowl, combine cream cheese, confectioner's sugar and cinnamon.

3. Spread cheese mixture equally on each tortilla chip and arrange on a serving platter. Top with berries.

Mandarin Orange Cupitas

Makes 4 cupitas

Ginger and orange team up for a delicious frozen dessert. Whip this up at the last minute, top with coconut and enjoy!

Variation
Substitute 4 scoops of vanilla bean ice cream and top with ¼ cup (60 mL) minced crystallized ginger.

1 cup	canned mandarin orange segments, drained	250 mL
½ cup	sweetened shredded coconut	125 mL
4	scoops ginger ice cream	4
4	corn cupitas (page 337)	4

1. In a medium bowl, combine oranges and coconut. Set aside.

2. Place 1 scoop of ice cream in each cupita. Freeze for at least 1 hour until chilled or for up to 4 hours. Place on serving plates and top with orange mixture.

Pecan Crunch Tacos

*These little tacos remind
me of holiday flavors.
Rich and nutty, they melt
in your mouth!*

• Candy/deep-fry thermometer

¼ cup	butter, softened	60 mL
⅓ cup	packed brown sugar	75 mL
⅓ cup	finely chopped pecans	75 mL
2 tbsp	quick-cooking rolled oats	30 mL
12	wonton wrappers	12
	Vegetable oil	
2 cups	confectioner's (icing) sugar (approx.)	500 mL

1. In a large bowl, mash together butter, brown sugar, pecans and oats until crumbly. Refrigerate until firm but not hard, about 30 minutes.

2. Place filling equally across one edge of each wonton wrap. Brush opposite end with water to dampen. Starting at edge closest to filling, roll up and secure with a toothpick.

3. Fill a deep-fryer, deep heavy pot or deep skillet with 3 inches (7.5 cm) of oil and heat to 350°F (180°C). Using tongs, gently place 3 to 4 wontons at a time in the hot oil and deep-fry, turning once, until golden brown and crispy, 2 to 3 minutes. Drain on paper towel. Roll in confectioner's sugar. (You may not use it all.) Transfer to a serving platter.

Cocktails

Michilada

Pronounced Mee chil ada, *this cool cocktail takes the beer with a twist of lime to the next level. Adding fresh citrus juices to your favorite beer creates a light and refreshing cocktail.*

Tip

There are a variety of Mexican beers on the market, such as Corona, Pacifico, Tecate and Dos Equis just to name a few. They all vary in taste so try them and find your favorites.

- Collins glass

	Cracked ice	
¼ cup	freshly squeezed lime or orange juice	60 mL
1	bottle (12 oz/341 mL) Mexican beer (see Tip, left)	1
1 or 2	lime or orange slices	1 or 2

1. Fill glass half full with cracked ice. Add lime juice. Top with beer. Garnish with floating lime slices and serve. Add remaining beer to the glass as needed.

Mexicola

Cuba libre, from which this drink is derived, meaning "Free Cuba," has become a national favorite. My friends and I like it with tequila rather than the usual rum. It gives it a nice kick and a sharper taste. A twist of lime blends the two flavors.

- Collins glass

	Cracked ice	
1 oz	silver tequila	30 mL
	Cola	
1 tbsp	freshly squeezed lime or orange juice	15 mL
1	lime wedge	1

1. Fill glass three-quarters full with cracked ice. Pour tequila over cracked ice. Top with cola and a twist of lime.

Prioska

The bittersweet taste of a Brazilian cocktail is a perfect match for any taco entrée or appetizer. This cocktail is a cousin to the Latin Caipirinha, which is made with rum. It is known as a Caipiroska. I call my version Prioska. It is light and refreshing with a bittersweet taste coming from the rind of the lime and the sugar combination.

Variation

Substitute a splash of cranberry juice for the club soda.

- Rocks highball glass
- Shaker

1 to 2	fresh limes (depending on size), each cut into 4 wedges	1 to 2
2 tsp	superfine sugar	10 mL
1½ oz	vodka	45 mL
2 cups	cracked ice	500 mL
	Club soda	

1. Place 3 lime wedges and sugar in a highball glass and gently mash with a wooden spoon or muddling stick.

2. Pour vodka over mixture.

3. Fill glass to rim with ice. Pour vodka mixture into a shaker. Shake well and strain back into glass. Top with remaining cracked ice and a splash of soda. Garnish with remaining lime wedge. Let cocktail stand for 2 to 3 minutes before serving.

Sangria

Makes 12 cocktails

Sangria is a delicious wine-based punch made with red wine and seasonal fruit. This cocktail will add a Spanish fiesta spirit to any gathering.

• 1 pitcher

1	bottle (750 mL) dry red wine, such as Cabernet Sauvignon, Shiraz, Merlot or Zinfandel	1
1 tbsp	granulated sugar	15 mL
	Juice of 1 orange	
	Juice of 1 lemon	
1	orange, thinly sliced	1
1	lemon, thinly sliced	1
2	peaches, diced	2
1 cup	sparkling water	250 mL
	Ice	

1. In a large pitcher, combine wine, sugar, orange juice and lemon juice. Add orange slices, lemon slices and peach chunks. Refrigerate overnight to ensure flavors infuse. Just before serving, stir in sparkling water. Serve in tall glasses half full of ice.

Summer Sangria Spritzer

Makes 24 cocktails

I enjoy white wine in the summer and this is the perfect fruity spritzer for a hot afternoon or a mid-morning brunch. Serve it in a large glass pitcher or punch bowl.

Tip
Sauvignon Blanc is a good selection for this sangria.

1/3 cup	brandy	75 mL
1/3 cup	peach schnapps	75 mL
2	bottles (each 750 mL) dry white wine (see Tip, left)	2
1 tbsp	granulated sugar	15 mL
1	orange, thinly sliced	1
1	lemon, thinly sliced	1
1	peach, peeled and diced	1
1	bottle (12 oz/375 mL) sparkling water	1

1. In a large pitcher, combine brandy, schnapps, wine and sugar, stirring until sugar is dissolved. Add orange slices, lemon slices and diced peach and refrigerate overnight. Serve in wine goblets with fruit in each one and top each with sparkling water.

Tequila Shots

Shooting tequila is a ritual we cherish in the West but it's not for the faint of heart or the averse to alcohol. A little salt, a shot of tequila and a little lime all add to the mystery. Tequila should not choke you or taste bad. There are some fine tequilas that are just right for sipping or shooting. Select a smooth aged tequila. Here is the popular and historical methodology.

Salt
Tequila shot
Lime wedge

1. Line up salt, tequila shot and lime wedge. Yell, "Uno, dos, tres!" Lick the area between your forefinger and thumb.

2. Pour salt on the wet spot. Lick salt and quickly drink (or shoot) the tequila. Grab your lime wedge and bite into it, squeezing as much juice into your mouth as possible. Enjoy!

Tequila Grand

This tall cool thirst quencher has a balance of flavors from various fruits. It is light and tangy.

• Collins glass

	Cracked ice	
1½ oz	silver tequila	45 mL
½ cup	cranberry cocktail	125 mL
	Orange-flavored liqueur, such as Triple Sec, Cointreau or Grand Marnier	
	Unsweetened pineapple juice	
	Freshly squeezed orange juice	

1. Fill glass half full with cracked ice. Pour tequila and cranberry juice over top. Add a splash of liqueur and stir. Top with a splash each pineapple and orange juice.

Tequila Sunrise

I love serving these for brunch or an early tailgate party on game day. They are smooth and go well with my breakfast tacos. The pomegranate syrup is a sweet natural alternative to the traditional splash of grenadine.

Variation

If you are pressed for time, replace Pomegranate Simple Syrup with 1 tbsp (15 mL) grenadine for a traditional Tequila Sunrise.

• Collins or highball glass

	Cracked ice	
1½ oz	gold tequila	45 mL
6 tbsp	fresh squeezed orange juice	90 mL
1 tbsp	Pomegranate Simple Syrup (see recipe below)	15 mL
1	lime wedge	1

1. Fill glass with cracked ice. Top with tequila and orange juice. Slowly add syrup. Let settle on bottom of glass. Serve with lime wedge.

Pomegranate Simple Syrup
Makes 1½ cups (375 mL)

2 cups	unsweetened pomegranate juice	500 mL
¼ cup	superfine sugar	60 mL
1 tbsp	freshly squeezed lemon juice	15 mL

1. In a small pot, combine pomegranate juice and sugar and bring to a boil over medium heat, stirring, until sugar is dissolved. Add lemon juice. Reduce heat and boil gently until reduced by about one-third and syrupy. Let cool to room temperature. Transfer to an airtight container and refrigerate for up to 5 days.

Chardonnay Margarita

Makes 4 cocktails

This is a luscious frozen cocktail for wine lovers. It is a perfect margarita with a lighter alcohol content and flavor. The lime, orange and wine blend well in this frosty drink.

Tip

A rich full-bodied Chardonnay works well with the recipe, or try a Sauvignon Blanc for a crisp lighter flavor.

- Blender
- Margarita glasses

½ cup	Chardonnay (see Tip, left)	125 mL
6 oz	frozen limeade concentrate	175 mL
½ cup	freshly squeezed orange juice	125 mL
3 cups	cracked ice	750 mL
2	limes, cut into quarters	2
	Kosher salt	
1	orange, sliced into quarters	1

1. In a blender, process wine, limeade and orange juice for 1 minute. Slowly add ice and blend to a slushy consistency.

2. Rub rims of each glass with lime wedge and dust with salt. Shake off any excess salt. Fill each glass with margarita mixture. Garnish with a twisted orange slice.

Margarita Martini

Makes 1 cocktail

According to many, this martini is closer to the original margarita than all the frozen fruity renditions we see today. It is tart, refreshing and potent.

Tip

To make an orange peel twist: Using a slice of orange, remove the center and as much of the white pith as possible, leaving the orange strip of peel. Wrap the peel around a straw. Let set for 6 to 8 minutes. Remove from straw. It will have a loose curly shape.

- Shaker
- Martini glass

	Cracked ice	
1 oz	silver tequila	30 mL
1 oz	orange-flavored liqueur, such as Triple Sec, Cointreau or Grand Marnier	30 mL
2 tbsp	freshly squeezed lime juice	30 mL
1	orange peel twist (see Tip, left)	1

1. Fill a shaker half full with cracked ice. Pour in tequila, liqueur and lime juice. Shake well and strain into a martini glass. Garnish with orange twist.

Chile Rita

I like my drinks with a kick of flavor that reminds me what I am drinking. This combination of chile and tequila laced with a sweet syrup is so delicious. This is my version of a famous margarita served at a local eatery. It is a fruity spicy flavor that is unforgettable.

Tips

Transfer remaining jam mixture to a sealed jar and refrigerate for up to 2 weeks.

Use a high-quality prepared liquid margarita mix with a medium sweet-sour balance.

• Margarita glass

¾ cup	boysenberry or raspberry jam	175 mL
1 tsp	hot pepper flakes	5 mL
2	lime wedges	2
	Kosher salt	
	Cracked ice	
1 oz	silver tequila	30 mL
½ cup	liquid margarita mix (see Tips, left)	125 mL

1. In a small pot, combine jam and hot pepper flakes and heat over medium-low heat, stirring, until jam is melted. Strain through a colander or strainer into a bowl to remove seeds and flakes. Let cool to room temperature.

2. Rub rim of glass with lime and dust with salt. Shake off any excess salt. Fill glass half full of ice. Add tequila and 1 tbsp (15 mL) of jam mixture. Top with margarita mix. Garnish with remaining lime wedge.

Grapefruit Fresco Margarita

Makes 1 cocktail

Grapefruit has that sweet tart taste that blends well with tequila. This margarita is refreshing and full of flavor.

Tip

To save time, buy prepared grapefruit sections found in the produce section of many supermarkets.

- Highball glass
- Shaker

2	lime wedges	2
	Kosher salt	
1 oz	silver tequila	30 mL
1 to 2	grapefruit sections, chopped	1 to 2
	Orange-flavored liqueur, such as Triple Sec, Cointreau or Grand Marnier	
1 tbsp	freshly squeezed grapefruit juice	15 mL
1 tbsp	liquid margarita mix (see Tips, page 368)	15 mL
	Cracked ice	
	Sprig of mint	

1. Rub rim of glass with lime wedge. Dust with salt. Shake off any excess salt.

2. Pour tequila and chopped grapefruit into a shaker and add a splash of orange liqueur. Top with grapefruit juice and margarita mix. Fill shaker half full of ice and shake. Pour into rimmed glass. Garnish with sprig of mint and lime wedge.

Margarita Classico

Frozen margarita is perfectly balanced — not too tart and not too sweet. The combination of beer, tequila and liqueur makes for a smooth frosty margarita.

Tip
For a thicker frozen margarita, reduce light beer to ½ cup (125 mL) and add more ice for desired consistency.

Variations
Green Apple Margarita: Drizzle ½ oz (15 mL) green apple liqueur over each frozen margarita and garnish with a thin slice of Granny Smith apple.

Peach Margarita: Add 2 oz (60 mL) peach schnapps to the margarita mixture and blend. Garnish with fresh chopped peaches.

Mango Margarita: Add ½ cup (125 mL) fresh mango chunks to margarita mixture and blend. Garnish with fresh mango slices.

- Margarita glasses
- Blender

1	lime, cut into 5 wedges	1
	Kosher salt	
¾ cup	frozen limeade concentrate	175 mL
¾ cup	silver tequila	175 mL
1½ oz	orange-flavored liqueur, such as Triple Sec, Cointreau or Grand Marnier	45 mL
¾ cup	light beer	175 mL
5 cups	cracked ice, divided	1.25 L

1. Rub rim of each glass with a lime wedge. Dust with salt. Shake off any excess salt.

2. In blender, blend limeade, tequila, liqueur, beer and 3 cups (750 mL) of the ice until slushy, 2 to 3 minutes. Add more ice, if desired. Pour into each glass and garnish each with a lime wedge.

Pink Cadillac Margarita Punch

Makes 12 cocktails

When I entertain I serve this margarita more than any other. The sweet grenadine takes the tartness away, creating a smooth cocktail you can enjoy all evening.

Tip
Use a high-quality prepared liquid margarita mix with a medium sweet-sour balance.

Variation
Substitute ½ cup (125 mL) cranberry cocktail or pomegranate juice for the grenadine.

- 1 punch bowl
- Highball glasses

1	bottle (1.75 L) margarita mix (see Tip, left)	1
1½ cups	gold tequila	375 mL
⅓ cup	grenadine	75 mL
4 to 5	limes, divided	4 to 5
	Cracked ice	
	Kosher Salt	

1. In a punch or serving bowl, combine margarita mix, tequila and grenadine. Cut 2 of the limes into thin slices and add to mixture. Add lots of cracked ice.

2. Cut the remaining limes into wedges. Rub rim of each glass with a lime wedge and dust with salt. Shake off any excess salt. Fill each glass with ice. Top with punch and garnish with remaining lime wedges.

Pomegranate Margarita

Makes 1 cocktail

Fresh pomegranate juice layered with citrusy orange and lime creates the perfect balance in this special margarita.

- Shaker

2	lime wedges	2
	Kosher salt	
	Cracked ice	
1 oz	silver tequila	30 mL
½ oz	orange-flavored liqueur, such as Triple Sec, Cointreau or Grand Marnier	15 mL
¼ cup	unsweetened pomegranate juice	60 mL
	Club soda	

1. Rub rim of glass with a lime wedge. Dust with salt. Shake off any excess salt.

2. Fill a shaker half full of ice. Add tequila, liqueur and pomegranate juice. Shake for 30 to 45 seconds. Strain into glass. Top with club soda and garnish with remaining lime wedge.

Bloody Mary Bar

Makes 12 cocktails

I have tasted many Bloody Marys and I have loved them all. With so many different ingredients, the options are endless. Create a special little area at your party where guests can go wild and make the perfect Bloody Mary, whatever the flavors may be!

- Blender
- 1 pitcher
- Collins glasses

2 cups	Tomato Table Salsa (page 302) or store-bought	500 mL
1	can (48 oz/1.36 L) tomato juice	1
	Cracked ice	
1¼ cups	vodka	300 mL
2 tbsp	Worcestershire sauce	30 mL
1 tbsp	prepared horseradish	15 mL

1. In a blender, purée salsa until smooth.

2. In a pitcher, combine salsa purée and tomato juice and refrigerate until chilled, for at least 30 minutes or up to 4 hours.

3. Fill a Collins glass half full with cracked ice. Pour in 1 oz (30 mL) of vodka. Top with tomato mixture. Add ½ tsp (2 mL) of the Worcestershire sauce and ¼ tsp (1 mL) of the horseradish into each Bloody Mary. Add garnish as desired (see below).

Bloody Mary Bar

Set out small bowls of any of the following for garnish: whole pickled garlic cloves, hot pepper flakes, cracked black peppercorns, kosher salt, ground cumin, garlic powder, celery sticks, baby dill pickles, yellow chile peppers, jalapeños, snow peas, sugar snap peas, chunks of cucumber, chopped green onions, Greek olives, chopped roasted New Mexico or Anahiem green chile (page 250), pickled okra, minced cilantro and a variety of hot sauces, such as Fiesta Taco Sauce (page 324), Salsa Verde (page 300), Cilantro and Chile Salsa (page 305).

Cowboy Coffee with Kahlúa Cream

This coffee toddy is rich with buttery flavor. It is a wonderful addition to any brunch or perfect for an after-dinner drink.

¾ cup	prepared medium blend coffee	250 mL
2 oz	butterscotch schnapps	60 mL
2 tbsp	whipped cream	30 mL
	Coffee-flavored liqueur	

1. Pour hot coffee into a coffee mug. Add schnapps and stir. Top with whipped cream and drizzle with liqueur.

Dulce de Leche Martini

*This is a seductively sweet caramel cocktail inspired by the dulce de leche (*Dool-say deh Le-chay*) candies you will find in Mexico. It makes a wonderful after-dinner drink, especially after feasting on tacos!*

Tip
Test the different caramel sauces on the market. I like one flavored with a hint of salt.

- Shaker
- Martini glass

	Cracked ice	
½ oz	rum	15 mL
2 tbsp	heavy or whipping (35%) cream	30 mL
2 tbsp	caramel sauce (See Tip, left)	30 mL

1. Fill a shaker half full of cracked ice. Pour in rum. Add cream and caramel sauce. Shake well. Pour liquid and ice into a martini glass.

Mambo Martini

This martini is like taking a sip of a cool refreshing daiquiri. Fresh lime always bodes well with Mexican food and spicy flavors.

- Shaker
- Chilled martini glass

	Ice	
1½ oz	light rum	45 mL
¼ cup	freshly squeezed lime juice	60 mL
1 tsp	superfine sugar	5 mL

1. Fill a shaker half full of ice. Pour in rum, lime juice and sugar. Shake and strain into chilled martini glass.

Mojito de Mexico

The mojito cocktail, Cuba's oldest cocktail, usually made with rum is tantalizing with tequila. Muddling the fresh mint and lime adds an intense flavor to this cocktail.

- Muddling stick
- Tall glass

8	mint leaves, divided	8
1 tbsp	granulated sugar	15 mL
1	lime, sliced into quarters	1
2 oz	silver tequila	60 mL
	Cracked ice	
	Club soda	

1. In a glass, add 7 mint leaves, sugar and lime. Muddle until sugar is almost dissolved and flavors are blended. Add tequila and fill with ice. Top with club soda and stir. Garnish with remaining mint leaf.

Cactus Colada

This drink has a tasty tropical flavor with a kick. Typically a Hawaiian cocktail, my cool colada gets a zing from a shot of tequila and a twist of lime, creating a Southwest surprise.

- Preheat oven to 350°F (180°C)
- Blender
- Collins glass

½ cup	sweetened flaked coconut	125 mL
1 cup	unsweetened pineapple juice	250 mL
½ cup	gold tequila	125 mL
½ cup	cream of coconut	125 mL
	Juice of 2 limes	
3 to 4 cups	cracked ice	750 mL to 1 L

1. Place coconut flakes on a baking sheet and bake in preheated oven until lightly browned, 6 to 8 minutes. Let cool completely.

2. In a blender, blend pineapple juice, tequila, cream of coconut, lime juice and 3 cups (750 mL) ice until ice is smooth, 2 to 3 minutes. Add more ice for a thicker consistency. Pour into serving glasses. Garnish each cocktail with toasted coconut.

Library and Archives Canada Cataloguing in Publication

Coffeen, Kelley
    300 best taco recipes : from tantalizing tacos to authentic tortillas, sauces,
    cocktails & salsas / Kelley Cleary Coffeen.

Includes index.
ISBN 978-0-7788-0267-9

    1. Tacos. 2. Cooking, Mexican. 3. Cooking, American--Southwestern style.
    4. Cookbooks I. Title. II. Title: Three hundred best taco recipes.

TX716.M4C617 2011   641.5972   C2010-907385-1

Index